The Evolution of Theory
in International Relations

THE EVOLUTION OF THEORY IN INTERNATIONAL RELATIONS

Essays in Honor of William T. R. Fox

edited by **Robert L. Rothstein**

University of South Carolina Press

Copyright © 1991 University of South Carolina

Published in Columbia, South Carolina, by the
University of South Carolina Press

Manufactured in the United States of America

Library of Congress Cataloging-in-Publication Data

The Evolution of theory in international relations ; essays in honor
of William T. R. Fox / edited by Robert L. Rothstein.
    p.   cm.
  Includes bibliographical references and index.
  ISBN 0-87249-762-3 (hard-cover acid free)
    1. International relations. I. Rothstein, Robert L. II. Fox,
William T. R. (William Thornton Rickert), 1912–
JX1395.E94 1991
327' .01–dc20   91–12846

CONTENTS

PREFACE

by Annette Baker Fox

How can a collaborator of Bill's who was also his wife of 53 years write objectively of his academic life? Clearly it is impossible. I cannot escape presenting a personal viewpoint, but subjectivity has its own virtues.

Political science brought us together as students at the University of Chicago when Bill was beginning his graduate work and I was an undergraduate. He taught me a great deal and this is one of the reasons that I, like many of the contributors to this volume, considered myself a student of his, mingling intellectual respect with great affection. Like other contributors, I felt richer for having been one of his colleagues.

Students at the university in the 1930s learned from those who composed the Chicago school of political science the need to be neutral observers. We also picked up the cautious optimism which prevailed despite the gloomy atmosphere of the Depression and the spread of fascism: We believed that social scientists might be able to contribute to the alleviation of the world's evils. Thus Bill, naturally cheerful and with an already well-developed social conscience, began to develop his scholarly vocation. Throughout his academic life he stressed that the future was only partly determined. Some choice was possible, the more rational the better. Social scientists could map the possible alternative avenues to follow and the consequences of choosing particular paths.

When Bill's intention to enter the Foreign Service was frustrated by Department of State penury, he turned in 1932 to the graduate study of international relations. At Chicago this meant international law and organization under Quincy Wright. From that monumental scholar Bill learned to cast his net very widely, both spatially and temporally, as he began to look at potential relationships across national boundaries and to understand their immense complexity. That the political process not only transcended such borders but was observable and comparable in every conceivable social group he learned from that unofficial dean of political scientists of the day, Charles E. Merriam.

It was Harold D. Lasswell who probably exerted the most seminal influence on Bill at the University of Chicago. Lasswell's counsel that sound political analysis is nothing less than correct orientation in the continuum which embraces the past, present and future, guided Bill from that period on. Although implementing Lasswell's instructions in very different ways than his mentor, Bill adopted "contemplative and manipulative attitudes toward political change" throughout his scholarly life.[1]

More down to earth, and equally important in molding Bill's approach to international relations, was his collaboration with Frederick Sherwood Dunn as associate director of the Yale Institute of International Studies from 1943 to 1950. Ted Dunn was a critically influential teacher for both of us. International relations was "politics in the absence of central authority." Behind state decisions were individuals who were making choices, and these choices might be clarified by policy-oriented theory. For me the approach was congenial. Ever the student adjusting to chance, I retooled from my chosen field of public administration to international relations. For Bill, it gave a moral underpinning to clear-headed investigations of policy implications while avoiding the oversimplifications and self-delusions of so-called peaceniks. Complexity stimulated his imagination as he stressed the relativity of power, at the same time observing that, as ethical values were likely to conflict with each other in the real world, decision makers should be enabled to self-consciously choose their ordering.

While teaching at Yale, Bill demonstrated that symbiotic relationship between theory and practice to which he often called attention. In *The Super-Powers*, a term he coined in this 1944 publication, he examined the significance for international relations of the rise of a new kind of state actor. The next year he served on the international staff of the United Nations Charter Conference in San Francisco, working on security provisions designed for a post-war world political system. In these activities he manifested his belief that if mankind is to exercise "some measure of rational control over [his] destiny, the limits of the possible and the consequences of the desirable have both to be investigated."[2]

Prior to his Yale years, Bill's attention had already been drawn to national security questions through his association at Princeton with Harold and Margaret Sprout and Edward Meade Earle. In 1950, shortly after Bill came to Columbia, General Dwight D. Eisenhower, then president of the university, persuaded Bill to direct the incipient Institute of War and Peace Studies. Bill somewhat reluctantly had to choose between devoting his full time to teaching and research and spending part of it administering an enterprise that encouraged others to follow policy-relevant studies of international relations. New opportunities arose to instruct, counsel, help manage university affairs, and advise various

---

1. Harold D. Lasswell, *World Politics and Personal Insecurity* (New York: Whitlesey House, 1935) pp.4-5.
2. William T.R. Fox, *The American Study of International Relations* (Columbia, SC: University of South Carolina Press, 1967) p.92.

public groups. The collegial environment not only provided ample occasion for Bill's conciliating skills, but also promoted that learning from colleagues which characterized Bill's whole academic life.

Learning and teaching were simultaneous. Generations of graduate students have attested to his generous attention to their individual concerns. Perhaps this was the most valuable contribution he could make to the understanding of international relations. He never completed the oft-revised examination of civil-military relations which he began early in his 38 years at Columbia, although he did draw on it for articles he published. He turned to other fields of inquiry including international aspects of developments in science and technology, arms control, the population explosion and the protection of human rights, approaching all as a meliorist social scientist.

When, 16 years after Bill came to Columbia, I joined him there to work together on a volume meant for a series devoted to the North Atlantic Treaty Organization (NATO), it was not just the military aspects that interested us. *NATO and the Range of American Choice*—the title exemplified Bill's approach—was happily completed without the collaboration ending in divorce. Frankness is sometimes easier when the co-authors are husband and wife. In writing this book we followed a procedure similar to that already adopted in joint articles published earlier. After we mapped the work with the imaginative points Bill conceived and I critiqued, we interviewed officials in various allied countries and I did the library research. Then I wrote the first rough draft, he drastically revised it, I revised his revision, he altered that revision, and I finally broke the cycle by impressing on him that the time had come to complete the work. Although Bill was an experienced and very meticulous editor as his students knew well, this book was professionally edited by Jane Schilling. With an uncanny instinct she spotted the places where we had fuzzed up a point on which we were not in full agreement and forced us to clarify the meaning, a very salubrious exercise.

At this time, in 1966, we were living in Rio de Janeiro where Bill taught in the foreign service academy under the Fulbright program. There he came face to face with the need to think about North-South relationships and about "global distributive justice." This international experience was one of several in foreign countries—England in 1955, Mexico in 1967, two stints at the Australian National University in Canberra, once in 1968 and then in 1979, a semester at Carleton University in Ottawa in 1971, and after retirement from Columbia, at the University of Toronto in 1983. These sojourns broadened Bill's perspectives and mine and helped us "*to see orsels as ithers see us*" and to free us of "*mony a...foolish notion.*"

Bill regarded Canada as an ideal international relations laboratory. It is a foreign country yet similar to the United States, a country where common attributes could be held constant while assessing the relevance of the differences observed. With his encouragement I became a "Canadianist" and so was prepared to serve when he arranged for the Canadian Studies Program for social science graduate teaching and research at Columbia from 1977 to 1984. Also, we were both members of two working committees on Canada-United States relations, one at the Council on Foreign Relations, the other at the Atlantic Council of the United States. In these groups we saw once again that transnational personal ties are often fundamental to transgovernmental relations. Bill's crowning work in this field was *A Continent Apart: The United States and Canada in World Politics*, published in 1985 and based on his Claude T. Bissell lectures at the University of Toronto.

Bill's concept of the North Atlantic of the Two, facing the outside world in a stable though asymmetrical relationship, was the theme for what was to have been a joint presentation at a conference in Amsterdam in November 1988. I had to write it alone, following his ideas, as I have also written this preface. These were difficult tasks without his invaluable participation, but like other contributors to this volume, this student and colleague has carried on, grateful for his guidance.

INTRODUCTION:
The Evolution of the Theoretical Debate

by Robert L. Rothstein

This book is dedicated to the memory of Professor William T. R. Fox. All of the contributors shared a desire to offer testimony of our respect, our admiration, and our affection for a man and a scholar who inspired and encouraged a generation of students and colleagues. We hope that this collection of essays is an appropriate testimonial, one that Bill himself would have appreciated, and—one hopes, in light of the results—greatly valued.

Bill was fond and of describing himself as a "pragmatic meliorist"and was, throughout his career, concerned with improving the conduct of world affairs and more carefully articulating the normative dimension of national and international policies. But Bill was also intensely concerned with the theoretical development of the discipline of international relations. And it is to this dimension of scholarly activity that this collection is addressed.

Bill was a remarkably undogmatic and open scholar. He did not demand from his students commitment to any particular theory, or ideology, or vision of what ought to be. He asked only for commitment to scholarship, a willingness to work, and an ability to make and defend an argument according to the best available standards and evidence. Indeed, when one looks at the contributors to this issue, there is ample, if indirect, testimony to Bill's openness: the group spans the ideological spectrum, theoretical commitments extend from efforts at "grand' theory to detailed (but theoretically informed) discussions of particular issues, and there is throughout, either explicitly or implicitly, a concern with normative issues.

This very diversity, however, also creates a problem of its own. How can such a diverse group produce a collection of essays that is coherent, integrated, and of general interest to an equally diverse readership? Of course, one might fudge the issue by arguing that any collection by this particular group of scholars is bound to be intrinsically interesting, perhaps even valuable, but this is an inherently unsatisfactory response. In any event, in my editorial capacity, I have attempted to diminish the problems created by diversity—without at the same time losing its benefits—by asking each author to take an evolutionary view of theoretical development in general or of a particular problem or issue that he or she has worked on. My hope is that in a small way this approach might provide a kind of "rolling" perspective on the way in which theory and theorizing have developed (or not developed) in our shared discipline over the past three or four decades.

No single substantive theme dominates this collection, which should not be surprising since we are not committed to a single theoretical vision or to the analysis of a single issue or perspective. Still, it does seem to me that several themes, or perhaps meta-themes, do emerge in this collection. Insofar as this judgment is correct—and I accept full responsibility if it is not—the meta-themes implicitly reflect perceptions, judgments, and intuitions about some of the central theoretical or conceptual concerns of our discipline.

The first meta-theme concerns the very value of either theory or theorizing in international relations. Certainly the skepticism that is prevalent in at least part of our discipline about what so many dedicated efforts to theorize have produced, or indeed can produce, is not without merit. Nevertheless, while ambitions have had to be scaled back (at least for most of us) and more modest goals have become the norm, there is after all some benefit in this— in knowing more about the limits and the possibilities of the theoretical enterprise in a particular context. In any case, the contributors to this volume do not seem to share the skepticism about theorizing that has emerged elsewhere. Indeed, the contributors seem to believe that the abandonment of the quest for theory would leave the discipline in shambles. That the quest is difficult and unlikely to result in more than partial and contingent answers to the questions that concern us does not mean that we can or should retreat into the seductive realm of policy advice, especially if such advice reflects only personal opinions and judgments. Put differently, perhaps one can say that the value of theorizing, especially from the perspective of providing some of the "glue" that holds the discipline together, is as great as the value of the theory itself, at least as long as the weak theories that we have produced do not cumulate into a strong theory. Theorizing is not unimportant because it is inadequate or unsatisfactory.

That we now can see many roads to increased understanding of the nature of our discipline and of the theories that might provide some provisional answers to the questions that concern us is strikingly evident in the pages that follow. For example, Waltz makes an eloquent and elegant case for neorealism and the dominance in some security issues of the configuration of structural power. Whether one agrees with this argument or not, whether one agrees that security confrontations between the major powers can be explained solely or primarily at the structural level (which is, after all, an interpreted, not necessarily a deterministic, level) or that security itself can any longer be so narrowly conceived, may not be as important as Waltz's inestimable contribution in generating a debate about fundamental theoretical and practical questions.

In what is a formidable challenge to the "causal centrality of structured power," Haas argues that international events are governed by "human self-reflection and by self-conscious striving for improvement." Haas sees causality running from the nation to the system and contends that progress has occurred or is occurring because our conceptions of what constitutes political problems and solutions have been and are informed by scientific reasoning. This provocative, original, and certainly controversial argument has, in a sense, one of the major virtues of Waltz's argument: it forces the reader to question, perhaps even to "revision," what he or she takes for granted about the key questions in our discipline. Moreover, if we are moving to a world political system in which questions of how and why to cooperate are at least as important as questions of conflict, Haas's emphasis on the role of consensual knowledge may become increasingly influential. Although it is written from a different perspective, perhaps Henkin's analysis of the human rights debate ought to be noted here. There may at least be a philosophical convergence between Haas and Henkin in that Henkin sees some movement from "state values," to "human values," and argues that the human rights idea has provided a principal countercurrent to the traditional emphasis on state values, an idea that has penetrated into international law and politics. There is also some parallel in the need to deal creatively with the tension between state and human values in Henkin and the tension between knowledge and structural power in Haas.

Many of the other contributors provide additional comments or perspectives on the evolution of the theoretical debate. Thus Puchala's striking and insightful comments on the behavioral movement, which are particularly evocative for those who lived through that earlier "great debate," raise significant questions about the kind of theory that we can produce and kind of analysis that is likely to be fruitful. He criticizes behavioralism as an "enticing detour through pseudo-science" and argues that our "rather impressive" theoretical output has come mainly from scholars who have focused on "unobservable wholes"—in effect, from scholars who have not worried about whether they were being "scientific" but rather have tried to provide "plausible meanings" for international events through the use of intuition, conceptualizing, and symbolizing. Perhaps these comments are too harsh on the behavioralists, in that they ignore some of the latent benefits of behavioralism (especially in making us all more aware of the critical questions involved in producing grounded theory), but Puchala's sophisticated analysis deserves wide and careful reading.

A number of other contributors also provide evidence of a continuing commitment to the effort to theorize, to catch "changing reality" in some kind of explanatory framework. For example, Jervis offers an acute and finely balanced analysis of the advantages and disadvantages of formal modeling and case studies as approaches to theory, an issue that has been central to much of the discipline's methodological debate. Snyder provides one of the best analyses of a structural theory of alliances that this writer has seen, thus greatly advancing our understanding of an important component of the theoretical mosaic. Zacher seeks to explicate the basis of mutual interests that makes international regulation more or less likely and simultaneously seeks to go beyond the state-centric perspective of realism by emphasizing mutual interests and cooperation. Rothstein attempts to put the effort to explain North-South within the context of the kind of weak theories that dominate in international relations and argues that thinking of the South as an international social movement—not merely a coalition—may help to understand that "great debate" of the 1970s. And Hansen, in her analysis of William T. R. Fox's scholarly production, emphasizes his sustained commitment to the need to produce a theoretical structure for our discipline.

As many have noted, most scholars of international relations, whatever their theoretical perspective, also have an abiding concern with practical issues of policy. Indeed, many scholars have either worked for one or another administration or in one or another political campaign or written about an immediate policy issue. Yet there is almost no direct comment on policy issues in the pages that follow, no effort to tell policymakers what they ought to do or to provide insights or guidance derived from our "superior wisdom." This does not imply, however, an indifference to the problems of the "real world." Rather, it seems to me to reflect an awareness of what we can or cannot do with the kind of weak theories that we produce, none of which are strong enough or contain enough of the relevant details of the policy world to permit explicit guidance. We cannot legitimately usurp the functions of the practitioner but we can be useful critics and gadflies and we can provide important help in devising appropriate ways to think about issues or put them in an appropriate analytical context. And of course as educators we can play a significant role in structuring the ways in which future practitioners organize their universe of discourse. The rough divide between the realm of theory and the realm of policy advice has many gray areas, areas in which the connections between the two realms may be relatively closer, but the need to be modest about the practical implications that can be drawn from weak theories should be apparent—or, perhaps I should say, is apparent to this writer.

There is in the pages that follow relatively little direct concern with the issue of methodology per se, although it is certainly discussed in Puchala, Jervis, and (from a different perspective) Zimmerman. One reason for this may be, as I have already noted, that one consequence of the behavioral movement—perhaps more important than its efforts to make us "scientific"—has been to increase sophistication about the limits of some advanced methodologies and the possibilities of some traditional methodologies; the long and bumpy road to theory is not likely to follow one methodological direction. In addition, to some extent, traditionalism is "in" again, in part because of the failures of behavioralism, in part because of rising concern with practical problems as U.S. power declines and some international economic regimes seem at risk, and in part because in some areas (political economy, domestic-external linkages) theorizing is rudimentary. But apart from these considerations, the extraordinary changes that are occurring in the international system, not only in the security realm but also in rising concern with the need to establish the grounds for cooperation in economic, social, and ecological realms, have meant that the discipline itself is confronted with a profound need to rethink prevailing conceptual frameworks—in effect, what we can take for granted in discussing international events and developments. We need to think carefully about what questions we need to ask and what questions we might be able to answer and both sets of questions may require a new theoretical vision—prior to any concern with appropriate methodologies.

A second meta-theme concerns the relationship between change and continuity. This perennial and apparently insoluble debate has taken on new urgency because of the rise of interdependence, the shocking and unanticipated events that seem to have transformed the East-West "relationship of major tension" into a relationship of major uncertainty, and the increasing demands for democratization (in many cases by default, as a protest against failed authoritarian regimes) in so many countries—among other things. But as the debate on, and response to, interdependence has indicated, the changes that were and are occurring can be interpreted in many ways. Thus decreased autonomy could seem to justify demands for increased multilateral cooperation, or cooperation among smaller groups, or an effort to reduce dependence or shift its costs elsewhere, or simply further study of whether or how much interdependence was growing—and what ought to be done about it. And changes in the external environment that were only partially linked to interdependence (slower growth, shifts in the world oil market), as well as changes in administration in the major developed countries (which led to a focus on getting domestic policies "right" and merely "managing" interdependence), also affected perceptions and policies.

A theory of change, or even a coherent framework to discuss and analyze change, would obviously be an enormous intellectual advance. But neither is likely, certainly not in the current environment, because the complexities are vast and perhaps beyond our means to resolve. In any case, while several of the essays that follow grapple with the problem of change from a variety of perspectives, none really provides a theory or a framework that would diminish our difficulties. Perhaps Haas's optimistic and indeed visionary argument about the progress that has occurred because of the power of scientific reasoning (a secular trend that is progressive, but one that does not deny the variations along the trend line caused by the misuse of knowledge) comes closest to providing a framework for thinking about change, but it does not provide much help in understanding how to respond to specific changes. Still, the central point is that there is more explicit concern with the problem of change in our theoretical analyses and it seems unlikely that we will be able to improve our understanding of change unless this concern becomes more deeply embedded in our attempts to theorize. The outcome of this effort will not be grounded theory but it may be greater sophistication about the nature of the international world, new or different visions of reality, and a more complex set of questions that we ask about our domain of concern.

Apart from Haas, the essays by Zimmerman, Puchala, and Rothstein are explicitly concerned with the problem of change. Zimmerman's discussion of the Soviet Union as an "ordinary state" is even more salient now as the Soviet Union moves, or seems to be moving, toward a more market-oriented economy and some kind of democratization. But Zimmerman also focuses on the "revisionist's dilemma," how to transform a system in which one has a stake—a system in which tinkering is insufficient, revolution seems too dangerous, but the conditions for political and economic reform are difficult to discern or control. Rothstein focuses on the same problem in a North-South context, as the South sought to transform a system from which some states in the South greatly benefitted, but without any very persuasive way of showing that the new order would be superior to the old for either North or South. However, Rothstein also seeks to analyze the way a variety of changes affected interpretations of North-South and are likely to continue to do so in the future. And Puchala in his fine essay seeks to indicate how theory may be our main guide as we seek to track an ever-changing reality. These are certainly small and tentative steps along the road to increased understanding of change but perhaps they suggest that the tension between continuity and change will become a more important component of our efforts to theorize or even to provide a more sophisticated guide to what is transpiring in world politics.

A final meta-theme, which may exist only in the mind of the editor, concerns direction or perhaps what it is we are seeking to achieve in the theoretical enterprise at this time. The great debates of the past, between classical realism and behavioralism in the 1950s and 1960s and between interdependence (and the political economy focus on cooperation) and neorealism in the 1970s and 1980s, have never been definitively resolved. Indeed, advocates of all these "schools" or approaches still have fervent adherents producing serious and, in some cases, distinguished and useful work. And of course new schools have arisen that supplement or challenge any or all of the older schools of thought, not least the psychological approaches of scholars such as Alexander George and Robert Jervis and the more formal, deductive modeling of a number of (usually) younger scholars. The diversity of aproach is enormous and apparently increasing and the likelihood of consensus seems to be diminishing. A key question, to which there are only very tentative answers, is whether there is a shared goal that, amidst diversity, provides a degree of unity for all these very different theoretical endeavors.

It seems to me that one possible answer is that we are in quest of a post-realist conceptual framework for international relations. Of course, advocates of classical realism or neorealism might well object in whole or in part and others might object to the potential confusion implicit in adding another term—post-realism—to the debate when there is still some uncertainty about realism and neorealism and the differences between them (which Waltz does much to clarify in his contribution). Still, as security concerns seem to be partially shifting (perhaps to Third World conflicts and the diffusion of dangerous military technologies), as the rise of new issues on the international agenda and the intrusion of domestic politics into international calculations continues, and as the quest for multilateral cooperation escalates in importance—even for conservative administrations that insist it will suffice to get domestic policies "right"—neither the minimalist vision of the neorealists, which seeks to explain a few critical security decisions by focusing on traditional calculations of power and interest, nor the grand schemes of the world systems approach (as structural as the neorealists) seem likely to suffice. But what ought to be included, or what ought we to be thinking about, to create a more plausible framework to understand international events?

There is no simple, clear answer to this question and indeed many of the attempted answers (or speculations) are largely an extrapolation of current fashions or the latest headlines. One reasonably safe guess is that domestic-external linkages will continue to be a central area of investigation and that the foreign policy and foreign economic policy component of international relations will become even more crucial. Perhaps this also suggests that ancient questions about the effects of forms of government on international (and of course domestic) behavior will become increasingly prominent, not least in reference to questions about war and peace and relative economic performance. In addition, it seems highly probable that much analytical effort will be expended on redefining the security *problematique* in regard to the shifting meaning of security and the security dilemma, the broadening of the idea of security itself, and perhaps a rising concern with regional security issues in the "new" Europe and the Third World.

More speculatively, a post-realist conceptual framework for international relations may also require at least a partial paradigm shift, a shift in what we take for granted about the nature of our field. I do not mean to imply that the security concern will disappear or that it should. But I do think that a post-realist framework must also include increased concentration on the international system as a policymaking system where the quest for agreement is as important as, and in some cases more important than, the quest for power or the balancing of power. This implies a focus not only on the production of international public goods but also much stronger conceptualizations of the nature of policymaking in a complex and not entirely independent policy environment. We shall need to think more deeply about bargaining in incremental systems, the possibilities of linkages and logrolling, and the utility of different coalition strategies—classic issues within the domestic polity.

Finally, in a variation of the argument that Ernst Haas makes in the concluding essay, one might also surmise that the changes that have occurred as a result of interdependence and other developments suggest that the power of ideas and the subjective component of international relations will become more important. The pressure of international norms—such as democracy, multilateral cooperation, and liberalized markets—may become even more consequential for domestic and international policymaking. Of course, some of these norms may conflict (for example, popular pressures for consumption against the competitive demands of the market), others may be dropped or accepted only rhetorically if they do not produce anticipated results quickly enough, and there will be many ambiguities and uncertainties in the application of general norms to specific circumstances. Still, the impact of these norms and perhaps others of more limited appeal (such as religious fundamentalism) may greatly change the fabric of international relations and assessment of how these norms are interpreted (individually and collectively) and applied may become central analytical concerns. In any case, normative concerns are bound to become increasingly salient in a world where some issues require multilateral cooperation that produces asymmetrical costs and benefits.

The Evolution of Theory
in International Relations

WILLIAM T.R. FOX AND THE STUDY OF WORLD POLITICS

by Elizabeth C. Hanson

In one of the earliest published volumes devoted to the subject of international relations theory, William T.R. Fox wrote, "International Relations has to be viewed as a subject which is something more than contemporary history if it is to evolve as a legitimate academic specialty or to yield results relevant to the major choices which governments and opinion leaders must make in world politics."[1] In a career which parallels the evolution of the discipline, Bill Fox helped to shape international relations as a major academic field and to demonstrate the relevance of its theoretical investigations to policy making.

His legacy was the cumulative effect of his contributions as a scholar, editor, administrator and especially as teacher and mentor. He was associate director of the Yale Institute of International Studies from 1943 to 1950. As the first managing editor of the institute's publication, *World Politics*, he provided the impetus and direction for the first major quarterly journal in the field. It was significant that he chose a name for the journal that conveyed a broader conception of the field than a label such as "international politics" would have done. Subsequently, he was a founding editor of *International Organization*. He was director of the Institute of War and Peace at Columbia University for a quarter of a century. During his career he participated in many research committees and conferences concerned with the research agenda of the field. Notable examples were the Committee on International Relations Research and the National Security Policy Research Committee of the Social Science Research Council, the latter of which he chaired from 1953 to 1964.

Fox's influence as teacher and mentor on the discipline of international relations was enormous. Scores of students who participated in his seminars now fill high academic or policy-making positions. These former students bear no indelible stamp branding them as products of W.T.R. Fox's tutelage. On the contrary, they are an exceedingly diverse group in their research interests, methodologies and paradigmatic orientations. The research areas investigated by the small selection of former students who have contributed to this volume have illustrated this diversity. These include North-South relations, systemic theory, Soviet

---

1.   Preface in W.T.R. Fox, ed., *Theoretical Aspects of International Relations* (Notre Dame, IN: University of Notre Dame Press, 1959) p.ix.

politics, politics of international commodity trade and international crisis behavior. The fact that his students over the years have moved in such different directions can be attributed in large part to Fox's extraordinary ability to foster critical and independent thinking about international relations. His style as a scholar and the breadth of his substantive interests also contributed to this outcome.

Three aspects of his scholarly contribution deserve special attention. Most important to this observer was his effective advocacy of a "pragmatic meliorist" approach to world politics. Secondly, he was a perceptive chronicler of the study of international relations in the United States, and he made a strong case for its relevance to public policy. It is unlikely that anyone has written so frequently over so long a period of time about the state of the field.[2] Thirdly, he was a keen observer of change in the international system and of its implications for the study of international relations and the conduct of foreign policy. He anticipated well in advance some of the directions in which the discipline was to move, and his formulations of certain concepts, such as power and security, are now widely accepted.

The first part of this essay will focus on Fox's "pragmatic meliorist" approach and how this philosophical orientation shaped his views about the policy relevance of international relations theory. The second part will examine his writings on contemporary issues.

The Pragmatic Meliorist Approach to World Politics

It is clear from Fox's writings, particularly his autobiographical essay, that intellectual influences from four sources played a major role in shaping his basic world view.[3] The first came from his graduate training at the University of Chicago in the 1930s with Charles Merriam, Harold Lasswell, Quincy Wright and Jacob Viner, whom he has described as "pluralist pragmatists" and "utopians of science and reason."[4] Their faith in the power of human reason to improve the world accorded with his optimistic temperament. Their instrumental view of power and their vision of a pluralist world system formed the basis of a model of world

2. Six articles, written between 1949 and 1966, were compiled in W.T.R. Fox, *The American Study of International Relations* (Columbia, SC: University of South Carolina Press, 1968).
3. W.T..R. Fox, "A Middle Western Isolationist-Internationalist's Journey toward Relevance," in Joseph Kruzel and James N. Rosenau, eds., *Journeys through World Politics: Autobiographical Reflections of Thirty-four Academic Travelers* (Lexington, MA: D.C. Heath and Company, 1988) pp.233-235.
4. *Ibid.*, p. 234; W.T.R. Fox, "Pluralism, the Science of Politics, and the World System," *World Politics* 27, no. 4 (July 1975) pp.597-611.

politics, which he later refined and modified in response to changing events and to the intellectual environments of Princeton and Yale.

The onset of World War II and his association with Edward Mead Earl and Harold Sprout at Princeton encouraged him to modify his "war as pathology" attitude which he had brought from Chicago, and to give geopolitics and national security a great deal more attention. At his next teaching post, the Yale Institute of International Studies, these influences took on the distinctive shape which Fox labeled the "pragmatic meliorist" or "range of choice" approach.[5] Finally, Fox's thinking was also influenced by the writings of those he criticized as "doctrinal realists," such as E.H. Carr and Hans Morgenthau.

The essential elements of Fox's pragmatic meliorist approach are scattered throughout his writings. Together they form a coherent picture of how the world works and how it might work better. Four aspects of this approach will be considered: his conception of politics, his instrumental view of power, his attitude toward the capacity of human beings to shape their future and his belief in the potential of social science for increasing rationality in public policy making.

Politics, Power and Security

"There will always be politics," Fox frequently reminded his students, "except in Heaven and Hell and other perfect dictatorships." World politics is a struggle for scarce values in a world of inequality and continuous but uneven change. Political leaders are always advancing more claims than the world political system can satisfy, and unmet demands generate conflict. Hence "conflict, and the political processes for adjusting conflicting claims for scarce values, are at the center of the study of international relations."[6] What is significant is the equal emphasis which Fox put on conflict and the adjustment of conflict as the appropriate focus for the discipline. Indeed, the article which most clearly presents this perspective is entitled "World Politics as Conflict Resolution."

As convinced as he was of the inevitability of the struggle for scarce values, he also believed that the intensity of the struggle could be moderated. Social scientists can be socially useful in finding ways to allocate scarce values more efficiently, "that is, with the least waste and the greatest creativity in the allocating process."[7] Greater efficiency means more people get more of what they want more of the time. The

---

5. *Ibid.*, p.240.
6. W.T.R. Fox, "World Politics as Conflict Resolution," in Robert O. Matthews, Arthur C. Rubinoff and Janice G. Stein, eds., *International Conflict and Conflict Management* (Scarborough, Ont.: Prentice-Hall of Canada, 1984) p.8.
7. Fox, "A Middle Western Isolationist-Internationalist's Journey toward Relevance," p.237.

social scientist may help to increase the efficiency of the allocative process by, for example, finding ways to lessen nonfunctional confrontations; by identifying alternative courses of action and the consequences of each for values and goals; and by helping policy makers understand that other groups besides one's own have needs and aspirations which must to some extent be met if political conflict is to be moderated.[8] The pragmatic meliorist views world politics not simply as a way of allocating scarce values but "as a process which is capable of producing as well as distributing the values for the attainment of which the actors in the world system are variously contending and collaborating."[9]

A second aspect of Fox's world view is his instrumental view of power, based on Bertrand Russell's definition of power as the "capacity to produce intended effects."[10] Fox believed that it was important to distinguish between the pursuit of power as a means to some other end and the pursuit of power as an end in itself. "For me," he wrote in his autobiographical essay, "the distinction between acquiring capacity to produce intended effects and the mindless accumulation of capacity to cause unintended and perhaps unwanted effects is fundamental."[11] His concern was with the uses of power, the "purposeful mobilization of potential," and with the calculations that statesmen must make about the choice of "least-cost means" for achieving foreign policy goals.[12] "Useless power," or "the power to produce unintended effects" he called the "Typhoid Mary" kind of power.[13] The question is which accumulations of power, to promote which foreign policy purposes, are worth which sacrifices.[14] In an essay on "Growing Points in the Study of International Relations," he observed with approval the shift in the discipline away from the tendency to view power as an essence—as something to be determined by adding up the various components—to an understanding of power as a relationship. He remarked that "contemporary students of power recognize the relativity of power of a particular state to its goals and to the goals and capabilities of competitors, as well as the non-additivity of power factors."[15]

---

8. *Ibid*.:; *American Study of International Relations*, pp.66-67.
9. Fox, "E. H. Carr and Political Realism: Vision and Revision," *Review of International Studies* II (1985) p. 14.
10. Fox, "A Middle Western Isolationist-Internationalist's Journey toward Relevance," p.234; Bertrand Russell, *Power: A New Social Analysis* (London: Allen & Unwin, 1938).
11. *Ibid.*, p. 234
12. *Ibid.*, p. 240.
13. Fox, "E. H. Carr and Political Realism," p. 6.
14. *Ibid.*, p.11.
15. Fox, *The American Study of International Relations*, p. 103.

The quest for power is not the same as the quest for security. Power is relational; one state's gain is another state's loss. But "one state's security is not necessarily every other state's insecurity. Greater security, like greater prosperity, but unlike dominant power, is an objective toward which it is at least conceivable that all states can move simultaneously."[16] If it is assumed that most statesmen most of the time seek security rather than hegemony and that power is regarded as a means to attain security, there is at least a possibility that there could be an all-round increase in security.[17]

Utopianism, Realism, and the Range of Choice

Like Raymond Aron, Stanley Hoffman and other scholars in international relations, Fox tended naturally to "think against."[18] He often identified what he considered to be two extreme positions and their shortcomings and then attempted to bring the two together at some midpoint. Hence his critiques had a dialectical quality and aimed at a kind of intellectual synthesis. His pragmatic meliorist position emerged from his critiques of the excessive voluntarism of "utopian internationalists" on the one hand and the "simplistic determinism" of political realists on the other.[19] The former, who dominated Anglo-American thinking about international affairs in the 1930s, were much too optimistic about the possibilities for building supranational institutions and a peaceful world order. They vastly underestimated the complexity of political change in a system of states without government. The realist model of the world of states in perpetual struggle for survival, on the other hand, was much too pessimistic about the possibilities for harmonizing contending interests and achieving positive change.

Fox was particularly critical of the deterministic aspects of political realism which he discerned in the first edition of E. H. Carr's *Twenty Years' Crisis*.[20] In an essay devoted to Carr, Fox praised the British scholar's relentless efforts to expose the hollowness of Anglo-American utopian thinking which prevailed in the inter-war era and admired his grasp of the sweeping systemic changes that were occurring. But Fox focused his attention on the portion of the original 1939 edition that was

---

16.   Fox, *The Superpowers: The United States, Britain, and the Soviet Union, Their Responsibility for Peace*(New York: Harcourt, Brace, 1944) p.11.
17.   *Ibid.*; Fox, "E.H. Carr and Political Realism," p.13.
18.   Stanley Hoffman, "A Retrospective," in Kruzel and Rosenau, eds., *Journeys Through World Politics*, p.269.
19.   The best summary of these two positions may be found in Fox, "E. H. Carr and Political Realism."
20.   E. H. Carr, *Twenty Years Crisis* (MacMillan: London, 1939)

subsequently deleted in 1946 which suggested that if European power relationships in 1938 had made the loss of Czechoslovakia's independence inevitable, it was preferable that this outcome be the result of negotiation rather than war.[21]

This apparent defense of the Munich settlement implied that "policy was simply a skillful adjustment to history, with as few broken heads as possible, to the basic changes that are going to occur anyway."[22] Implicit in this version of peaceful change was the assumption that "the biggest and meanest dog will get the meatiest bone whatever mere mortals managing the affairs of state may think they are doing."[23] It exemplified, Fox believed, an attitude toward the historical process which narrowly restricted the range of choice in foreign policy and ignored the ability of policy makers to "change purposely." The passing of the European Age may have been inevitable, but whether the continent was ruled by a Nazi regime or organized into a common market was not.[24]

Between the excessive voluntarism of those who believe any future is possible and the excessive involuntarism of "those who believe in appeasement at any cost or in an unending struggle with the forces of darkness," Fox advocated his pragmatic meliorist position. The challenge, he maintained, was to distinguish between those aspects of world politics that are relatively fixed, those that are changing but uncontrollable, and those that may be manipulable. It is the "margin of manipulable choice" which should be the focus of attention of both scholars and policy makers. "Rational political action consists in achieving the best possible reconciliation of the desirable and the possible."[25]

The Policy Relevance of International Relations Theory

Fox strongly believed that the study of international relations could help policy makers act with greater rationality by illuminating the range of choice open to them and the different consequences that flow from various alternative courses of action. Scholarly theorizing can reveal incompatibilities in policy goals and indicate ways to reformulate those goals to avoid these incompatibilities. It can point to more economical ways of implementing objectives and it can help to redefine apparently conflicting national interests. Fox summarized his view about the relevance of the study of international relations studies in his

---

21. Fox, "E. H. Carr and Political Realism," p. 4; Carr, p. 278.
22. Fox, "The Uses of International Relations Theory," in *Theoretical Aspects of International Relations*, pp. 29-30.
23. Fox, "E. H. Carr and Political Realism," p. 9.
24. *Ibid.*, p. 6.
25. This is a recurring theme in Fox's work. See, for example "The Uses of International Relations Theory," p. 46.

autobiographical essay as follows: "Given a future that is partly but only partly determined and means to shape that future that are substantial but far from unlimited even for major actors in world politics, policy-relevant IR studies delimit the range of choice, clarify the consequences of alternative choices within that range, identify least-cost means for achieving chosen foreign policy ends, and point to ways of minimizing irrationality in the foreign policy decision process."[26]

Theories affect the world political process whether or not the particular theorist intends to do so and sometimes in ways that are not anticipated. Theories can clarify choice, thus delimiting what is possible or expanding the range of alternatives when they indicate courses of action not previously imagined. Theorists render a disservice to policy makers when they make the range of choice seem greater or smaller than it actually is.[27] Hence it is important for international relations scholars to make implicit theories more explicit so that these theories can be subjected to critical analysis and their relevance for public policy considered. "The study of world politics does not have to be policy-oriented to be policy-relevant," Fox wrote in an essay in honor of Harold Lasswell, "nor to be purged of policy relevance to be theoretically significant."[28] Lasswell, he suggested, was probably one of the most theoretical and at the same time one of the most practical scholars of world politics.

Although Fox was convinced that the theoretical activity of international relations scholars was policy relevant, he was skeptical about their efforts to provide complete prescriptions for immediate policy decisions. "Policy-relevant studies that clarify choice are not the same as policy-oriented studies that prescribe choice," he wrote in his autobiographical essay.[29] The scholar generally does not have access to the up-to-date information or contacts that government insiders will have. When an international relations scholar tries too hard to become immediately useful, he may become merely a "peddler of 'current events' or an apologist for the reigning priests of high policy, "thus abandoning his role as a social scientist.[30] The academic international relations scholar should think within a longer time frame and a wider context than the policy maker responsible for day to day decisions can manage. Ordering

---

26. Fox, "A Middle Western Isolationist-Internationalist's Journey toward Relevance," p. 240.
27. Fox, "The Uses of International Relations Theory," p. 31.
28. Fox, "Harold D. Lasswell and the Study of World Politics: Configuration Analysis, Garrison State and World Commonwealth," in Arnold A. Rogow, ed., *Analysis, Garrison State, and World Commonwealth* (Chicago: University of Chicago Press, 1969 p. 378.
29. Fox, "A Middle Western Isolationist-Internationalist's Journey toward Relevance," p. 240.
30. Fox, "The Uses of International Relations Theory," p. 32.

concepts and analytical models enable the theorist to transcend the limits of class, culture and nation to some extent.[31]

Doctrinal Realism vs. Empirical Realism

Fox's critical synthesis style makes him difficult to categorize. In many respects he seems to be a realist. He saw international politics, like all politics, as a continuous and ubiquitous struggle for scarce values. This struggle on the international level has a special character because it is "politics carried on in the absence of government." The unmitigated threat of violence poses problems of security for sovereign states and requires them to take appropriate measures and pursue policies to ensure their survival. The use of force remains the ultimate means of deciding among competing claimants and of promoting and protecting the state, its institutions and values. In such a system states, acting from self-interest, struggle for power to preserve their security.[32]

In 1944 when Fox wrote his first book, *The Super-Powers*, he was concerned about a possible post-war resurgence of utopian internationalist thinking which sought an escape from power politics to some new system of regulating inter-state relations. In the first chapter, entitled, "In Defense of Talking About Power," he sought to debunk the "peculiarly American notion" that "problems in a world of power politics can be solved by creating a world of no-power politics."[33] Although he continued throughout his career to warn against excessively optimistic, voluntaristic visions of the future, by the 1960s he seems to have perceived a greater danger from the opposite extreme. He saw that World War II and a generation of realist literature had convinced most people that world peace through the establishment of supra-national institutions was unlikely and that some kinds of future are beyond reach. Most scholars, as well as statesmen, had come to recognize the limits to change. He noted in his essay on Carr that "The need in the 1980s is to devote as much effort to determining what can be done as what cannot."[34]

Fox undoubtedly considered himself a realist, and a large portion of his professional attention focused on issues of national security. From his earliest publications, however, he took a position that differed from realist theorists in the tradition of E.H. Carr and Hans Morgenthau on three fundamental issues: the possibilities for positive change in interna-

---

31. Fox, "Pluralism, the Science of Politics, and the World System," p.608; *The American Study of International Relations*, p.69.
32. A good summary of these views may be found in Fox, "World Politics as Conflict Resolution."
33. Fox, *The Super-Powers*, p.4.
34. Fox, *The American Study of International Relations*, p. 66; see also "E. H. Carr and Political Realism," p. 12.

tional relations; the role of moral principle in foreign policy making; and the importance of non-state actors. His criticisms of realist theory led him to develop over time a conceptual distinction between "doctrinal realists" and "empirical realists," which he suggested in earlier writings but did not fully articulate until 1985 in the essay on E.H. Carr.[35]

Fox described doctrinal realists as excessively pessimistic and deterministic in their overemphasis on conflict, the struggle for power and the limits to choice in foreign policy making. Theirs was, he maintained, a Hobbesian view of the world in which eternal conflict is structurally determined and there is no escape from the security dilemma—"a world of states and an unending struggle for survival with no possibility of harmonizing contending interests."[36]

The empirical realist, on the other hand, stresses both the inevitability of competing claims to scarce values among states and the possibilities for harmonizing those contending interests. He does not expect denial of national interest but tries to find opportunities to reconcile national and international interests to promote all-round gains in security and welfare. Fox includes in his broad category of empirical realists the "neo-realists," who attempt to address their predecessors' failures to explain cooperation. The high cost of pure conflict in an interdependent world leads selfish actors to adhere to certain norms and decision-making procedures rather than acting solely on the basis of short-term calculations of self-interest.[37] The pragmatic meliorist is also an empirical realist but one without any "doctrinal hang-up about acknowledging that there may be shared values whose existence permits national interests to be harmonized at least between some states some of the time."[38] Although he did not explicitly claim membership in this category of pragmatic meliorist-empirical realists, it is clear from his writings that he considered himself to be among them.

Fox regarded the doctrinal realist's view of world politics to be as much an oversimplification of reality as that of the utopian internationalists of the 1930s. He considered their policy implications to be similar. The prescriptions of both failed to provide "a discriminating basis for identifying the margin of choice in foreign affairs and the values which could or should be promoted at the margin."[39] The realism of E.H. Carr on the eve of World War II called for adapting to inevitable changes in power, while the doctrinal realism of the 1950s and 1960s—with its

---

35. Fox, "E. H. Carr and Political Realism."
36. *Ibid.*, p.9.
37. *Ibid.*, p.13.
38. *Ibid.*
39. *Ibid.*, p.7.

emphasis upon the inevitable, unending, unmitigated struggle for power—also implied a restricted range of choice for policy makers.[40]

Fox believed that the doctrinal realist's perspective was grounded in a view of historical necessity that obscures the complexity and importance of the foreign-policy maker's actions and discourages efforts to effect positive change. The empirical realist's assumption that there is an area of manipulable choice in foreign policy making and that the interests of states can sometimes be harmonized focuses attention on the decision maker's choices and on the political process for adjusting conflicting claims among states. The assumption of choice makes policy making much more difficult since it requires "agonizing analyses of hard choices among disparate values."[41] The task of adjusting conflicting claims among states is also extraordinarily difficult, involving painful negotiation and rigorous intellectual analysis. To emphasize the laborious nature of this political process Fox frequently invoked in his lectures and his writings Max Weber's description of politics as "a slow boring of hard boards."[42]

The doctrinal realist's conception of the national interest as the sole criterion of foreign-policy making also oversimplified the decision-making process in Fox's view. In a remarkable exchange with Hans Morgenthau on the topic of national interest and moral principles in foreign policy, which was published in the *The American Scholar* in 1948, Fox argued that there was no way of determining the national interest except in terms of some explicitly declared set of value preferences.[43] He took issue with Morgenthau's argument that the statesman must choose between moral principle and the national interest as the ultimate standard of decision, that between these two conceptions of foreign policy there can be no compromise. Fox argued, to the contrary, that there could be no escape from compromise.

True, national survival must be placed at the top of the hierarchy of foreign policy objectives, but the self which is to be preserved is not merely the physical entity. "The camel's nose of moral principle is already under the tent," he pointed out, "when one admits that it is territorial integrity plus basic institutions which must 'in the national interest' be protected."[44] Moral principle necessarily enters into any formulation of the national interest, and the values inherent therein must

---

40. *Ibid.*, p.9.
41. *Ibid.*
42. See, for example, W.T.R. Fox, "The Reconciliation of the Desirable and the Possible," *American Scholar* 18, no. 1 (Winter 1948-49) p.213.
43. *Ibid.*, pp.212-216; Hans J. Morgenthau, "The Reconciliation of the Desirable and the Possible," *American Scholar* 18, no. 1 (Winter 1948-49) p.213.
44. *Ibid.*, p.214.

be part of the calculation about which values will be sacrificed to achieve other equally important values. Furthermore, survival is not always at stake, in which case judgments must be made about an array of other foreign policy objectives, some of which may be incompatible: "It is in weighing the risks and the gains—the value losses and the value increments to the self in whose name one is acting, i.e, the nation-state—that judgments about the possible emerge. It is in formulating this judgment that one arrives at a conception of the national interest."[45] Thus, the "reconciliation of the desirable and the possible," which is the policy maker's chief task, will always be some form of compromise.

Fox parted company with the doctrinal realists not only over the range of choice and the role of moral principle in foreign-policy making but also over their definition of the field. In an essay on the impact on the field of international relations of the Chicago School, named after a group of political scientists at the University of Chicago in the 1930s, Fox contrasted their "inclusive pluralist net" with the "exclusive simplifying assumptions" of those who took a "power approach," namely Morgenthau, Nicholas Spykman and Raymond Aron.[46] The three "brilliant simplifiers" considered only the power of states in pursuit of national interest and were primarily concerned with strategy and diplomacy in the relations among the greatest powers. This model is static and restrictive, Fox argued. It fails to take account of the activities of non-state actors; to address such important issues as trade barriers, resource scarcity, population pressures and Third World demands for higher living standards; and to explain some of the major transformations of the last half century.[47] Scholars of the Chicago School, on the other hand, were concerned with all groups that participated in the political process. Merriam, in particular, considered nation-states to be only one class of political associations that were related to each other and to various sub-, trans- and supra-national associations.[48] What Fox found most remarkable about the Chicago School was that its shift in basic organizing concepts from institutions to politics, groups, process and power in political science had the effect of expanding "international relations" (i.e., inter-state relations) to "world politics."[49]

---

45.   *Ibid.*
46.   Fox, "Pluralism, the Science of Politics, and the World System," pp. 599-601.
47.   *Ibid.*, pp. 600-601 and Fox, "A Middle Western Isolationist-Internationalist's Journey toward Relevance." p. 241.
48.   Fox, "Pluralism, the Science of Politics, and the World System," pp. 598.
49.   *Ibid.*, p. 597.

This pluralistic view of the world political system as "a seamless web spun by a wide variety of nation-state, domestic, transnational and supra-national actors" shaped Fox's conception of the field and underlay the scholarship and teaching of his entire career.[50] In his autobiographical essay he wrote, "Labels are not important in themselves, but through the whole of my fifty-year journey toward relevance I have continued to believe that 'world politics' connotes more exactly than 'international relations' the boundaries of my intellectual concerns."[51] He noted that World War II and the Cold War had obscured the limitations of the state-centric model but that something resembling the Chicago School perspective seemed to resurface with the reduction in tensions during the 1970s. International political economy, neo-realism, regimes and a variety of other contemporary terms implicitly or explicitly recognized the transnational, not merely interstate, character of world politics. In closing this essay, one of his last, he acknowledged that it was essential to understand the behavior of great powers in a world of states, but he insisted that "putting people back into our model world of states is more difficult, but no less essential."[52]

Pragmatic Meliorism and Contemporary World Issues

Force, Peace and Security

Much of Fox's scholarly work focused on, in his words, "the peacetime role of force, and especially American force, in promoting and maintaining national and international security."[53] His first book, *The Super-Powers: The United States, Britain and the Soviet Union—Their Responsibility for Peace*, which he wrote in 1944, was about "armed power in the post-war world."[54] The thrust of the book was that these three powers have special responsibilities for whatever peace and order were established after the war. Clearly, it was a Concert of Europe model of the post-war order, although he never used that term. He argued that the organization of post-war Europe required not disarmament but the collaboration of the superpowers and the exercise of their power in a responsible and moderate way, that is, as a means to security, not domination. The task was not "to emasculate the surviving great powers,"

---

50. Fox, "A Middle Western Isolationist-Internationalist's Journey toward Relevance," p. 236.
51. *Ibid.*, p.241.
52. *Ibid.*, p.242.
53. Fox, "A Middle Western Isolationist-Internationalist's Journey," p. 241.
54. Fox, *The Super-Powers*, p. 10.

he wrote. It was "to seek a definition of the national interest of each in such terms that each will find it possible to collaborate with the others to maintain a stable and just world order."[55]

Fox erred in his prediction that Britain would be one of the superpowers, but he correctly anticipated the "two-sidedness" of world politics after 1945.[56] He pointed out that it had taken World War II to demonstrate the true strength of American and Soviet power, and that the end of the war was likely to bring into sharper relief these two aggregations of power. "It will be commonplace after this war, he predicted,"to speak of the United States and the Soviet Union as the 'Big Two' whose falling-out will be the curtain-raiser for the Third World War."[57] The greatest danger, he believed, was not that either of the two would deliberately and directly seek conflict with each other because it would be clear that such a conflict would be a catastrophe to both. Even in this pre-nuclear era he estimated that the victory of one over the other would "involve the sacrifice of other values for the loss of which military victory would hardly compensate."[58] He saw the greatest danger in the possibility of the two powers being drawn indirectly or reluctantly into a war—either by involvement in a third-party conflict or by the leadership of one country becoming convinced that conflict with the other was inevitable. It is notable that a group of scholars writing 45 years later considered these two scenarios, now called "catalytic" and "pre-emptive war," respectively, to be the most likely way in which a nuclear war between the United States and the Soviet Union might begin.[59]

Fox's attitude toward the Soviet Union at the end of World War II was a good example of his pragmatic meliorism. He believed that Soviet cooperation in maintaining peace was possible; it was "neither to be assumed nor to be rejected in advance."[60] He acknowledged that the Soviet Union might embark upon expansionist policies but suggested that the United States could avoid policies which were most likely to encourage the Soviet Union in that direction. It was important for the

---

55. *Ibid.*, p.9.
56. Fox, "A Middle Western Isolationist -Internationalist's Journey toward Relevance," p. 239; Fox. "The Superpowers Then and Now," *International Journal* 35, No. 3 (Summer, 1980) pp.417-436.
57. Fox, *The Super-Powers*, p.101
58. *Ibid.*, p.100.
59. Albert Carnesdale, et al, *Living with Nuclear Weapons* (New York: Bantam Books, 1983) pp.53-59.
60. Fox, *The Super-Powers*, p.85.

United States to try "to understand Soviet objectives and to discover the extent to which these objectives can be reconciled with American objectives."[61] His hopes for superpower collaboration turned out to be too optimistic, but he insisted in 1979 that the idea "could not be dismissed in advance as impractical."[62]

In his exchange in the *American Scholar* in 1948 he criticized those who, on the one hand, refused to consider any of the Soviet Union's security concerns and those who, on the other hand, advocated unlimited concessions. The challenge to American policy makers, he insisted, was to steer some middle course between these two extremes, to find the right mix between firmness and conciliation.[63]

Fox took a similar pragmatic approach to other post-war issues, notably the international control of atomic energy and the establishment of the United Nations. He argued in both cases that since a world authority which could enforce its will on the major powers was not attainable by any desirable means, any workable, acceptable proposals for organized international cooperation would have to reflect the existing balance of interests.[64] Accordingly, he criticized the Baruch plan for requiring the Soviet Union to surrender its veto on enforcement measures for control of atomic weapons.[65] Great Power veto rights on international peace and security issues were an inescapable fact, whether there was a formal provision for it or not. For the same reasons he defended the great power veto in the United Nations Security Council.[66] In an article assessing the United Nations after five years he suggested that the organization had been "oversold" by the creation of expectations that it

---

61. *Ibid.*, p.84.
62. W.T.R. Fox, *Foresight and Hindsight: 1939-79* (Canberra, Australia: Australian National University, 1980) p.21. This is the published version of the Arthur Yencken Memorial Lectures, 20 and 27 July 1979 at the Australian National University.
63. Fox, "The Reconciliation of the Desirable and the Possible," p.213.
64. See for examples the following works: Fox, "Collective Enforcement of Peace and Security," *American Political Science Review* 39, no. 3 (October 1945); "The Super-Powers at San Francisco," *The Review of Politics*, (January, 1946); "Atomic Energy and International Relations," in William F. Ogburn, ed., *Technology and International Relations* (Chicago: University of Chicago Press, 1949); "The International Control of Atomic Weapons," in Bernard Brodie, ed., *The Absolute Weapon* (New York: Harcourt, Brace and Company, 1946); 'The Struggle for Atomic Control," (New York: Public Affairs Committee, 1947); "The United Nations in the Era of Total Diplomacy," *International Organization* 5, no. 2 (1951).
65. Fox, "The Struggle for Atomic Control," p.13.
66. Fox, "The United Nations in the Era of Total Diplomacy," pp.266-267.

would provide an escape from power politics. The result was cynicism and disillusionment when the U.N. became an arena for great power rivalry and a political forum for Afro-Asian nations.[67]

Civil-Military Relations and American Security

With the onset of the Cold War, Fox focused his attention on American national security policy, particularly the relationship between civilian and military leadership in the formulation of policy. His many articles on this subject stressed the need for peacetime military preparedness in an age of increasingly sophisticated military weapons.[68] Preparedness meant that resources to deter aggression, as well as to protect the nation's security, must be mobilized and available well in advance of any actual war crisis. He argued that the complexity of weapons and the necessity for complete mobilization had lengthened the time required to build up military capabilities and these were needed as much to deter the aggressor as to defeat him.[69] Equally important to Fox was the need for an effective policy-making structure and process which integrated civilian and military perspectives and coordinated military planning for the use of force with foreign policy objectives.

In his writings Fox identified two constraints on American efforts to develop this kind of preparedness. The first was a set of attitudes about civil-military relations and national security policy which he called the "liberal-civilian mind."[70] According to this perspective, military preparedness in peacetime increases the likelihood of war and poses threats to a nation's liberties. The tendency to regard a strong army as a greater threat than any external enemy was "deeply rooted in our Anglo-American heritage," but was obsolete in the second half of the twentieth century, he maintained.[71]

The other constraint on effective policy making for national security was the absence of scholarly attention to the problem. In an article written in *World Politics* in 1955 he lamented the fact that scholarship and journalism did not play nearly as important a role in national security policy as in other policy areas. It was extremely important, he insisted, that political scientists devote more attention to "the process by which

---

67. *Ibid.*, p.271 and *American Study of International Relations*, p.62.
68. See, for example, Fox, "Civil-Military Relations Research: The SSRC Committee and its Research Survey," *World Politics* 6, no. 2 (1954); "Civilians, Soldiers, and American Military Policy," *World Politics* 7, no. 3 (1955); "Representativeness and Efficiency: Dual Problem of Civil-Military Relations," *Political Science Quarterly* 76, no. 3 (1961).
69. Fox, "Civilians, Soldiers, and American Military Policy," p.408.
70. *Ibid.*, pp.408-409; "Representativeness and Efficiency," pp.335-356.
71. Fox, "Civilians, Soldiers, and American Military Policy," pp.408-409.

technical military considerations and civilian policy considerations are fused to determine how big and what kind of military apparatus the United States is to have and where and for what purposes it is to be used."[72]

The real challenge in civil-military relations, as Fox viewed it, was not so much civilian supremacy as civilian competence to understand and evaluate technical military recommendations in light of non-military considerations.[73] The way to balance civilian and military influence was not to reduce military participation in high-level decisions but to improve civilian technical competence and understanding of military problems. At the same time members of the professional military must develop greater awareness of the policy implications of the various courses of action they are likely to recommend on technical grounds.[74] The role of universities and the press was critical in developing the kind of sophistication on national security issues that leaders and the attentive public needed to make discriminating responses to military recommendations.

The Calculus of Policy Making

Fox's concern for a more rational national security policy-making process led him to comment on a variety of other topics besides civil-military relations, such as arms control war termination, and NATO. To obtain results more in accordance with their intentions and expectations, Fox maintained, statesmen must perpetually engage in a process of weighing costs and gains to values from alternative policies and courses of action.[75] Cooperation in the competitive international political system is sometimes possible when cost-benefit calculations, independently arrived at by different actors, coincide. In an article which appeared in *Daedalus* in 1960, Fox discussed the criteria for evaluating arms control agreements and the conditions which were likely to facilitate or hinder their successful conclusion. The one overriding requirement for a feasible arms control proposal, Fox wrote, was "that each indispensable participant, using its own calculus, calculate that it gains more than it yields by entering and remaining within a system of control."[76] He considered this condition to be more important than the level of trust between the participants or any specific characteristics of the agreement.

---

72. *Ibid.*, p.402.
73. *Ibid.*, p.406.
74. *Ibid.*, p.366.
75. Fox, *American Study of International Relations*, p.70.
76. Fox, "Political and Diplomatic Prerequisites of Arms Control," *Daedalus*, (Fall 1960), p.1006.

Fox was also interested in the calculus of decision making which brings long, protracted wars to an end. "Least-cost, highest-return, earliest-termination strategies call for a continuing calculus," he wrote in an article on this subject in the last year of the Vietnam war. "On any reasonable estimate, sacrifices still to be endured must not appear disproportionate to gains still to be realized."[77] In a lecture given some years later, he explained how certain American attitudes regarding war made the difficult task of ending a large-scale, protracted limited war in the nuclear age almost impossible. The belief that "only crusades are worth fighting and that whatever is worth fighting for is worth whatever it costs," encourages the view that any particular war must be ended in such a way that it will "never again" have to be refought.[78] The "myth of the risen domino," that is, the view that a domino propped up in one part of the world will prevent dominoes from having to be propped up elsewhere, discourages any calculations about "how much if any further sacrifice would be likely to yield gains commensurate with that sacrifice." The "risen domino" perspective, he wrote, "leaves little opportunity to consider that those who have not yet died will be the ones who really 'die in vain.'"[79]

Conflict Resolution and International Security

The great challenge to statesmen, diplomats and scholars in the 1980s, Fox asserted in his autobiography, is "to discover how to have less violence less of the time while still preserving and promoting the values that in the past they have believed worth fighting a war to maintain."[80] The problem with the doctrinal realists, he wrote in his essay on E.H. Carr, is that they can explain why there is conflict from time to time in the multiple sovereignty state system, but they do not shed much light on why these conflicts are sometimes settled peacefully.[81] Fox's scholarly interest in conflict resolution led him to study not only the conditions under which protracted war might be terminated but also the political processes by which allied states resolve their conflicting claims. In his work on the North Atlantic Treaty Organization and the "stable but unequal" relationship between the United States and Canada he con-

---

77. Fox, "The Cause of Peace and Conditions of War," *The Annals of the American Academy of Political and Social Science* 392 (November 1970) p.11.
78. Fox, *Foresight and Hindsight*, p.36.
79. *Ibid.*, p.37.
80. Fox, "A Middle Western Isolationist-Internationalist's Journey toward Relevance," p.238.
81. Fox, "E. H. Carr and Political Realism," p.13.

sidered two factors to be particularly important. One was a certain moderation in the exercise of U.S. power by resisting temptations to dominate the relationship. The other was the growth of trans-national and trans-governmental interest groups which tend to dilute government to government confrontation and help to make collaboration self-sustaining.[82]

Although Fox devoted a great deal of attention to problems of North American and Western security, he also thought in the broader terms of international security. The "depressing extrapolation of trends" in population growth, the exhaustion of unrenewable natural resources, and the widening gap between the rich and poor countries posed serious threats to the security of the planet, he warned in the Arthur Yencken Lectures in Australia; but these extrapolations are "best treated as hypotheses to be disconfirmed by appropriate national and international action."[83] He believed that new institutions and better political skills were necessary to deal with these challenges, as well as an increased willingness on the part of the industrialized countries to work with, rather than merely dictate solutions to, the developing countries in their search for economic security.[84] He suggested that North-South relations might one day require the same unremitting attention as East-West relations had in the past and warned that the material benefits of technological innovation must be shared with the developing countries. "A world of plenty may or may not be a world of peace," he wrote in his article on science, technology and international politics, "but unless certain minimum aspirations of less advantaged peoples are met, the prospects for peace and order will be dim indeed."[85]

The Relevance of W.T.R. Fox

For nearly a half century Fox analyzed the world scene—sometimes with hindsight, sometimes with foresight.[86] Viewed retrospectively, his wise, sound and sensible analyses have stood the test of time remarkably well. His pluralist conception of "world politics" anticipated the transnationalist literature of the 1970s. He foresaw the emergence of the

---

82. Fox, *A Continent Apart: The United States and Canada in World Politics* (Toronto: University of Toronto Press), 1985, p.111; W.T.R. Fox and Annette Baker Fox, *NATO and the Range of American Choice* (New York: Columbia University Press, 1967) pp.295, 299, 306-307.
83. Fox, *Foresight and Hindsight*, p.68.
84. *Ibid.*, p.68-86; "A Middle-Western Isolationist-Internationalist's Journey toward Relevance," p.242.
85. Fox, "Science, Technology and International Politics," *International Studies Quarterly* 12, no. 1 (March 1968) p.15.
86. See a summary of these views in *Foresight and Hindsight*.

superpower, a new kind of actor in the post World War II international system, and the book which introduced the idea contributed a new word to the English language. This work did more than coin a phrase. It added a new concept to the subject of international relations and pointed to a significant transformation in the international system. Fox was one of a small number of international relations scholars who examined the reciprocal relationship of science and international politics.[87] He was a keen observer of technological innovation and its implications for the international system. He was one of the first international relations scholars to write about the impact of nuclear weapons on international politics and the first major book on the subject, *The Absolute Weapon*, edited by Bernard Brodie, contained an essay by Fox. He wrote about all-round gains in security and about policy making as the rational calculation of gains and losses from alternative courses of action long before the terminology of positive-sum games, payoffs and cost-benefit analyses permeated the literature of international relations.

The various elements of Fox's pragmatic meliorist orientation which have been extracted from his collection of scholarly works may be summarized with the following set of propositions. Politics is a continuous and ubiquitous struggle for scarce values; hence conflict is and will continue to be a pervasive feature of international relations. The protection and promotion of values requires the ability and willingness to use force, since war is the ultimate method of resolving conflict. Military capabilities, like other elements of power, must be geared toward policy objectives. Policy making requires rational calculations about choices among alternative courses of action and the implications of each for the values to be promoted. World politics is not "an iron fund of values to be contested"; it can sometimes be a positive-sum game with all-round gains in the pursuit of certain values, such as security.[88] International conflict can be moderated at times by increasing the options available or by reinterpreting the national interest. Science and technology can help to expand the range of choice and reduce sources of conflict by increasing some of the scarce resources to be allocated. Social scientists can increase the rationality of policy making by helping to clarify the range of choice available and the consequences of alternative courses of action.

These propositions and the world view they comprise reflect an unresolved tension in the American study of international relations. The

---

87. See Fox, "Science, Technology and Politics."
88. *Ibid.*, p.14.

discipline took on a highly normative character as it emerged in the curricula of American universities, and a strong voluntaristic tradition, which Fox described, has persisted in its scholarship .[89] A recent collection of autobiographies of leading scholars in international relations reinforces that point. One of the editors observes at the end of the volume that a characteristic widely shared among the contributors was a "genuine concern for the real world," the "normative hope of being able to make a difference."[90] This characteristic may be a distinguishing feature of the discipline, he suggests. Yet, the realist image of a system of sovereign states competing for power, security and other scarce values remains the dominant paradigm, with all of its implications for the limits to change. Fox articulated this tension throughout his scholarly career. His focus on the "margin of manipulable choice" was an effort to steer a middle course between the excesses of voluntarism and determinism. His pragmatic meliorism combined the optimism of an activist with the skepticism of a scientist. His work assures us that even if change is possible only at the margins, it is worth making the effort.

89. W.T.R. Fox and Annette Baker Fox, "The Teaching of International Relations in the United States," *World Politics* 13, no. 3 (April 1961) pp.339-359.
90. Joseph Kruzel, "Reflections on the Journeys," in Kruzel and Rosenau, eds., *Journeys through World Politics*, p.502.

REALIST THOUGHT AND NEOREALIST THEORY

by Kenneth N. Waltz[1]

Exploring various ways to forward the study of international politics was one of William T.R. Fox's many interests. In 1957, he organized a series of seminars that brought together a number of established scholars, among them Paul Nitze, Hans Morgenthau and Charles Kindleberger, along with such younger scholars as Robert W. Tucker, Morton Kaplan and Martin Wight, to discuss problems in the study of international-political theory and its relation to the behavior of states. A volume edited and co-authored by Bill was the tangible product of the colloquium.[2] As one of the many students and colleagues who benefitted from Bill's ideas, encouragement, and support, I offer this essay as a small contribution toward clarifying some problems in the framing and applying of international political theory.

I begin by looking at a theoretical breakthrough in a related field: economics. Realists and neorealists represent two of the major theoretical approaches followed by students of international politics in the past half century or so. They encountered problems similar to those the Physiocrats began to solve in France in the middle of the eighteenth century. Students of international politics have had an extraordinarily difficult time casting their subject in theoretical terms. Looking first at an example of comparable difficulties surmounted in a related field may be instructive.

How Economic Theory Became Possible

Difficulties common to earlier economists and twentieth-century political scientists are revealed by examining Sir Josiah Child's *A New Discourse*, written mainly in the years 1668 to 1670.[3] Child dealt with a striking question. Why, he wondered, did the prosperity of the Dutch surpass that of the English? In casting about for an answer, he seized on what seemed to be a compelling fact: namely, that the Dutch rate of interest had been lower than the English rate. The reasoning used to

1.   I should like to thank David Schleicher for his help on this paper
2.   William T.R. Fox, co-author and ed., *Theoretical Aspects of International Relations* (Notre Dame, IN: University of Notre Dame Press, 1959).
3.   Josiah Child, *A New Discourse of Trade*, 4th ed. (London: J. Hodges, 1740). See also William Letwin, *Sir Josiah Child, Merchant Economist* (Cambridge, MA: Harvard University Press, 1959).

establish the causal role of the rate of interest is correlative and sequential. Child tried to show that the prosperity of various countries varies inversely with prevailing rates of interest. He then established the causal direction by arguing that the expected changes in the level of prosperity followed upon changes in rates of interest.

Child's work is the kind of pre-theoretical effort that provides stimulus to, and material for, later theories. That is its merit. It is, however, the kind of work that can neither provide satisfactory explanations nor lead to the construction of theory. We can profit by noticing why this is so. Child tried to establish a necessary relation between the rate of interest and the level of prosperity. Other economists picked different factors as their favorite causes—the accumulation of bullion, the fertility of the population or the soil, the industry of the people, the level of rents, or whatever. But none was able to show why the relation between the chosen factor or factors and the condition to be accounted for necessarily held. Child, for example, could not supply an answer to this now obvious question: Why doesn't a rise in interest rates attract capital, ultimately lowering its price as with commodities? He could not say whether the association he claimed to have found was causal or coincidental. He could not say whether other factors in play may have caused interest rates and national prosperity to move in opposite directions. Innumerable explanations for the observed relation were available. Pre-physiocratic economists could only cast about for sequences and associations that seemed to pertain within or across countries. They could at best hope to formulate plausible explanations of particular outcomes. They had no way of relating the parts of an economy to one another and to the economy as a whole.

The first step forward was, as it had to be, to invent the concept of an economy as distinct from the society and the polity in which it is embedded. Some will always complain that it is artificial to think of an economy separate from its society and polity. Such critics are right. Yet the critics miss the point. Theory is artifice. A theory is an intellectual construction by which we select facts and interpret them. The challenge is to bring theory to bear on facts in ways that permit explanation and prediction. That can only be accomplished by distinguishing between theory and fact. Only if this distinction is made can theory be used to examine and interpret facts.

In the pre-theoretic era of economics, more and more information became available in the form of reported, or purported, facts, and more and more attempts were made to account for them. But differences of explanation remained unreconciled and explanations of particular processes and outcomes did not add up to an understanding of how a national economy works. In a remarkable survey in which the historical development, the sociological setting, and the scientific qualities of economic thought are brought together, Joseph Schumpeter described the best economic literature of that earlier time as having "all the freshness and fruitfulness of direct observation." But, he added, it also "shows all the helplessness of mere observation by itself."[4] Information accumulated, but arguments, even perceptive ones about propositions that might have been developed as theories, did not add up to anything more than ideas about particulars occasioned by current controversies.

Child was better than most economists of his day, although not as good as the best. The most creative economists were frustrated by the condition that Schumpeter described. The seventeenth-century economist Sir William Petty, for example, felt the frustration. Schumpeter described him as creating "for himself theoretical tools with which he tried to force a way through the undergrowth of facts."[5] To eliminate useless and misleading "facts" was an important endeavor, but not a sufficient one. What blocked the progress of economic understanding was neither too little nor too much knowledge but rather the lack of a certain kind of knowledge.

The answers to factual questions pose puzzles that theory may hope to solve and provide materials for theorists to work with. But the work begins only when theoretical questions are posed. Theory cannot be fashioned from the answers to such factual questions as: What follows upon, or is associated with, what. Instead, answers have to be sought to such theoretical questions as these: How does this thing work? How does it all hang together? These questions cannot usefully be asked unless one has some idea of what the "thing" or the "it" might be. Theory becomes possible only if various objects and processes, movements and events, acts and interactions, are viewed as forming a domain that can be studied in its own right. Clearing away useless facts was not enough; something new had to be created. An invention was needed that would permit economic phenomena to be seen as distinct processes, that would permit an economy to be viewed as a realm of affairs marked off from social and political life.

This the Physiocrats first achieved. Francois Quesnay's famous economic table is a picture depicting the circulation of wealth among the productive and unproductive classes of society, but it is a picture of the

---

4.   Joseph Schumpeter, *Economic Doctrine and Method: An Historical Sketch*, R. Aris, trans. (New York: Oxford University Press, 1967) p.24.
5.   *Ibid.*, p.30.

unseen and the unseeable.[6] Certain cycles are well-known facts of economic life—cycles of sowing and harvesting, of mining, refining, forging, and manufacturing. But such a direct simplification of observable processes is not what Quesnay's table presents. It presents, instead, the essential qualities of an economy in picture form. The Physiocrats were the first to think of an economy as a self-sustaining whole made up of interacting parts and repeated activities. To do so, they had to make radical simplifications—for example, by employing a psychology that saw people simply as seeking the greatest satisfaction from the least effort. They invented the concepts they needed. Their notion of a "social product" can well be described as the intellectual creation of the unobservable and the nonexistent. No one can point to a social product. It is not an identifiable quantity of goods but is instead a concept whose validity can be established only through its role in a theory that yields an improved understanding of the economy.

The Physiocrats developed concepts comprising innumerable particularities and contingencies without examining them. Among these concepts were the durable notions of distribution and circulation. The quaint and crude appearance of some physiocratic ideas should not obscure the radical advance that their theory represented. Economists had found it hard to get a theoretical hold on their subject. In pre-physiocratic economics, as Schumpeter said, "the connecting link of economic causality and an insight into the inner necessities and the general character of economics were missing. It was possible to consider the individual acts of exchange, the phenomenon of money, and the question of protective tariffs as economic problems, but it was impossible to see the total process which unfolds itself in a particular economic period. Before the Physiocrats appeared on the scene, only local symptoms on the economic body, as it were, had been perceived." Only the parts of an economy could be dealt with. It was therefore necessary again in Schumpeter's words, "to derive an explanatory principle from each separate complex of facts—as it were in a gigantic struggle with them—and it was at best possible merely to sense the great general contexts."[7]

International Politics: Beyond the Theoretical Pale

What the Physiocrats did for economics is exactly what Raymond Aron and Hans Morgenthau, two of the most theoretically self-conscious

---

6. Francois Quesnay was the foremost Physiocrat. His *Tableau Oeconomique* was published in 1758.
7. Schumpeter, *op. cit.*, pp.42-44, 46.

traditional realists, believed to be impossible for students of international politics to accomplish. Aron drew a sharp distinction between the study of economics and the study of international politics. The latter he assigned to the category of history, which deals with unique events and situations, and of sociology, which deals with non-logical actions and searches for general relations among them. In contrast to economics, Aron said international politics suffers from the following difficulties:

- Innumerable factors affect the international system and no distinction can be made between those that are internal and those that are external to it.
- States, the principal international actors, cannot be endowed with a single aim.
- No distinction can be drawn between dependent and independent variables.
- No accounting identities—such as investment equals savings—can be devised.
- No mechanism exists for the restoration of a disrupted equilibrium.
- There is no possibility of prediction and manipulation with identified means leading to specified goals.[8]

Do the reasons cited eliminate the possibility of devising a theory of international politics? If so, then economics would have been similarly hampered. Aron did not relate obvious differences between economics and politics to the requirements of theory construction. He merely identified differences, in the confident belief that because of them no international-political theory is possible.

Morgenthau's theoretical stance is similar to Aron's. Morgenthau dealt persuasively with major problems and with issues of enduring importance. He had the knack of singling out salient facts and constructing causal analyses around them. He sought "to paint a picture of foreign policy" that would present its "rational essence," abstracting from personality and prejudice, and, especially in democracies, from the importunities of popular opinion that "impair the rationality of foreign policy."[9] He was engaged, as it were, "in a gigantic struggle" with the facts, seeking "to derive an explanatory principle" from them. Like Petty, he forged concepts that might help him "force a way through the undergrowth of facts," such concepts as "national interest" and "interest

---

8. Raymond Aron, "What is a Theory of International Relations?" *Journal of International Affairs* 21, no. 2 (1967) pp.185-206.
9. Hans J. Morgenthau, *Politics Among Nations*, 5th ed. (New York: Alfred A. Knopf, 1972) p.7.

defined as power." Like Child, Morgenthau and other realists failed to take the fateful step beyond developing concepts to the fashioning of a recognizable theory.

Morgenthau described his purpose as being "to present a theory of international politics."[10] Elements of a theory are presented, but never a theory. Morgenthau at once believed in "the possibility of developing a rational theory"and remained deeply skeptical about that possibility. Without a concept of the whole, he could only deal with the parts. As is rather commonly done, he confused the problem of explaining foreign policy with the problem of developing a theory of international politics. He then concluded that international political theory is difficult if not impossible to contrive.[11] He was fond of repeating Blaise Pascal's remark that the history of the world would have been different had Cleopatra's nose been a bit shorter, and then asking, "how do you systemize that?"[12] His appreciation of the role of the accidental and the occurrence of the unexpected in politics dampened his theoretical aspirations.

Neorealism's response is that, while difficulties abound, some that seem most daunting lie in misapprehensions about theory. Theory obviously cannot explain the accidental or account for unexpected events. Theories deal in regularities and repetitions and are possible only if these can be identified. As a realist, Morgenthau maintained "the autonomy of politics," but he failed to develop the concept and apply it to international politics.[13] A theory is a depiction of the organization of a domain and of the connections among its parts.[14] A theory indicates that some factors are more important than others and specifies relations among them. In reality, everything is related to everything else, and one domain cannot be separated from others. Theory isolates one realm from all others in order to deal with it intellectually. To isolate a realm is a precondition to developing a theory that will explain what goes on within it. The theoretical ambitions of Morgenthau, as of Aron, were forestalled by his belief that the international political domain cannot be marked off from others for the purpose of constructing a theory.

---

10. *Ibid.*, p.3.
11. Morgenthau, *Truth and Power* (New York: Praeger, 1970) pp.253-258.
12. Morgenthau, "International Relations: Quantitative and Qualitative Approaches," in Norman Palmer, ed., *A Design for International Relations Research: Scope, Theory, Methods, and Relevance* (Philadelphia: American Academy of Political and Social Science, 1970) p.78.
13. Morgenthau (1972), *op. cit.*, p.12.
14. Ludwig Boltzman, "Theories as Representations," excerpt, Rudolph Weingartner, trans., in Arthur Danto and Sidney Morgenbesser, eds., *Philosophy of Science* (Cleveland, OH: World, 1960).

In summarizing Aron's argument, I have put the first three points in sequence because they are closely interrelated. The single word "complexity" suggests the impediment that concerns him. If "economic, political, and social variables"[15] enter into the international system, as surely they do, if states have not one but many goals, as surely they have, if separating dependent from independent variables and distinguishing effects from causes is an uncertain undertaking, as surely it is—then one can never hope to fashion a theory.

Complexity, however, does not work against theory. Rather, theory is a means of dealing with complexity. Economists can deal with it because they long ago solved Aron's first problem. Given the concept of a market—a bounded economic domain—they have been able to develop further concepts and draw connections among them. Because realists did not solve the first problem, they could not satisfactorily deal with the next two. Men have many motives. If all or very many of them must always be taken into account, economic theory becomes impossible. "Economic man" was therefore created. Men were assumed to be single-minded, economic maximizers. An assumption or a set of assumptions is necessary. In making assumptions about men's (or states') motivations, the world must be drastically simplified; subtleties must be rudely pushed aside, and reality must be grossly distorted. Descriptions strive for accuracy; assumptions are brazenly false. The assumptions on which theories are built are radical simplifications of the world and are useful only because they are such. Any radical simplification conveys a false impression of the world.

Aron's second and third points must be amended. Actors cannot realistically be endowed with a single aim, but we can only know by trying whether or not they can usefully be so endowed for purposes of constructing a theory. Political studies are not different from other studies in the realm of human affairs. We can make bold assumptions about motives, we can guess which few of many factors are salient, we can arbitrarily specify relations of dependence and independence among variables. We may even expect that the more complex and intricate the matters being studied are the stronger the urge "to be simple-minded" would become.[16]

If international politics is a recalcitrant realm for the theorist, then its special difficulties lie elsewhere than in the first three of Aron's points. Are they perhaps found in the last three? As the fourth of Aron's

---

15.   Aron, *op. cit.*, p.198.
16.   "To be simple-minded" is Anatol Rapoport's first rule for the construction of mathematical models. See his "Lewis F. Richardson's Mathematical Theory of War," *Journal of Conflict Resolution* 1, no. 3 (1957) pp.275-276.

impediments to theory, I have listed the absence of "accounting identities" or, as others have put it, the lack of a unit of measure and a medium of exchange in which goals can be valued and instruments comparatively priced. Political capability and political effect, whether or not conceived of simply in terms of power, cannot be expressed in units, such as dollars, that would have clear meaning and be applicable to different instruments and ends. Yet one finds in Adam Smith, for example, no numbers that are essential to his theory. Indeed, one finds hardly any numbers at all, and thus no "accounting identities." That supply equals demand or that investment equals savings are general propositions or purported laws that theory may explain. Stating the laws does not depend on counting, weighing, or measuring anything. As Frank Knight well and rightly wrote:

> Pure theory, in economics as in any field, is abstract; it deals with forms only, in complete abstraction from content. On the individual side, economic theory takes men with (a) any wants whatever, (b) any resources whatever, and (c) any system of technology whatever, and develops principles of economic behaviour. The validity of its "laws" does not depend on the actual conditions or data, with respect to any of these three elementary phases of economic action.[17]

In politics, not everything can be counted or measured, but some things can be. That may be helpful in the application of theories but has nothing to do with their construction.

The fifth and sixth difficulties discovered by Aron seem to tell us something substantive about politics rather than about its amenability to theory and its status as science. In classical economic theory, no mechanism—that is, no agent or institution—restores a lost equilibrium. Classical and neoclassical economists were microtheorists—market and exchange relations emerge from the exercise of individual choice. The economy is produced by the interaction of persons and firms; it cannot be said to have goals or purposes of its own.[18] Governments may, of course, act to restore a lost equilibrium. So may powerful persons or firms within the economy. But at this point we leave the realm of theory and enter the realm of practice—or "sociology" as Aron uses the term. "Any concrete study of international relations is sociological," he avers.[19] The

---

17. Frank Hyneman Knight, *The Ethics of Competition and Other Essays* (London: George Allen & Unwin, 1936) p.281.
18. See also James M. Buchanan, "An Individualistic Theory of Political Process," in David Easton, ed., *Varieties of Political Theory* (Englewood Cliffs, NJ: Prentice-Hall, 1966) pp.25-26.
19. Aron, *op.cit.*, p.198.

characteristic attaches to concrete studies and not simply to the study of international politics.

Aron identifies science with the ability to predict and control.[20] Yet theories of evolution predict nothing in particular. Astronomers do predict (although without controlling), but what entitles astronomy to be called a science is not the ability to predict but the ability to specify causes, to state the theories and laws by which the predictions are made. Economic theory is impressive even when economists show themselves to be unreliable in prediction and prescription alike. Since theory abstracts from much of the complication of the world in an effort to explain it, the application of theory in any realm is a perplexing and uncertain matter.

Aron's first three problems can be solved, although in the realm of theory all solutions are tentative. Aron's last three difficulties are not impediments to the construction of theory but rather to its application and testing.

International Politics: Within the Theoretical Pale

The new realism, in contrast to the old, begins by proposing a solution to the problem of distinguishing factors internal to international political systems from those that are external. Theory isolates one realm from others in order to deal with it intellectually. By depicting an international-political system as a whole, with structural and unit levels at once distinct and connected, neorealism establishes the autonomy of international politics and thus makes a theory about it possible.[21] Neorealism develops the concept of a system's structure which at once bounds the domain that students of international politics deal with and enables them to see how the structure of the system, and variations in it, affect the interacting units and the outcomes they produce. International structure emerges from the interaction of states and then constrains them from taking certain actions while propelling them toward others.

The concept of structure is based on the fact that units differently juxtaposed and combined behave differently and in interacting produce different outcomes. International structures are defined, first, by the ordering principle of the system, in our case anarchy, and second, by the distribution of capabilities across units. In an anarchic realm, structures are defined in terms of their major units. International structures vary with significant changes in the number of great powers. Great powers

---

20. *Ibid.*, p. 201. See also Morgenthau (1970), *op. cit.*, p.253.
21. Neorealism is sometimes referred to as structural realism. Throughout this essay I refer to my own formulation of neorealist theory. See esp. chs. 5-6 of *Theory of International Politics* (Reading, MA. Addison-Wesley, 1979).

are marked off from others by the combined capabilities (or power) they command. When their number changes consequentially, the calculations and behaviors of states, and the outcomes their interactions produce, vary.

The idea that international politics can be thought of as a system with a precisely defined structure is neorealism's fundamental departure from traditional realism. The spareness of the definition of international structure has attracted criticism. Robert Keohane asserts that neorealist theory "can be modified progressively to attain closer correspondence with reality."[22] In the most sensitive and insightful essay on neorealism that I have read, Barry Buzan asks whether the logic of neorealism completely captures "the main features of the international political system." He answers this way:

> "The criticisms of Ruggie, Keohane, and others suggest that it does not, because their concerns with factors such as dynamic density, information richness, communication facilities, and such like do not obviously fit into Waltz's ostensibly 'systemic' theory."[23]

One wonders whether such factors as these can be seen as concepts that might become elements of a theory? "Dynamic density" would seem to be the most promising candidate. Yet dynamic density is not a part of a theory about one type of society or another. Rather it is a condition that develops in greater or lesser degree within and across societies. If the volume of transactions grows sufficiently, it will disrupt a simple society and transform it into a complex one. Dynamic density is not part of a theory of any society. Rather it is a social force developing in society that under certain circumstances may first disrupt and then transform it.[24] The "such likes" mentioned by Buzan would not fit into any theory. Can one imagine how demographic trends, information richness and international institutions could be thrown into a theory? No theory can contain the "such likes," but if a theory is any good, it helps us to understand and explain them, to estimate their significance and to gauge their effects. Moreover, any theory leaves some things unexplained, and no theory enables one to move directly and easily from theory to application. Theories, one must add, are not useful merely because they may help one

---

22. Robert O. Keohane, "Theory of World Politics: Structural Realism and Beyond" in Keohane, ed., *Neorealism and Its Critics* (New York: Columbia University Press, 1986) p.191.
23. Barry Buzan, "Systems, Structures and Units: Reconstructing Waltz's Theory of International Politics," unpublished paper (April 1988) p.35.
24. John G. Ruggie, "Continuity and Transformation in the World Polity," in Keohane, ed., *op. cit.*, pp.148-152; Waltz, "A Response to my Critics," pp.323-326. Waltz (1979), *op. cit., pp.126-128.*

to understand, explain, and sometimes predict the trend of events. Equally important, they help one to understand how a given system works.

To achieve "closeness of fit" would negate theory. A theory cannot fit the facts or correspond with the events it seeks to explain. The ultimate closeness of fit would be achieved by writing a finely detailed description of the world that interests us. Nevertheless, neorealism continues to be criticized for its omissions. A theory can be written only by leaving out most matters that are of practical interest. To believe that listing the omissions of a theory constitutes a valid criticism is to misconstrue the theoretical enterprise.

The question of omissions arises because I limit the second term that defines structure to the distribution of power across nations. Now and then critics point out that logically many factors other than power, such as governmental form or national ideology, can be cast in distributional terms. Obviously so, but logic alone does not write theories. The question is not what does logic permit, but what does this theory require? Considerations of power dominate considerations of ideology. In a structural theory, states are differently placed by their power and differences in placement help to explain both their behavior and their fates. In any political system, the distribution of the unit's capabilities is a key to explanation. The distribution of power is of special explanatory importance in self-help political systems because the units of the system are not formally differentiated with distinct functions specified as are the parts of hierarchic orders.

Barry Buzan raises questions about the adequacy "of defining structure within the relatively narrow sectoral terms of politics."[25] It may be that a better theory could be devised by differently drawing the borders of the domain to which it will apply, by adding something to the theory, by subtracting something from it, or by altering assumptions and rearranging the relations among a theory's concepts. But doing any or all of these things requires operations entirely different from the mere listing of omissions. Theory, after all, is mostly omissions. What is omitted cannot be added without thoroughly reworking the theory and turning it into a different one. Should one broaden the perspective of international-political theory to include economics? An international political-economic theory would presumably be twice as good as a theory of international politics alone. To fashion such a theory, one would have to show how the international political-economic domain can be marked off from others. One would first have to define its structures and then develop a theory to explain actions and outcomes within it. A political-

---

25. Buzan, *op. cit.*, p.11.

economic theory would represent a long step toward a general theory of international relations, but no one has shown how to take it.

Those who want to disaggregate power as defined in neorealist theory are either calling for a new theory, while failing to provide one, or are pointing to some of the knotty problems that arise in the testing and application of theory. In the latter case, they, like Aron, confuse difficulties in testing and applying theory with the problem of constructing one.[26] Critics of neorealist theory fail to understand that a theory is not a statement about everything that is important in international-political life, but rather a necessarily slender explanatory construct. Adding elements of practical importance would carry us back from a neorealist theory to a realist approach. The rich variety and wondrous complexity of international life would be reclaimed at the price of extinguishing theory.

Neorealism breaks with realism in four major ways. The first and most important one I have examined at some length. The remaining three I shall treat more briefly. They follow from, and are made possible by, the first one. Neorealism departs from traditional realism in the following additional ways: Neorealism produces a shift in causal relations, offers a different interpretation of power, and treats the unit level differently.

Theory and Reality

Causal Directions

Constructing theories according to different suppositions alters the appearance of whole fields of inquiry. A new theory draws attention to new objects of inquiry, interchanges causes and effects, and addresses different worlds. When John Hobson cast economics in macrotheoretical terms, he baffled his fellow economists. The London Extension Board would not allow him to offer courses on political economy because an economics professor who had read Hobson's book thought it "equivalent in rationality to an attempt to prove the flatness of the earth."[27] Hobson's figure was apt. Microtheory, the economic orthodoxy of the day, portrayed a world different from the one that Hobson's macrotheory revealed.

Similarly, the neorealist's world looks different from the one that earlier realists had portrayed. For realists, the world addressed is one of interacting states. For neorealists, interacting states can be adequately

---

26. See, for example., Joseph S. Nye, Jr., "Neorealism and Neoliberalism," in *World Politics* 40, no. 2, (January 1988) pp.241-245; Keohane, *op. cit.*, pp.184-200; Buzan, *op. cit.* pp.28-34.

27. John Maynard Keynes, *The General Theory of Employment, Interest, and Money* (London: Macmillan, 1951) pp.365-6.

studied only by distinguishing between structural and unit-level causes and effects. Structure becomes a new object of inquiry, as well as an occasion for argument. In the light of neorealist theory, means and ends are differently viewed, as are causes and effects. Realists think of causes running in one direction, from interacting states to the outcomes their acts and interactions produce. This is clearly seen in Morgenthau's "Six Principles of Political Realism," which form the substance of a chapter headed "A Realist Theory of International Politics."[28] Strikingly, one finds much said about foreign policy and little about international politics. The principles develop as Morgenthau searches for his well-known "rational outline, a map that suggests to us the possible meanings of foreign policy."[29] The principles are about human nature, about interest and power, and about questions of morality. Political realism offers the perspective in which the actions of statesmen are to be understood and judged. Morgenthau's work was in harmony with the developing political science of his day, although at the time this was not seen. Methodological presuppositions shape the conduct of inquiry. The political-science paradigm was becoming deeply entrenched. Its logic is preeminently behavioral. The established paradigm of any field indicates what facts to scrutinize and how they are interconnected. Behavioral logic explains political outcomes through examining the constituent parts of political systems. When Aron and other traditionalists insist that theorists' categories be consonant with actors' motives and perceptions, they are affirming the preeminently behavioral logic that their inquiries follow.[30] The characteristics and the interactions of behavioral units are taken to be the direct causes of political events, whether in the study of national or of international politics. Aron, Morgenthau and other realists tried to understand and explain international outcomes by examining the actions and interactions of the units, the states that populate the international arena and those who guide their policies. Realism's approach is primarily inductive. Neorealism is more heavily deductive.

Like classical economists before them, realists were unable to account for a major anomaly. Classical theory held that disequilibria would be righted by the working of market forces without need for governmental intervention. Hobson's, and later in fuller form John Maynard Keynes's, macroeconomic theory explained why in the natural course of events recovery from depressions was such a long time coming.[31] A similarly

---

28. Morgenthau (1972), *op. cit.*, pp.4-14.
29. *Ibid.*, p. 5.
30. See Waltz (1979), *op. cit., pp. 44, 47, 62*.
31. In his *General Theory*, Keynes gives Hobson full credit for setting forth the basic concepts of macroeconomic theory.

big anomaly in realist theory is seen in the attempt to explain alternations of war and peace. Like most students of international politics, realists infer outcomes from the salient attributes of the actors producing them. Governmental forms, economic systems, social institutions, political ideologies—hese are but a few examples of where the causes of war and peace have been found. Yet, although causes are specifically assigned, we know that states with every imaginable variation of economic institution, social custom, and political ideology have fought wars. If an indicated condition seems to have caused a given war, one must wonder what accounts for the repetition of wars even as their causes vary. Variations in the quality of the units are not linked directly to the outcomes their behaviors produce, nor are variations in patterns of interaction. Many, for example, have claimed that World War I was caused by the interaction of two opposed and closely balanced coalitions. But then many have claimed that World War II was caused by the failure of some states to right an imbalance of power by combining to counter an existing alliance. Over the centuries, the texture of international life has remained impressively, or depressingly, uniform even while profound changes were taking place in the composition of states which, according to realists, account for national behavior and international outcomes. Realists cannot explain the disjunction between supposed causes and observed effects. Neorealists can.

Neorealism contends that international politics can be understood only if the effects of structure are added to traditional realism's unit-level explanations. More generally, neorealism reconceives the causal link between interacting units and international outcomes. Neorealist theory shows that causes run not in one direction, from interacting units to outcomes produced, but rather in two directions. One must believe that some causes of international outcomes are located at the level of the interacting units. Since variations in unit-level causes do not correspond to variations in observed outcomes, one has to believe that some causes are located at the structural level of international politics as well. Realists cannot handle causation at a level above states because they fail to conceive of structure as a force that shapes and shoves the units. Causes at the level of units interact with those at the level of the structure and because they do so explanation at the level of units alone is bound to mislead. If one's theory allows for the handling of both unit-level and structure-level causes, then it can cope with both the changes and the continuities that occur in a system.

Power as Means and End

For many realists, the desire for power is rooted in the nature of man. Morgenthau recognized that given competition for scarce goods with no one to serve as arbiter, a struggle for power will ensue among the competitors, and that consequently the struggle for power can be explained without reference to the evil born in men. The struggle for power arises because people want things and not necessarily because of the evil in their desires. This he labels one of the two roots of conflict, but even while discussing it he pulls toward the "other root of conflict and concomitant evil"—the *animus dominandi*, the desire for power. He often considers man's drive for power as a datum more basic than the chance conditions under which struggles for power occur.[32]

The reasoning is faithful to Hobbes for whom the three causes of quarrels were competition, diffidence (i.e., distrust), and glory. Competition leads to fighting for gain, diffidence to fighting to keep what has been gained, glory to fighting for reputation. Because some hunger for power, it behooves others to cultivate their appetites.[33] For Morgenthau, as for Hobbes, even if one has plenty of power and is secure in its possession, more power is nevertheless wanted. As Morgenthau put it:

> Since the desire to attain a maximum of power is universal, all nations must always be afraid that their own miscalculations and the power increases of other nations might add up to an inferiority for themselves which they must at all costs try to avoid.[34]

Both Hobbes and Morgenthau see that conflict is in part situationally explained, but both believe that even were it not so, pride, lust, and the quest for glory would cause the war of all against all to continue indefinitely. Ultimately, conflict and war are rooted in human nature.

The preoccupation with the qualities of man is understandable in view of the purposes Hobbes and Morgenthau entertain. Both are interested in understanding the state. Hobbes seeks a logical explanation of its emergence; Morgenthau seeks to explain how it behaves internationally. Morgenthau thought of the "rational" statesman as striving ever to accumulate more and more power. Power is seen as an end in itself. Nations at times may act aside from considerations of power. When they do, Morgenthau insists, their actions are not "of a political nature."[35] The claim that "the desire to attain a maximum of power is universal" among nations is one of Morgenthau's "objective laws that have their roots in human nature."[36] Yet much of the behavior of nations contradicts it. Morgenthau does not explain why other desires fail to moderate or

32. Morgenthau, *Scientific Man vs. Power Politics* (Chicago: University of Chicago Press, 1946) p.192.
33. Thomas Hobbes, *Leviathan*.
34. Morgenthau (1972), *op. cit.*, p.208.
35. *Ibid.*, p.27.
36. *Ibid.*

outweigh the fear states may have about miscalculation of their relative power. His opinions about power are congenial to realism. They are easily slipped into because the effort to explain behavior and outcomes by the characteristics of units leads realists to assign to them attributes that seem to accord with behavior and outcomes observed. Unable to conceive of international politics as a self-sustaining system, realists concentrate on the behavior and outcomes that seem to follow from the characteristics they have attributed to men and states. Neorealists, rather than viewing power as an end in itself, see power as a possibly useful means, with states running risks if they have either too little or too much of it. Weakness may invite an attack that greater strength would dissuade an adversary from launching. Excessive strength may prompt other states to increase their arms and pool their efforts. Power is a possibly useful means, and sensible statesmen try to have an appropriate amount of it. In crucial situations, the ultimate concern of states is not for power but for security. This is an important revision of realist theory.

A still more important one is neorealism's use of the concept of power as a defining characteristic of structure. Power in neorealist theory is simply the combined capability of a state. Its distribution across states, and changes in that distribution, help to define structures and changes in them as explained above. Some complaints have been made about the absence of efforts on the part of neorealists to devise objective measures of power. Whatever the difficulties of measurement may be, they are not theoretical difficulties but practical ones encountered when moving from theory to its practical application.

Interacting Units

For realists, anarchy is a general condition rather than a distinct structure. Anarchy sets the problem that states have to cope with. Once this is understood, the emphasis of realists shifts to the interacting units. States are unlike one another in form of government, character of rulers, types of ideology, and in many other ways. For both realists and neorealists, differently constituted states behave differently and produce different outcomes. For neorealists, however, states are made functionally similar by the constraints of structure, with the principal differences among them defined according to capabilities. For neorealists, moreover, structure mediates the outcomes that states produce. As internal and external circumstances change, structures and states may bear more or less causal weight. The question of the relative importance of different levels cannot be abstractly or definitively answered. Ambiguity cannot be resolved since structures affect units even as units affect structures. Some have thought that this is a defect of neorealist theory. It is so, however, only if factors at the unit level or at the structural level determine, rather than merely affect, outcomes. Theories cannot remove the uncertainty of politics, but only help us to comprehend it.

Neorealists concentrate their attention on the central, previously unanswered question in the study of international politics: How can the structure of an international-political system be distinguished from its interacting parts? Once that question is answered, attention shifts to the effects of structure on interacting units. Theorists concerned with structural explanations need not ask how variations in units affect outcomes, even though outcomes find their causes at both structural and unit levels. Neorealists see states as like units; each state "is like all other states in being an autonomous political unit." Autonomy is the unit-level counterpart of anarchy at the structural level.[37] A theory of international politics can leave aside variation in the composition of states and in the resources and technology they command because the logic of anarchy does not vary with its content. Realists concentrate on the heterogeneity of states because they believe that differences of behavior and outcomes proceed directly from differences in the composition of units. Noticing that the proposition is faulty, neorealists offer a theory that explains how structures affect behavior and outcomes.

The logic of anarchy obtains whether the system is composed of tribes, nations, oligopolistic firms, or street gangs. Yet systems populated by units of different sorts in some ways perform differently, even though they share the same organizing principle. More needs to be said about the status and role of units in neorealist theory. More also needs to be said about changes in the background conditions against which states operate. Changes in the industrial and military technologies available to states, for example, may change the character of systems but do not change the theory by which their operation is explained. These are subjects for another essay. Here I have been concerned not to deny the many connections between the old and the new realism but to emphasize the most important theoretical changes that neorealism has wrought. I have been all the more concerned to do this since the influence of realist and behavioral logic lingers in the study of international politics, as in political science generally.

---

37. On page 95 of *Theory of International Politics,* I slipped into using "sovereignty" for "autonomy." Sovereignty, Ruggie points out, is particular to the modern state. See his "Continuity and Transformation," in Keohane, ed., *op. cit.,* pp.142-148

WOE TO THE ORPHANS OF
THE SCIENTIFIC REVOLUTION

by Donald J. Puchala

When, in 1967, the Department of Public Law and Government at Columbia University voted to change its name to the Department of Political Science, I enthusiastically joined the majority. Several of my more senior colleagues, William T.R. Fox among them, questioned this change of academic symbolism. They argued, wrongly I thought, that inserting the designation "science" into the department's title signalled a veering toward a philosophy of knowledge that had not yet adequately proven its efficacy in the study of human affairs. "Public Law" and "Government" were after all only objects of study, while "Political Science" was a prescribed way to study, and there was some risk, my senior colleagues explained, in favoring, even by a choice of symbols, one pathway to understanding over others. But as Bertrand Russell had poetically underlined quite some time before, whatever, "presents itself as empiricism is sure of widespread acceptance, not on its merits, but because empiricism is the fashion."[1] And so, political science was embraced by Columbia University.

As it turned out, the name change failed to elevate the Columbia department in Albert Somit's prestige rankings. Most of the department's members were insufficiently *avant garde* or especially "scientific" in their methods of scholarship.[2]

Actually, most of the members of the Columbia department were specialists in international relations and remained largely unbothered by the "scientific revolution" in political science. One result of the agnosticism of these scholars regarding science as applied to the study of human affairs was that they missed most of what Neal and Hamlett described as the "enthusiastic, well-financed, faddist, nationally-oriented" academic circus that was the field of international relations in the United States during the 1960s and 1970s.[3]

The more significant result of ignoring the scientific revolution was that the Columbia specialists in international relations produced, or had

---

1. Poem by Bertrand Russell, reproduced in *Challenges to Empiricism* Harold Morik ed. (Indianapolis: Hackett Publishing Company, 1980) p. vii.
2. Albert Somit and Joseph Tanenhaus, *American Political Science: A Profile of a Discipline* (New York: Atherton Press, 1964) pp.28-41.
3. Fred Warner Neal and Bruce D. Hamlett, "The Never-Never Land of International Relations," *International Studies Quarterly* 13, no.3 (September 1969) p.283.

a hand in producing, several of the most highly respected, and still widely read, contemporary works in the theory of international relations. These included, among others, Kenneth Waltz's *Man, the State and War*, Hedley Bull's *The Anarchical Society*, Louis Henkin's *How Nations Behave*, and Raymond Aron's *Peace and War*. At the time, the other large island of relative indifference toward scientism in international relations (or "behavioralism" as the movement was alternatively designated) was Harvard University. There Stanley Hoffmann held court, Joseph Nye held an assistant professorship, Steven Krasner held a degree, and Robert Keohane held a return ticket. The place held by this Harvard cast in the field of contemporary international relations theory needs no reiteration here.

Being indifferent to scientism is not the same as disparaging science. Each of the scholars I have mentioned probably identifies himself as a social scientist and, indeed, the theoretical work of each qualifies as science. But none of what I would consider to be the most insightful works of contemporary international relations theory seem to have resulted from commitments to epistemologies of logical positivism, operationalism or empirical verifiability that rest at the philosophical core of behavioralism. If there are epistemological commitments underlying the theoretical accomplishments of thinkers like Robert Keohane, Joseph Nye, Kenneth Waltz, Hedley Bull, Raymond Aron, Stanley Hoffmann, Hans Morgenthau, Ernst Haas and, most recently, Andrew Schmookler, they would seem to be either a traditional kind of empiricism reminiscent of David Hume or John Locke, or something akin to Kantian transcendentalism. About this, more will be said later.

What needs to be acknowledged here, however, is that important contributions to the theory of international relations have also been made by scholars centrally identified with both scientism and behavioralism. Harold Lasswell, Morton Kaplan and Karl Deutsch are certainly prominent among these. But, as I will attempt to show in a moment, the greatest *theoretical* contributions were made by these scholars not when they were performing as positivists, but rather when they were thinking as metaphysicians.

The thesis of this essay is that striving for enhanced theoretical understanding in the discipline of international relations has not been entirely the "elusive quest" recently portrayed by Yale H. Ferguson and Richard W. Mansbach, although one can sympathize with their consternation and accept much of what they offer to account for it.[4] To the extent

---

4. Yale H. Ferguson and Richard W. Mansbach, *The Elusive Quest: Theory and International Politics* (Columbia, SC: The University of South Carolina Press, 1988) pp.32-48.

that there has been an elusive quest, it has taken the form of a two-decade detour (heralded as a short-cut) through pseudo-science. This way turned out to be fraught with quicksands that swallowed most of the unwitting intellectual pilgrims. However, not everyone took the detour. Some travelers found their way back, and our theoretical understanding of international relations is presently the better for this.

The 20-Year Detour

Michael Haas's fine essay on "International Relations Theory," published in 1970, captured the exuberance of the behavioral revolutionaries then emerging from Yale, Michigan, Northwestern and elsewhere, who were well-armed—that is, statistically trained, computer literate, and Hempel-Popper-primed—to transform international relations into a true science. "Although advocates of earlier emphases are still active," Haas asserted with some confidence, "the behaviorist school is certainly the most important source of innovation today." "The behaviorist," he explained, "defines knowledge as the sum of all tested propositions." Haas expected that "in years to come it will be imperative to link theory and research much more intimately in order for the field of international relations as a whole to yield tested propositions that may be pyramided into the edifice of a theoretical science... Since a strictly *empirical science* would only consist of almanacs of raw data or isolated findings, in a *theoretical science* there must be an analytical structure capable of generalizing beyond data to predict relationships within as yet unexperienced situations."[5] Oran Young agreed, saying that "one important conception of theory focuses on highly and deductively interdependent propositions dealing with specified classes of phenomena."[6] At the time, I also shared this vision of international relations as a deductive science. For there it was: an edifice of ever-broadening and deepening knowledge about international relations, built up in pyramid fashion, tested proposition added onto tested proposition until the masses of verified facts amounted to umbrella statements about particular realms of international behavior as, for example, crisis behavior, escalation or integration. Such umbrella statements would constitute "middle-gauge" theories, and these would then be heaped and summed to ultimately arrive at a general theory of international relations. From such a general theory, indeed, from the

---

5.   Michael Haas, "International Relations Theory," in Michael Haas and Henry S. Kariel, eds., *Approaches to the Study of Political Science* (Scranton, PA: Chandler Publishing Company, 1970) pp.446-448.
6.   Oran R. Young, "Aron and the Whale: A Jonah in Theory," in Klaus Knorr and James N. Rosenau, eds., *Contending Approaches to International Politics* (Princeton, N.J.: Princeton University Press, 1969) p.131.

middle-gauge levels of the propositional pyramid, it would be possible to explain particular events by deducing (albeit probabilistically) from discovered laws of human behavior. Knowing such laws would also make it possible to predict future happenings within statistically determined intervals of confidence.

Nor was there much doubt in the ranks of the aspiring scientists of international relations that these propositional pyramids could be built because systematic, replicable observations were the handles, as one young scholar put it to me, for "grabbing the world where it is grabbable." Many, like J. David Singer and Charles McClelland, for example, believed that social reality was almost universally "grabbable" and that data could be generated, or "made" as was said in the vernacular of the time, that would render observable just about anything that the social scientist needed to observe. Nor were the scientists of international relations predisposed to forego opportunities that the new room-sized computers presented for the systematic storage, rapid retrieval and statistical and visual scrutiny of data.

The "scientific revolution" in the discipline of international relations began in the early 1960s. It was in full swing by 1969 when it was highlighted by the publication of J. David Singer's *Quantitative International Politics*.[7] Yet by the mid-1980s, Ferguson and Mansbach observe, "the scientific revolution" had been "all but abandoned as a goal" because among other things it had "precious few results to show for decades of work and countless dollars spent."[8] Even a most sympathetic reviewer of the behaviorist literature in international relations would have to share this view, particularly regarding the scientists' early aspirations for building propositional pyramids into empirical theories.

Still, proponents of scientism in international relations continue to ply their trade. Interestingly, the intellectual genre, while largely ignored in the United Kingdom and France, has caught on in West Germany and Scandinavia as well as in Eastern Europe and the Soviet Union, where "science" has an important ideological connotation. However in the United States, today's proponents of scientism in international relations are mostly the second- and third-generation students of the early enthusiasts. They organize panels at meetings of the International Studies Association, talk about such things as the pitfalls in coding *The New York Times* and finally settling the debate between Waltz and Deutsch and Singer about stability and polarity (which took place in 1964!). They cite one another profusely in their books and journal articles, but they tend

---

7.   J. David Singer, "Data-Making in International Relations," *Behavioral Science* 10 (January 1965) pp.68-80.
8.   Ferguson and Mansbach, *op. cit.*, pp.220-221.

to be cited less and less frequently outside of their intellectual subculture. Their readership in journals such as *The Journal of Conflict Resolution* has also fallen off noticeably. Alas, these are the orphans of the scientific revolution in international relations.

What Went Wrong? The Critics and Their Claims

From the beginning, scientism as applied to the study of international relations raised hackles. The crescendo of criticism rose over time in direct proportion to the revolution's failure to revolutionize knowledge in the discipline. The behaviorists were labelled "number crunchers." They were accused of being uninterested in philosophy and unmindful of history, which in F. Parkinson's estimation was "the greatest potential danger to the field of study of international relations."[9] When they ventured to make policy prescriptions on the basis of their work, as the Peace Researchers sometimes did, they were panned for being irresponsible, and when they abstained from policy involvement they were pilloried for being irrelevant.[10] Some outspoken critics, like Hedley Bull, argued that the behavioralists could not answer any questions about international relations that were worth asking. "If by a scientific theory of international relations," Bull wrote in 1975, "we mean one which is... strictly empirically verifiable, then in my view no strictly scientific theory can come to grips with the central issues of the subject... which concern the value premises of international conduct."[11]

In the midst of this came Oran Young's harsh review of Bruce Russett's, *International Regions and the International System.* Young memorably referred to Russett as the "industrious tailor to a naked emperor," and criticized him for "purist induction," which meant running everything against everything else in the hopes that something interesting might emerge.[12] *International Regions*, frankly, was not one of Russett's better efforts, but neither was it the worst case of purist induction then running rampant in the literature. "There is, in much of this," Neal and Hamlett summarized for the critics,

> a commendable effort to be objective... But the result seems to be more one of avoiding the real problems of international relations—theory at the expense of philosophy, data collection at the expense of analysis, quan-

9. F. Parkinson, *The Philosophy of International Relations: A Study in the History of Thought* (Beverly Hills, CA: Sage Publications, 1977) p.186.
10. Neal and Hamlett, *op. cit.*, pp.296-305.
11. Hedley Bull, "New Directions in International Relations Theory," *International Studies* 14, no.2 (April-June, 1975) p.279.
12. Oran R. Young, "Professor Russett: Industrious Tailor to a Naked Emperor," *World Politics* 21, no.3 (April 1969) pp.486-511.

tification at the expense of meaning. While the objective is to be scientific, what is achieved is often merely technical.[13]

I have allowed several of the critics of scientism as applied to international relations to speak here for themselves, partly to convey the spirit of the anti-behavioral attack, and partly to signal its superficiality. There was nothing fundamental in the criticism, nothing, that is, that could not be responded to by telling the critics that they simply did not understand what science as applied to international relations entailed.

In fact, criticism had the effect of encouraging the behavioralists to work harder and plow deeper in the intellectual fields they had chosen to till. For one thing, the behaviorists were not without a philosophy. They espoused logical positivism and it carried great authority *among scientists.* Secondly, the behavorists were not ignoring history. They were coding it! Instead of "crunching numbers" they were comparing sampled social-political reality to established, interpretable, intuitively meaningful statistical models. Correlation and regression models, even when reduced to rudimentary linear and bivariate forms, are not outlandish departures from the common sense of how things go together in the world. Rather than engaging in "purist induction," most of the more sophisticated behavioralist scholars, like Singer for example, were in fact trying to build the propositional pyramids of progressively higher-level theory that was their scientific goal. Several behavioralist scholars are still trying to do this.[14]

Deeper Issues of Epistemology

I, however, am no longer looking to build an empirical theory of international relations by testing and heaping propositions or by otherwise working methodically from the parts to the whole of the social-political realities in which I am interested. This is because I am now reasonably convinced that no general theory will, or even can, emerge from such a piecemeal theory-building effort. Scientific theories are simply not born by inducing wholes from parts.[15]

Behavioralism in international relations has not been overwhelmed by its critics; it has instead hit an epistemological iceberg that has been floating in its intellectual waters since the beginning. In its rush to "go scientific" in the early 1960s, practitioners of behavioralist international relations rather uncritically adopted from political science the logical

---

13. Neal and Hamlett, *op. cit.*, p.294.
14. For an especially impressive effort, see Michael P. Sullivan, *Power in Contemporary International Politics* (Columbia, SC: University of South Carolina Press, 1990).
15. Paul K. Feyerabend, "Science Without Experience," in *Challenges to Empiricism, op. cit.*, p.163.

positivistic epistemology that political science, in its haste to move away from public law and government, rather uncritically adopted from sociology. How critical or uncritical the sociologists were is not clear to me, though it is most likely that they adopted their logical positivism from psychology, which in its ambitions to be a true science of the mind embraced logical positivism to ape the natural sciences, where the sense-dependent, observation-bound pathway to knowledge was obviously producing exhilarating results.

Simply and briefly put, the positivist believes that knowledge about the world can only be gained from sensory experience, that complex ideas (or facts) about the world are arrived at by combining simpler ideas, but that all complex ideas ultimately can be traced back to component simpler ideas acquired by sensory experience. What the positivist does not believe is also significant. He does not believe that alternative pathways to knowledge—that is, ways other than through sensory experience and the amalgamation of simple experience-born facts—are possible, or indeed necessary. He does not therefore believe in metaphysics, or knowledge of reality gained through reasoning or contemplation (or in religion which instills knowledge of reality via revelation). Seeing, for the positivist, is believing, and that which cannot be observed (or otherwise sensed) cannot be real. In Susanne Langer's phrasing is sophisticated:

> The only philosophy that rose directly out of a contemplation of science is positivism, and it is probably the least interesting of all doctrines, an appeal to common sense against the difficulties of establishing metaphysical or logical first principles.

> Positivism, the scientists' metaphysic, entertains no doubts and raises no epistemological problems; its belief in the veracity of sense is implicit and dogmatic knowledge from sensory experience was deemed the only knowledge that carried any affidavit of truth; for truth became identified, for all vigorous modern minds, with empirical fact. And so, scientific culture succeeded... An undisputed empiricism—not skeptical, but positivistic—became its official metaphysical creed, experiment its avowed method, a vast hoard of "data" its capital, and correct prediction of future occurrences its proof.[16]

It was this positivism that behavioral international relations bought wholesale in the 1960s, without acknowledging, possibly without recog-

16. Susanne K. Langer, *Philosophy in a New Key* (Cambridge, MA.: Harvard University Press, 1960) pp.14-16.

nizing, that positivism's entire epistemological edifice was at that very time being challenged by the work of important figures in the field of the philosophy of knowledge such as Ernst Cassirer, Susanne Langer, Paul Feyerabend, Hilary Putnam and Thomas Kuhn.[17] In fact, as Harold Morick explained in the introduction to the 1980 symposium, *Challenges to Empiricism*, "one of the main themes of philosophy and theory of science in the last 20 years is the critical assessment of the foundations of contemporary empiricism."[18] Positivism's orthodoxy was shaken by a variety of tugs and pulls from those who made a profession of studying pathways to the truth. Langer raised pragmatic questions: in what sense could science claim to be building knowledge from sensory experience, when most of the phenomena being studied were not being experienced? Were not the findings of science revealed as "readings" on instruments rather than as sensed objects. If so, are our "sense data" not actually symbols of objects, and do we therefore need an epistemology based on the meaning of symbols rather than on the interpretation of sensed objects?[19] Other critics have challenged the positivists' notion of generalization via induction: Does observation lead to theoretical intuition through the amalgamation of simple understandings into complex ideas and ultimately into laws, or does prior intuition inspire and organize observation? To the extent that the latter is the case, what are the sources of prior intuition? Need intuitions come from prior observations, or can physical and human reality be known through reason and introspection much in the way that the ethereal realm of mathematics is accessed? Reflecting on the development of natural science, Feyerabend, for example, emphasized that "progress was often made by following theory, not observation, and by rearranging our observational world in conformance with theoretical assumptions." Further noting that "in the struggle for better knowledge theory and observation enter on an equal footing," Feyerabend concludes that, "empiricism, insofar as it goes beyond the invitation not to forget considering observations, is...an unreasonable doctrine, not in agreement with scientific practice."[20]

There is more. Most fundamental, and most damaging to logical positivism is the question of whether there is an *unobservable* reality, natural, social or otherwise, that is nonetheless *knowable*. Philosophers of every age, beginning perhaps with Plato, have of course believed in the unobservable but knowable, or in its linguistic variant the knowable

---

17. Langer, *ibid.*, pp.20-25 *et passim*; Ernst Cassier, *The Philosophy of Symbolic Forms* (New Haven: Yale University Press, 1957), 3, pp.105-204 *et passim*; others mentioned have representative pieces in Morick, ed., *Challenges to Empiricism*.
18. Morick, ed., *op. cit.*, p.1.
19. Langer, *op. cit.*, pp.21-22.
20. Feyerabend, *op. cit.*, p.163.

but verbally unexplainable (due to the constraints of the discursive nature of human languages). What intrigues me, and what might bother positivists practicing in the social sciences who wish to think about it, is that many of the central concepts of our human-oriented disciplines denote unobservables which we nevertheless hope are knowables. "State," "society," "international system," "international interdependence," "global economy," "world revolution," "security community," and the like are bread-and-butter notions for those of us who make a profession trying to say intelligent things about world affairs. Yet, none of these are observable as wholes, and they never will be observable as wholes. This is quite a different problem from much that has been encountered in the natural sciences, where initial unobservables like atomic particles, chromosomes, genes, moons around Neptune and chemical reactions at the molecular level, frequently become observable as observational techniques are improved. By contrast, social wholes are not likely to become more empirically accessible once we have figured out better ways to look at them. Of course, natural science, in its theoretically most ambitious endeavors, like the quest for a Unified Theory in physics, is also dealing with unobservables; here problems of "knowability" are similar to those facing social scientists. But social scientists tend to run into unobservability at much lower levels of abstraction.

Logical positivism as applied to international relations could resolve the problem of unobservable wholes if it could assure us that the nature of unobservable wholes could be induced from the nature of observable parts, and that the wholes are in no sense greater than or different from the sum of their respective parts. Frankly, I am skeptical on both of these counts. One can accept that in physics and chemistry, where elements and reactions seem to be universally invariant, it is possible to infer something about the universe by observing happenings on Earth or in other parts of the cosmos. One can even suppose that in archeology or paleontology the nature of wholes can be induced from the study of parts, though within limits, as we cannot really be certain what a Brontosaurus looked like. And surely, the limits of parts/wholes inferences must be even greater regarding social structures and processes where there is apparently great variability across time and space, because unlike the physical universe or the dead and fixed worlds of archaeology and paleontology, social wholes change their nature. There is also always considerable uncertainty about whether parts observed are actually elements of the wholes inferred. Some philosophers, like Susanne Langer whose work I find to be extremely insightful, tell us that our attempts to infer or otherwise know about social wholes from observed parts have been futile and therefore probably misguided from the start:

> The physical sciences found their stride without much hesitation; psychology and sociology tried hard and seriously to 'catch the tune and keep the step,' but with mathematical laws they were never really handy. Psychologists have probably spent almost as much time avowing their empiricism, their factual premises, their experimental techniques, as... making general inductions. They still tell us that their lack of laws and calculable results is due to the fact that psychology is but young. When physics was as old as psychology is now, it was a definite systematic body of highly general facts, and the possibilities of its future expansion were clearly visible.[21]

Other philosophers like Ernst Cassirer tell us that the problem is that we cannot simply combine observation-generated facts together to get at the nature of the unobservable social wholes because the formulas for making the combinations are not to be found in the facts themselves:

> Our technical instruments for observation and experimentation have been immensely improved, and our analyses have become sharper and more penetrating. We appear, nevertheless, not yet to have found a method for the mastery and organization of this material... Our wealth of facts is not necessarily a wealth of thoughts. Unless we succeed in finding a clue... to lead us out of this labyrinth, we can have no real insight into the general character of human culture; we shall remain lost in a mass of disconnected and disintegrated data which seem to lack all of conceptual unity. [22]

Most dramatically, philosophers like Louis Arnaud Reid warn us that we should not seek knowledge about unobservable wholes by trying to sum up observation-generated facts, because such knowledge would be false, since the wholes are different from the sums of their parts:

> It is the old difficulty of the wood and the trees. The man who trusts in propositions alone to bring him truth may completely miss, in his preoccupation with parts, the significance of the whole, particularly if that whole is of a higher sort than one of mere aggregation. Propositions can only be summed and synthesized into syllogisms, and the man who takes them for more than they are worth is likely to take reality as a mere heap or the mere syllogistic synthesis which it is not. This is often admitted, and the need of imagination, of a wholeness of outlook for the man of science, is frequently pointed out.[23]

---

21. Langer, *op. cit.*, p.16.
22. Ernst Cassirer, *An Essay On Man* (New Haven: Yale University Press, 1962) p.22.
23. Louis Arnaud Reid, *Knowledge and Truth* (London: Macmillan, 1923) p.219.

Admittedly, and as noted, the scientific revolution in international relations is not over for everybody. Indeed it cannot be ended or superseded until the behaviorists and their critics resist attributions like "number crunchers" and "traditionalists" and center their debate on the epistemological issues that separate them. These issues are absolutely fundamental. Until this dialogue about philosophies of knowledge takes place, the proponents of the alternative epistemological schools will continue to talk past one another, or as is more the present case, they will simply not talk to each other at all.

For me, however, the scientific revolution is over. While I continue to be inspired by and try to emulate the careful designs and rigorous approaches to research problems that the behavioralists favor, I can no longer picture myself positivistically proposition-testing my way to international relations theory.

The Metaphysicists Among Us

Whatever form the *quest* for theory in international relations may have taken during the last three decades, the actual development of theory has been rather impressive. As noted, the theoretical accomplishments have been made largely by those who did not make the detour toward scientism. To evaluate and appreciate this theoretical development, one must step away from logical positivism, because by positivism's gauge very few "empirically verified, general propositions" have been discovered. Moreover, using anything that has been discovered as a starting point for deductions down to and through lower levels of generality remains fraught with considerable intellectual danger. Robert Keohane worries about this. "If we took literally [science philosopher Imre Lakatos's] requirements... all actual theories of international politics... would fail the test."[24]

However, there may not be as much cause for concern as Keohane believes. Neither empirical verifiability in a strict sense nor prediction by rigorous deduction are actually what theorizing in international relations has been about. The value of international relations theory should really not be assessed in terms of satisfying the requirements of natural science.

Successful international relations theorists are those among our intellectual brethren who have tried to gain knowledge of the "unobservable wholes" of human affairs, and who have done this innovatively and

---

24. Robert O. Keohane, "Theory and World Politics: Structural Realism and Beyond," in Paul R. Viotti and Mark V. Kauppi, eds., *International Relations Theory* (New York: Macmillan, 1987) p.129.

convincingly enough to compel us to take them seriously. They can be considered successful because their work has been either plausible, provocative or elegant enough to capture our serious attention, to inspire our careful criticism, to fire our imagination and to redirect our research. Those generally recognized as leading international relations theorists today have earned their stature through accomplishments in wholistic image-building—feats of imagination, if you will—and not necessarily by exhibiting extraordinary prowess at working systematically through empirical problems. The theorists are first and foremost conceptualizers, symbolizers, synthesizers and abstract organizers. Kenneth Boulding might call them experts in eiconics.[25]

What they have been doing as theorists in their writing is painting for us bold-stroked, broad-brushed pictures of social reality and telling us that the real world is like their pictures. It may be empirically unobservable, except in a partial and piecemeal way, and its wholeness may be different from or greater than the sum of its parts, but they, the theorists, know what it looks like.

If the theorists were as straightforward as they might be, and not as sensitive as they are about being branded "unscientific," they might explain that they believe their pictured worlds to be real because they emerged from human intuition, and relying on human intuition is a fully legitimate avenue to knowledge. "Great discoveries," Morton Kaplan explained in 1969, "when they do not occur accidentally or as a consequence of trial-and-error procedures, are the product of scientific intuition."[26] Indeed, intuition is the basic stuff from which metaphysics are made, if we appreciate that metaphysics properly deal with the nature of unobservable reality and not with the mystical matters that common parlance has attributed to this branch of philosophy. There is then more to *knowing* than empirically *seeing*, and it is in this alternative epistemological realm—call it imagining, image-making, symbolization or eiconics—that all abstract theorists, including the leading international relations theorists, operate.[27] This realm of the symbolic, incidentally, is

---

25. Kenneth Boulding, *The Image: Knowledge in Life and Society* (Ann Arbor: University of Michigan Press, 1956) pp.64-81. C.A.W. Manning also deals with the notion of theory as the pursuit of an understanding of social wholes in his discussion of "social cosmology." See *The Nature of International Society* (London: John Wiley & Sons, 1962) pp.64-77, 200-216. Manning also explicitly links his work to Boulding's and offers Kenneth Waltz's, *Man, the State and War* as an interesting example of eiconics employed in theorizing about international relations (p. 75). Waltz in fact uses a vocabulary of "images." See *Man, the State and War* (New York: Columbia University Press, 1959).
26. Morton Kaplan, "The New Great Debate," in Knorr and Rosenau, eds., *op. cit.*, p.42.
27. Susanne Langer, *op. cit.*, pp.26-102.

also where artists dwell philosophically. Conceivably, aesthetic criteria could be brought into the evaluation of the "pictures" that the abstract theorists verbally paint.[28] However, at this point let us not require that good international relations theory must be "beautiful"—"insightful" will do.

Some Big Pictures

What has been impressive in the development of theory in the field of international relations has been the flow of alternative images of reality projected by the theorists. Admittedly, those who have been looking for a cumulatively broadening and deepening understanding of international relations, or something akin to physicists' Unified Theory, would be understandably less impressed with this flow of alternative images than those, like me, who choose to experience the abstract theoretical litera-ture somewhat in the way one might experience a gallery full of fine art. If the works are worthy of inclusion in the collection, they probably all capture the truth in some manner, or at least they captured something that was true when they were composed. Each work, however, delivers a different intellectual experience, and the greater the variety of such experiences contained in the collection, the greater the overall value of the collection.[29] International relations theory has its old masters, like Thucydides and Machiavelli, its established contemporaries like Keohane and Nye, John Ruggie and Oran Young, and even an *avant garde* corps, like Andrew Schmookler, Fritz Kratochwil and Nicholas Onuf.

Lest the reader here suspect that I have been terminally stricken with the "humanist's disease," let me point out that the clash of alternative theories has always been an integral part of the advancement of science. "You can be a good empiricist," epistemologist Paul Feyerabend in-structs, "only if you are prepared to work with many alternative theories rather than with a single point of view."

This plurality of theories must not be regarded as a preliminary stage of knowledge which will at some time in the future be replaced with One

---

28. Reid, *op. cit.*, pp.222-238; See also, Richard Kostelanetz, "Contemporary American Esthetics," in Kostelanetz, ed., *Esthetics Contemporary* (Buffalo, NY: Prometheus Books, 1978) pp.20-24.
29. This "art gallery" metaphor should not be taken too literally, although it is in the realms of symbolization, abstraction and metaphysics that philosophy, science and art commingle. In deference to the aesthetically inclined, let me note that kind of experience one receives in an art gallery is of a different quality from what one receives in reading international relations theory.

True Theory. Theoretical pluralism is assumed to be an *essential feature* of all knowledge that claims to be objective.[30]

The intellectual danger in diminishing theoretical pluralism is that single perspectives tend to degenerate into dogma, much as political realism did during the first decades after World War II. Once these systems of thought have answered all of the questions that they initially raised, they create the illusion that there are no further questions to be asked. With regard to social theory, there is the additional danger that dogmatized thought systems could become political ideologies, as happened with the social-pathological "isms" of the twentieth century. These were snatched by latter-generation political activists from the lively pluralism of nineteenth-century political thought and used, in the guise of utopian schemes, to justify some of history's grandest-scale atrocities.[31] So-called "liberal economic theory" and "dependency theory" are today almost fully dogmatized, and the realities they purport to explain are crying out for alternative, innovative metaphysical treatments.

Surely it is both impossible and unnecessary to move through the entire gallery of images of the world that contemporary international relations theorists have projected. Let me, however, highlight a few that I find especially insightful, or that seemed to me to be particularly innovative and insightful during their heydays at the center of disciplinary attention. Some of the "still lifes" in the gallery of theories are intriguing. The realists are most prominent among theorists who have given us images of the *structure* of the international system. Some like Hans Morgenthau and Kenneth Waltz organize their anarchical worlds of states in terms of distributions of power and explain why, because of inherent equilibrating tendencies, these distributions tend to be relatively resistant to short-term change.[32] Nowhere, in all of the theoretical literature, for example, is the balance of power more elegantly presented than in Part IV of Morgenthau's *Politics Among Nations: The Struggle for Power and Peace.*

---

30. Paul K. Feyerabend, "How to be a Good Empiricist —A Plea for Tolerance in Epistemological Matters," in Morick, ed., *op. cit.,* p.166.
31. Paul Johnson, *Modern Times: The World from the Twenties to the Eighties* (New York: Harper and Row) pp.49-104, 261-309.
32. Kenneth Waltz, *Theory of International Politics* (Reading, MA: Addison-Wesley, 1979); Hans J. Morgenthau, *Politics Among Nations: The Struggle for Power and Peace* (New York: Alfred A. Knopf, 1967), 4th edition, pp.161-218.

Raymond Aron, in structuring his imagined world, adds a distribution of political ideologies to the distribution of power and invites us then to envisage various combinations of power polarity and ideological heterogeneity in a variety of differently structured international systems.[33] Morton Kaplan nurtures the image of anarchy, as he finds no "international political system" in his imagined world. But his anarchically interacting states or "national actors" are themselves rather intriguingly structured as hierarchies of nested systems and subsystems, all of these operating similarly and repetitively—homeostatically and anti-entropically—to maintain their structural integrities.[34] Kaplan's *System and Process in International Politics* has been rather harshly criticized for its portrayal of unreal worlds in the form of mythical models, but what the critics frequently miss is the extent to which, at a more abstract level, the system-subsystem-linked image taps insightfully into social-political reality and in fact explains a good deal of behavior at the different inter-systemic nodes.

Anarchy is a lesser *leitmotif* in Hedley Bull's picture of the international system inasmuch as he identifies, in addition to distributions of power and political fragmentation, an international society in the form of transactions, connections and other bonds among peoples. An edifice of internationally acknowledged laws and rules—all of which tend to constrain the extreme manifestations of anarchy.[35] In their *Power and Interdependence*, which remains, in my estimation, one of the most innovative contributions to contemporary theory in international relations, Robert Keohane and Joseph Nye imagine a world beyond anarchy. They add a variety of non-states to the inventory of structural elements in the international system, insert degrees of interdependence into the ordering of relationships among their elements, build in a more prevalent implicit and explicit rule structure in the form of regimes, and posit a pattern of structural variation according to issues or the substantive promptings to interaction.[36]

There are of course many more pictures of international structure contained in the literature of international relations theory—Immanuel Wallerstein's, Mansbach and Vasquez's and John Burton's, for example—but again, there is no need here to be comprehensive as the main

---

33. Raymond Aron, *Peace and War: A Theory of International Relations* (Garden City, N.Y.: Doubleday, 1966) pp.71-124.
34. Morton Kaplan, *System and Process in International Politics* (New York: Columbia University Press, 1957).
35. Hedley Bull, *The Anarchical Society: A Study of Order in World Politics* (London: Macmillan, 1977).
36. Robert O. Keohane and Joseph S. Nye, *Power and Interdependence: World Politics in Transition* (Boston: Little, Brown and Company, 1977) pp.3-62.

point is that the theorists are first and foremost image makers, and exciting images of the structure of the international system have flowed in some profusion.

The moving pictures are also fascinating. Since explaining systemic and intra-systemic change have remained central among the puzzles of our discipline, any number of theorists of contemporary international relations have directed their image- making toward the dynamics of international politics or international political economy. Harold Lasswell, always well ahead of his time, made a major effort to explain change in his *World Politics and Personal Insecurity*.[37] Here he offers an involved moving picture of simultaneous ideological and power polarization at the international level. He invites his readers to watch as international polarization and ideological differentiation first feed, and then feed upon, the anxieties of human beings, until tensions are ultimately released in the catharsis of great war. Raymond Aron paints a remarkably similar picture in his masterful discussion of "the dialectics of peace and war," except that he adds additional dynamics to explain relationships among technological change, socio-economic structural change and differential changes in the international capabilities of states.[38]

Robert Gilpin pictures a dynamic, homeostatic linking of national wealth, national power and international aggrandizement which, for benefiting states, tends to generate exponential ascents toward hegemony.[39] But the same dynamic also works in reverse: At a point near an ascending state's logistic plateau, the marginal power costs of maintaining international position begin to outweigh the marginal benefits, and accelerating exhaustion, exploited by ambitious and marauding rivals, sets in. From a systemic perspective, Gilpin gives us an elegant version of historically familiar cycles of the rise and fall of power.

Andrew Schmookler, in his amazingly erudite volume *The Parable of the Tribes*, offers an alternative image of the dynamics of national aggrandizement stemming from imperatives to maximize societal power

---

37. Harold Lasswell, *World Politics and Personal Insecurity* (New York: Free Press, 1965) [original copyright 1935] pp.3-72.
38. Raymond Aron, *op. cit.* pp.150-176.
39. Robert Gilpin, *War and Change in World Politics* (New York: Cambridge University Press, 1981).

in the interest of successful selection in the course of social evolution.[40] Altogether different kinds of international dynamics are pictured by Karl Deutsch, as he shows peoples evolving toward peaceful coexistence and commingling through communication, social learning and shifting political allegiances.[41] Different kinds of international dynamics are also displayed in the writings of David Mitrany, where international cooperation begets greater international cooperation, in the work of Amitai Etzioni, where international transactions beget international management, and in the work of Keohane and Nye, where international interdependence begets international rules.[42]

Again, many other theorists' images of the dynamics of international relations—those of A.F.K. Organski, Ernst Haas, Karl Polyani or Edward Morse, for example—could be displayed here, but the point is made. Unless the theorists paint their wholistic pictures for us, our world views, as Andrew Schmookler tells his readers, would tend "to be myopically mired in the magnifying-glass stage" where, "the parts are delineated in excruciating detail...[but] the whole is left for some invisible hand to assemble or is regarded as no more than the sum of its parts.[43]

The Origins of the Art

To me it is not entirely clear what the actual epistemological principles are that explain theorizing about international relations, except that they are not principles of logical positivism. Nor are they principles of pure rationalism, where adherents aver that reality can be known through powers of human reason uncomplemented by sensory experience.[44] Some pure rationalists continue to ply their trade in the field of international relations theory in the form of game theorists and kindred deductive model builders, and in fact in recent years there has been something of a resurgence of such efforts. The undertakings of the new generation modelers, however, are no more convincing than those of the game theorists of the 1960s, who, like Anatol Rapoport, Duncan Luce and Howard Raiffa, Morton Kaplan and Arthur Burns, subsequently and progressively modified their enthusiasms for deductively generated

---

40. Andrew Schmookler, *The Parable of the Tribes: The Problem of Power in Social Evolution* (Boston: Houghton Mifflin, 1984) pp.3-131.
41. Karl W. Deutsch, *et al.*, *Political Community and the North Atlantic Area* (Princeton: Princeton University Press, 1957).
42. David Mitrany, *A Working Peace System* (Chicago: Quadrangle Books, 1966) pp.29-33; Amitai Etzioni, "The Epigensis of Political Communities at the International Level," *American Journal of Sociology* 68 (1963) pp.407-421.
43. Andrew Schmookler, *op. cit.*, p.5.
44. R.S. Woolhouse, *The Empiricists* (New York: Oxford University Press, 1988) p.2.

mathematical models as vehicles for understanding international relations.[45]

The criticisms and self-criticisms of the deductive modelers from within the genre have dealt largely with uncertainties involved in assigning values to variables (like utilities in game matrices) *a priori*. Values and priorities tend to vary across individuals and groups as well as across time and space, so that what is *rational* for all players in a given game can never be posited with certainty. This makes the assigning of utilities a wholly speculative undertaking, and it makes the dynamic of the game indeterminate unless the identities of particular human players are stipulated. Once this is done, however, the model loses its generality and deductive interest.

From outside the genre the fundamental difficulty has been one of accepting that real world outcomes could ever be deduced from abstractly modeled relationships, or as Rapoport noted, mathematical decision theory has been used as "a prop for *rationalizing* decisions arrived at by processes far from rational," and that "in this role rational decision theory can become a source of dangerous fixations and delusions."[46] Or, as Philip Green expressed it, "this [game theoretic] definition of rational behavior... does not at first glance have any real-world relevance. Purely instrumental choice unhindered either by emotional or ideological blocks on the one hand, or by ignorance on the other, exists only in the abstract theory of games."

Most of theorists who have painted appealing and useful wholistic pictures of the structure and functioning of the international system have not been very explicit about the epistemological origins of their images. Many have not been at all self-conscious concerning epistemological matters; most have contended that they have been operating as scientists and have left it at that. Raymond Aron endorsed a philosophy of knowledge based on empirical generalization from historical experience that he called "historical sociology" and Stanley Hoffmann accepted its tenets.[47] In his criticisms of the behavioralists, Hedley Bull made clear that he too believed that wholistic pictures could be painted on the basis of empirical generalizations from history. Morton Kaplan contended that he was working deductively from the tenets of general systems theory, but I am inclined to agree with the critics who argued that Kaplan's three "real-looking" models—the balance of power and loose and tight bipolarity—were actually empirical generalizations from nineteenth cen-

45. Philip Green, *Deadly Logic: The Theory of Nuclear Deterrence* (Columbus, Ohio: Ohio State University Press, 1966) pp.93-102, 293-294.
46. Anatol Rapoport, *Strategy and Conscience* (New York: Schocken Books, 1969) p.83.
47. Philip Green, *op. cit.*, p.98.

tury European and twentieth century global history respectively, and the rest of the models were variations on these.

Overall, it would appear that the wholistic "pictures" of the international relations theorists emerge from combinations of experience (vicarious experience for the most part) and reasoning. Experience acquired by watching the world in various ways, particularly by reading history, produces countless perceptions to which the human mind adds form, order, relationship, cause and effect so as to transform the perceptions into cognitions in the nature of images and symbols. "There is such a thing as a sense of realities and possibilities of social activity, which can be developed from a study of the proper sort of history," historian Joseph Strayer suggests. "It is in acquiring, or seeking to acquire, this sense of social realities," he says, "that the historian ceases to be a scientist and becomes an artist."[48]

I like to call the product of such a process of imaginatively generalizing from long and varied experience not art but *intuition*. Immanuel Kant called it *transcendental logic*. "Our cognition," he wrote,

> has, on the part of the mind, two sources. Of these the first is he receptivity of impressions, and the second the spontaneity of notions... The first receives the crude appearances of sense, and the second works them up into the finished perception of the object... Thoughts, without a content of perceptions, are void; perceptions without the focus of notions, are blind.[49]

Langer calls the same process *symbolization* or *ideation*, and in slight contrast to Kant locates it prior to thought in the procedural chain of human understanding, saying that "it is not the essential act of thought that is symbolization, but an act essential to thought and prior to it."[50] To think about the world, we must first symbolize our raw impressions of it. We must symbolize in order to, as Cassirer would have it, transform our "wealth of facts" into a "wealth of thoughts," and we must symbolize the world in order to organize our empirical inquiries about it. Rather than emerging from empirical inquiry, theory, generated by intuition as here defined, launches it. Successful international relations theorists are masters of such intuition.

---

48. Joseph R. Strayer, "Introduction," in Jacques Barzun, *et al.*, *The Interpretation of History* (New York: Peter Smith, 1950) p.15.
49. James Hutchinson Stirling, *Text-Book to Kant: The Critique of Pure Reason* (Edinburgh: Oliver and Boyd, 1881) pp.169, 171.
50. Susanne Langer, *op. cit.*, p.41.

But What About Validity?

Since, Hedley Bull agrees, "the general propositions about this subject... derive from a scientifically imperfect process of perception and intuition," he concludes that "these general propositions cannot be accorded anything more than tentative and inconclusive status."[51] Positivistically speaking, Bull is correct. Ultimately, there is no way to empirically ascertain the validity of the images of reality that international relations theorists have conceived and projected. It should be born in mind, however, that there are respected epistemological traditions which do not insist that truth can be ascertained only through empirical verification. As emphasized above, positivistic approaches to verification will not work because the wholes are unobservable, and investigating the parts separately simply will not do.

More practically speaking, with regard to theorizing about the world in real time (which many theorists usefully do) realities in international relations do not last long enough to mount comprehensive, systematic and effective empirical assaults on them. This is especially the case where such efforts are conceived and designed to involve operationalizing, coding and testing all of the propositions the various theories propound or all of the aspects of the various theoretical pictures verbally painted to describe and explain contemporaneous international relations. Before we really got going empirically on "hegemonic stability," for example, the world had moved "beyond hegemony." Before that, "protracted conflict," turned into "multipolar equilibrium." And before our eyes in the 1980s we may have witnessed "the decline of the major powers" just as we had begun digging empirically into the nature and attributes of "the superpowers."

International reality is a moving target that theorists track reasonably well. But the dynamism befuddles empiricists who wish to be simultaneously absolutely right and absolutely relevant. Naturally, these reservations do not apply with regard to the empirical examination of immediate and distant eras past, but even here we run into the "wholes/parts" problem. There are no conceivable "grand experiments" that will, at a stroke, render true or false, adequate or wanting, the wholistic thought systems of social theorists in the way that, for example, Eddington's 1919 "light deflection" and Campell's 1922 "red shift" experiments unseated Newtonian physics and enthroned Einstein's theory of relativity.[52] To the extent that social science lacks philosophical

---

51. Hedley Bull, "International Theory: The Case for the Classical Approach," in Knorr and Rosenau, eds., *op. cit.*, p.20.
52. Paul Johnson, *op. cit.*, pp.2-3.

justification for inducing wholes from parts, and given that probabilism will not do because meaningful sampling from undefinable populations is impossible, the ultimate *empirical* validity of the theorist's big pictures must remain elusive. But again, positivistically *unverifiable* does not necessarily mean *untrue*.

As long as any positivistic juices continue to trickle within us, we will probably continue to worry about empirical verification and resist evaluating our theories in purely pragmatic terms. Perhaps there is something to be learned from our colleagues in the discipline of history who tend on the whole to be a good deal more modest about the contributions that generalization and interpretation can make to the understanding of human affairs.[53] They do not seek deductive laws, and they no longer seek teleological meanings, but they do look for generalizations about individual and collective behavior, about plausible causes and plausible effects, to help explain the chronologies they observe.

Contrasting historians' and scientists' uses of generalizations, philosopher of history W.B. Gallie observes, that applying generalizations to history is "basically different from applying them with a view to deducing, and in particular predicting, some future event. The latter use of generalizations," he continues,

> enables us to anticipate and even dispense with observation: the whole purpose of the former is to render possible, or set in motion again, certain kinds of 'progressive observation'... The whole point of explanations of this kind being that the event can now be followed as part of a still developing whole to which it belongs.[54]

Functionally speaking, this is precisely the role which theory plays in the understanding of international relations: It helps us follow events by setting them within a context of wholes of which they are parts. It does not, because it cannot in the absence of laws (probabilistic or otherwise) invite us to deduce, and it does not permit us to predict. Rather, theory helps us to understand events because it gives them context and meaning in terms of higher abstractions.

Perhaps we need not ask so emphatically whether a theory is "scientific," but rather whether it is useful. Does it give plausible meaning to events as they occur around us and perhaps as they have occurred in the past? Does it especially give new meaning to events that have confused

---

53. Not all historians, however, are quite this modest about the theoretical implications of their work and the aspirations of their discipline. See Joseph R. Strayer, *op. cit.*, pp.1-26.
54. W.B. Gallie, *Philosophy and the Historical Understanding* (New York: Schocken Books, 1964) p.90.

us, or identify new events that have eluded us? Does it order, or at least suggest an order to our experiences? Does it cue us to ask questions that we are not otherwise prompted to ask, and does it guide our search for answers to places where we are not otherwise predisposed to search? And we should also ask those among us who are the agents that make international events occur, whether the pictures painted by international realtions theorists improve this understanding of the realities surrounding them. Does this understanding ease the process of actually coping with international realities? The ultimate goal of international relations theory should be to enable respondents to give positive answers to these questions.

MODELS AND CASES IN THE STUDY OF INTERNATIONAL CONFLICT[1]

by Robert Jervis

The physicist might spend thousands of years studying the behavior of ocean waves on a beach in most meticulous detail; in the end he would be no wiser than before with regard to what is essential in wave motion. The really profound understanding of waves is quite independent of observing any real waves. For that matter, the most important waves in our lives are not even observable directly—I am referring to the waves which underlie our entire telecommunication system and also subatomic events. It is these kinds of essences which pure theory seeks. It goes without saying that ultimately the findings of theory must somehow be translated into real predictions and observations. But to demand this too soon is not wise.[2]

—Anatol Rapoport

The implication of these complexities of human and social reality is that the explanatory strategy of the hard sciences has only a limited application to the social sciences. Models, procedures, and methodologies created to explore a world in which clocklike...characteristics predominate will capture only a part of the much richer world of social and political interaction. Thus, a simple search for regularities and lawful relationships among variables—a strategy that has led to tremendous successes in the physical sciences—will not explain social outcomes, but only some of the conditions affecting those outcomes. Because the properties of political reality differ from those of physical reality, the properties of political regularities also differ from those of physical regularities. The regularities we discover are soft. They are soft because they are the outcomes of processes that exhibit plastic rather than cast-iron control. They are imbedded in history and involve recurrent "passings-through" of large numbers of human memories, learning processes, human goal-seeking impulses and choices among alternatives. The regularities we discover appear

---

1.   A preliminary version of this article was presented at the University of Chicago Dean's Symposium, 4-5 May 1989.
2.   Anatol Rapoport, "Various Meanings of Theory," *American Political Science Review* 52 (December 1958) p.988.

to have a short half-life. They decay quickly because of the memory, creative searching, and learning that underlie them. Indeed, social science itself may contribute to this decay, since learning increasingly includes not only learning from experience, but from scientific research itself.[3]

—*Gabriel Almond and Stephen Genco*

One of the recurring issues in the study of politics in general, and international politics in particular, is the extent to which analyses can and should be performed according to scientific methods.[4] Until recently, many of those who advocated a scientific approach to the study of international relations stressed the utility of quantitative data. Now more attention is given to deductive models,[5] shifting the focus away from the quality of the evidence to the structure and form of the arguments. Although we cannot resolve these debates once and for all, there is benefit in examining the advantages and disadvantages both of case studies and of rigorous models. Of course, this is not an either/or issue. Scholars can use both methods since, at least to some extent, they supplement each other.[6] But the arguments for each approach may be particularly interesting and fruitful because, as the quotations from the Rapoport and Almond and Genco studies remind us, they raise basic questions about the nature of the world in which we live.

The ambiguity in the concepts of case studies and, even more, of formal models should be acknowledged at the outset. A model is a formal, often mathematical representation of the variables that are believed to capture the main relationships in the phenomena that one is studying. Furthermore, these variables and relationships are posed in sufficiently general terms so that they can apply to a wide range of cases. Usually, they are quite parsimonious. That is, they omit large numbers of details that may be idiosyncratic to individual cases. Formal models then lend themselves to producing deductions and indeed this is the main point and virtue of the enterprise.

---

3. Gabriel Almond and Stephen Genco, "Clouds, Clocks, and the Study of Politics," *World Politics* 29 (July 1977) pp.493-4.
4. The literature is voluminous. See, for example, William T.R. Fox, ed., *Theoretical Aspects of International Relations* (Notre Dame: University of Notre Dame Press: 1959) and Klaus Knorr and James Rosenau, eds., *Contending Approaches to the Study of International Politics* (Princeton: Princeton University Press, 1969).
5. See, for example, Christopher Achen and Duncan Snidal, "Rational Deterrence Theory and Comparative Case Studies," *World Politics* 41 (January 1989) pp.143-70. The same issue carries three rebuttals and a synthesis: Alexander George and Richard Smoke, "Deterrence and Foreign Policy," Robert Jervis, "Rational Deterrence: Theory and Practice," Richard Ned Lebow and Janice Stein, "Rational Deterrence Theory: I Think, Therefore I Deter" and George Downs, "The Rational Deterrence Debate."
6. Downs, "The Rational Deterrence Debate."

Without going deeply into questions of definition, three points about formal models should be made. First, in recent years attention has focussed on rational-choice models. (Of course, rational choice is not itself unambiguous, although it is usually equated with maximizing subjective expected utility.) But other kinds of formal models are also possible. Well-developed psychological theories, like cognitive dissonance (now out of favor among psychologists) and prospect theory,[7] lend themselves to modeling. The attempts to reconstruct the belief systems of either individuals or groups, most formally in artificial intelligence, will, by most definitions, be non-rational-choice models.

Second, some of the criticisms of rational choice apply to all models. Most obvious is the charge that the costs of attempting to squeeze complex and changing phenomena into unyielding formulations sacrifice what we are trying to understand. Other criticisms are more ambiguous in their scope. Thus the argument, common in anthropology, that modeling assumes that people behave the same way throughout time and across cultures would not necessarily deny the possibility of building specific models to capture the behavior of peoples in specific cultures. Still other criticisms, such as that people are strongly driven by nonrational emotions, cut against rational choice but say nothing about the prospects for modeling based on other assumptions.

Third, to say that modeling, or even rational-choice modeling, is a powerful analytical tool is not to specify what the model is. As Herbert Simon and others have noted, much of the "work" of the argument in rational choice is being done by the often implicit substantive claims about what people seek and how they see the world, not by the abstract claim that people maximize.[8] For example, many of the substantive arguments about deterrence are not directly related to, and indeed may even be at odds with, arguments about modeling versus case studies. One can construct formal models based on the argument that credible threats are likely to maintain peace; one can equally well propose formal models

---

7. Amos Tversky and Daniel Kahneman, "Rational Choice and the Framing of Decisions," *Journal of Business* 59 (October 1986) pp.S251-78.

8. Herbert Simon, "Human Nature and Politics: The Dialogue of Psychology and Political Science," *American Political Science Review* 79 (June 1985) pp.293-304. Also see Jervis, "Realism, Game Theory and Cooperation," *World Politics* 40 (April 1988) pp.317-49.

based on the "spiral theory" that argues that threats are likely to increase conflict and lead to unnecessary wars.[9]

The concept of case studies is also ambiguous. One can distinguish between full-blown historical studies which go into very great detail and the shorter studies of, for instance, Lebow[10] and George and Smoke,[11] which cover about 10 cases. This approach is in turn different from that of my work in *Perception and Misperception*,[12] in which I use aspects of many cases to illustrate points and demonstrate the plausibility of arguments. Still another approach is found in studies that employ quantitative data in the form of coding large numbers of cases according to the authors' judgment as to how they score on certain variables (for example, who initiated the conflict, whether or not deterrence succeeded, what the ties were between the various countries, etc.) in order to estimate the contribution of a set of independent variables to the success or failure of a policy.[13]

In all these approaches scholars are making subjective, but presumably not arbitrary, judgments about historical cases. Indeed, it is hard to imagine any other kind of empirical evidence in this realm. It is unavoidable that the theories and generalizations will be vulnerable to disputes about historical interpretations of particular cases.[14] Developing data on large numbers of cases reduces the vulnerability of general conclusions to changes in the analysis of any one case, but raises other difficulties that I will discuss later.

Most political scientists resort to a version of what economists call "stylized facts." That is, they rely on "potted" history convenient to their arguments. Thus major cases become models in a somewhat different sense than I discussed earlier. I have in mind here the common use of the spiral or 1914 model as well as the World War II model. We use the former for a situation in which a policy of threats and deterrence magnifies conflict and leads to wars and in which a policy of reassurance and conciliation might have kept the peace. However, historical research

---

9. For further discussion, see Jervis, "Rational Deterrence."
10. Richard Ned Lebow, *Between Peace and War* (Baltimore: Johns Hopkins University Press, 1981).
11. Alexander George and Richard Smoke, *Deterrence in American Foreign Policy* (New York: Columbia University Press, 1974).
12. *Perception and Misperception in International Politics* (Princeton: Princeton University Press, 1976).
13. A good summary of this work is Jack Levy, "Quantitative Studies of Deterrence Success and Failure," in Paul Stern, et al., eds., *Perspectives on Deterrence* (New York: Oxford University Press, 1989).
14. See, for example, the argument between John Orme, "Deterrence Failures: A Second Look," *International Security* 11 (Spring 1987) pp.96-124 and Richard Ned Lebow, "Deterrence Failure Revisited," *International Security* 12 (Summer 1987) pp.197-212. Also see the discussion below.

has indicated that Germany was driven to expand before 1914, in part by domestic pressures, and probably could not have been conciliated. (Whether a better policy of deterrence would have worked is difficult to say.) Different problems arise with the World War II model. While few would argue that Hitler could have been appeased, this case does not neatly fit the deterrence mold because it seems unlikely that even a well-designed policy of threats and containment could have avoided war, although it could have led to fighting on more favorable terms. Here, then, the heuristic use of crucial historical cases has proven so attractive as to overwhelm a more accurate portrayal of the cases themselves.

Continuum of Approaches

Models cannot stand on their own without case studies by which to test their validity. The other side of this coin is that the use of case studies is impossible without the parallel use of theoretical ideas. Even "mere" description is impossible without guiding precepts as to what is important and how it is to be interpreted.

While neither pure modeling nor pure empiricism is sensible, it may be useful to think of approaches as lying on a continuum. At one end are deductive models, largely but not exclusively of the rational choice variety. In the middle would be work that reconstructs actors' beliefs and perspectives, but tries to group these into a fairly small number of categories and does so with an eye to probing general arguments. At the other end of the continuum would be work that tries to reconstruct the worldviews and behaviors of the participants through *verstehen*, sees knowledge as highly contextualized and is anti-positivist. A discussion of this end of the continuum is beyond my competence and so will be omitted.

Between the first two kinds of investigations is what might be called "soft rational choice," perhaps the most common approach in history and political science. In many discussions of particular cases much of the work goes into trying to figure out what goals and beliefs the actors could have had to account for what initially seems puzzling behavior. Take, for example, Donald Kagan's analysis of the Peloponnesian Wars. He notes that one view of an Athenian leader's actions "explains that behavior by incompetence or stupidity. Those qualities surely exist and often explain military and political behavior, but before resorting to such an explanation, a historian prefers to exhaust the other possibilities."[15] Later, he explains the Athenian rejection of a seemingly favorable Spartan

---

15. Donald Kagan, *The Fall of the Athenian Empire* (Ithaca, NY: Cornell University Press, 1987) p. 126.

proposal by pointing to the Athenians' belief that the Spartans could not be trusted.

This kind of approach is used all the time, both in scholarship and in everyday life. Indeed, it is almost what we mean by making sense of behavior. It differs from modeling by being quite informal and by not proposing generalizations. Although the implicit appeal to common sense implies that goals and beliefs have a great deal of consistency across time and culture, there is no explicit attempt to locate consistent perceptual and decision-making patterns or to relate behavior to first principles.

Advantages and Disadvantages of Each Approach

Some scholars suggest that different degrees of formalization are appropriate for different questions or at different stages of our understanding—formal theories generate propositions, they say, and empirical investigations test them. There is something to this, but while formal models can generate propositions, they do not have a monopoly in this respect. Case studies can and do yield general principles and expectations that can be tested in other contexts. Of course this implies a perspective that is not totally opposed to that of modeling in that it assumes a significant degree of consistency among cases.

A radically different line of argument would be that modeling and case studies are two very different ways of understanding political phenomena. Each has its own criteria for validity, and the two methods are not comparable. This would be similar to an extreme version of Kuhn's claims about paradigms, and could therefore be attractive to practitioners because it would allow members of each camp to simply ignore one another. However, it would also leave as inappropriate, as well as unanswered, all the questions about the strengths and weaknesses of each approach. Without arguing that either one or the other is always best, it does not seem wise to dissolve all of the issues.

A fairly standard argument, which I think is partly correct, is that the choice between case studies and modeling involves a trade-off between richness and rigor. That is, the logic in formal models is very clear, but to gain this we must sacrifice much about the particular case that is causally important. Thus a formal model will neither fit all cases nor will it give the specifics of how the outcome actually came about. Case studies, on the other hand, often cannot be generalized and, without a matched comparison, have difficulty establishing causation.

In international politics we are often interested in particular cases. Thus World Wars I and II are not events equal in importance to hundreds of others. Because they had such an impact on world politics, we want to know about their causes in great detail. Although we seek to establish generalizations and first principles, if they exist, we also want a full and rich account of these events.

Models and, even more so, large-scale statistical analyses often tell us that many cases will fit into one category and fewer into another. Similarly, my own work on misperception is couched in terms of propensities and tendencies. However, these approaches do not tell us when and why an individual case fits into the most common pattern. For some purposes, this is a major concern. For example, if threats usually produce the desired result, we want to know what distinguishes cases in which this is true from ones in which it is not. If it is true that when two *status quo* powers rely on policies of threats toward one another the usual result is a spiral of greater tensions and hostility, we still want to know what distinguishes these cases from ones in which the same general starting conditions are present but the outcomes are different.

The choice of approach is related in part to the specific subject matter. Thus it seems to me that analyses of bargaining lend themselves to modeling more than do studies of misperception. One can take the game of "chicken" and set up a model to determine when states should back down or stand firm. Doing so enables one to deduce the sorts of tactics that bargainers should follow.[16] Similarly, one can adopt a fairly deductive approach to the linked topics of signaling, how states project desired images, and the logical status of various kinds of past behavior as evidence for how the state will behave in the future, because logic and working from the first principles are powerful and likely to produce a first approximation as to how actors actually behave.[17] Misperception, by contrast, does not seem to yield to this kind of formalization, at least not until a tremendous amount of empirical research has been done. Thus the more recent work in cognitive science and artificial intelligence could not have been carried out without extensive case study and laboratory investigations. There simply is no way to take a few axioms and deduce much about how people are likely to perceive and misperceive. (This is not to say that deduction plays no role here. As I mentioned earlier, psychological theories have many testable, counter-intuitive implications.)

Modeling may then be more appropriate when the number of factors at work is fairly small (i.e., when the parsimony in the approach matches

---

16. See, for example, Jervis, "Bargaining and Bargaining Tactics," in *Coercion, NOMOS* 14, J. Roland Pennock and John Chapman, eds., (Chicago: Aldine-Atherton, 1972) pp.272-88 and Glenn Snyder, "'Prisoner's Dilemma' and 'Chicken' Models in International Politics," *International Studies Quarterly* 15 (March 1971) pp.66-103.

17. *The Logic of Images in International Relations* (Princeton: Princeton University Press, 1970). See also the second edition (New York: Columbia University Press, 1989).

the parsimony in the situation), when behavior is determined rather than contingent, when actors' beliefs do not vary greatly in ways that strongly influence behavior, when the same effects are not produced by different causes and when actors' behavior is not influenced by how they got to where they are (i.e., when behavior is not path-dependent, as it is likely to be when actors' memories are important).

Although analogies are dangerous, it is interesting that some biologists have argued that the approach of physics, which relies on parsimony and is driven by deduction, may be inappropriate for their subject matter. My own knowledge here is very limited, so let me present an extended quotation from Francis Crick:

> Physics is also different because its results can be expressed in powerful, deep, and often counterintuitive general laws. There is really nothing in biology that corresponds to special and general relativity, or quantum electrodynamics, or even such simple conservation laws as those of Newtonian mechanics: the conservation of energy, of momentum, and of angular momentum. Biology has its "laws," such as those of Mendelian genetics, but they are often only rather broad generalizations, with significant exceptions to them...
>
> What is found in biology is mechanisms, mechanisms built with chemical components and that are often modified by other, later, mechanisms added to the earlier ones. While Occam's razor is a very useful tool in the physical sciences, it can be a very dangerous implement in biology. It is thus very rash to use simplicity and elegance as a guide in biological research...
>
> To produce a really good biological theory one must try to see through the clutter produced by evolution to the basic mechanisms lying beneath them, realizing that they are likely to be overlaid by other, secondary mechanisms. What seems to physicists to be a hopelessly complicated process may have been what nature found simplest, because nature could only build on what was already there.[18]

Of course, this raises the crucial question of whether, or when, politics more closely resemble physics or biology, to which I will return shortly.[19]

Advantages of Modeling

Let me turn to the advantages and disadvantages of formal models, starting with the former. First, the requirement for explicitness makes the scholar think hard about exactly what she thinks is at work. If done well, it allows the reader to see the logic that would otherwise be vague or

---

18. *What Mad Pursuit* (New York: Basic Books, 1988) pp.138-40.
19. See Almond and Genco, "Clouds, Clocks, and the Study of Politics."

implicit. Much scholarship deals with problems by "hand-waving"— assertions that really do not confront the problems or alternative possibilities. Relationships that seem obviously true often are not, and the first step is to rigorously develop arguments about them. For example, it may seem clear that a state gains advantages by developing a larger and more flexible nuclear arsenal. Not only is this proposition unconfirmed by the thin and ambiguous empirical evidence,[20] but the reasoning that leads to it is flawed.[21] Similarly, it seems obvious that the side with greatest resolve will have an advantage in bargaining in the game of chicken, but at least one formalization suggests otherwise.[22] Hence, formalization can reveal that implications that seemed to follow from a theory in fact do not. For instance, I think most people took from Schelling's treatment of the chicken paradigm the point that in such situations each side would take advantage of all bargaining advantages to push the other very hard. A reconsideration (which did not involve much formalization) led to the conclusion that this is incorrect, that states in fact should not be expected to try to extract as many concessions from the other side as they might and that instead caution should usually prevail.[23]

Second, formalization can then lead to conclusions that the scholar did not suspect at the outset, or at least that others did not. Bruce Bueno de Mesquita's work implies that, all other things being equal, states are more likely to attack their allies than their adversaries (the reasoning is that the former can expect fewer countries to come to their assistance and that, in the absence of a war, relations with allies are more likely to deteriorate than are those with adversaries, which are bad to begin with).[24] Perhaps the best known examples of counterintuitive inferences are Riker's argument that actors should not seek to expand their coalitions beyond the minimum size that is necessary for victory[25] and Olson's argument

---

20. Richard Betts, *Nuclear Balance and Nuclear Blackmail* (Washington: Brookings Institution, 1987); McGeorge Bundy, *Danger and Survival* (New York: Random House, 1988).
21. Jervis, *The Illogic of American Nuclear Strategy* (Ithaca, NY: Cornell University Press, 1984), ch. 1; Jervis, *The Meaning of the Nuclear Revolution* (Ithaca, NY: Cornell University Press, 1989) chs. 1, 3 and 7.
22. Robert Powell, "Nuclear Brinkmanship with Two-Sided Incomplete Information," *American Political Science Review* 82 (March 1988) pp.155-74.
23. Jervis, *The Meaning of the Nuclear Revolution*, ch. 1.
24. Bruce Bueno de Mesquita, *The War Trap* (New Haven: Yale University Press, 1981).
25. William Riker, *The Theory of Political Coalitions* (New Haven: Yale University Press, 1962). Note, however, that this applies only in zero-sum situations, which in fact are extremely rare in politics.

that collective action should occur only under special circumstances.[26] Indeed, many conclusions might have come to the fore sooner had people taken some central and powerful ideas more seriously. For example, had we thought through the implications of Joseph Berliner's brilliant analysis of the incentives in the Soviet economic system,[27] we would have anticipated several of the recent revelations about the sorry state of that system and the misrepresentations that characterize it. We would have expected managers of coal mines to mix rocks with their product in order to meet their quotas and officials to bribe others to accept falsified figures.

Setting out a full representation of the forces that one thinks are at work can bring to light important propositions and relationships that are likely to be missed in more casual analysis. It is often said that if statesmen are rational, they will go to war only if they think they are more likely to win than to lose. However, putting the problem into a simple equation shows that it would be rational for a state to go to war even if it thought the chance of victory was much less than 50 percent if it believed the possible gains from victory were very great and the losses from defeat relatively small. Similarly, it is often said that a rational decision maker would go to war only if he or she thought the expected utility of doing so was greater than the value of the *status quo*. But again, a simple equation shows that it is necessary to compare the expected utility of fighting not with the *status quo*, but with the expected utility of not starting a war; it can be rational for a statesman to start a war whose expected utility is negative when the expected utility of not fighting is even worse. This also indicates that a state which is trying to influence another's war/peace calculations (i.e., seeking to deter it from war) will often be well served by trying to increase the value the other expects from staying at peace, a conclusion consistent with the case study literature which stresses the importance of reassurances. In the same way, a full model indicates that a crucial element in decisions to stay at peace, go to war, avoid risks or willingly run them will be strongly influenced by judgments about whether time is on the side of the state or its adversary.[28]

It was only by working through the implications of bargaining in the game of chicken, using a simple equation, that I realized certain tactics I had thought would benefit the state in fact would not do so because they

---

26. Mancur Olson, *The Theory of Collective Action* (Cambridge, MA: Harvard University Press, 1965).
27. Joseph Berliner, *Factory and Manager in the USSR* (Cambridge, MA: Harvard University Press, 1957).
28. This paragraph draws on John Mueller, *Retreat from Doomsday: The Obsolescence of Major War* (New York: Basic Books, 1989).

would increase the adversary's incentives to stand firm just as much as they did the state's.[29] Similarly, when I set out to write "Cooperation Under the Security Dilemma," I thought I had a list of conditions and strategies that increased the chances of cooperation. It was only after I sketched out the links between the "prisoner's dilemma" and the security dilemma that I realized I could use first principles to deduce the effects of the conditions and strategies I had collected and to generate additional ones. Instead of a list, I had the beginnings of a theory.[30]

Formally specifying a model can also remind one of the importance of a variable previously taken for granted. In many cases it is this function, rather than the derived conclusions, which is the model's most important contribution. By developing a formal representation of crisis stability, Robert Powell not only reached some counterintuitive and, I suspect, misleading conclusions, but brought out the role played by the state's belief that it can defuse the crisis by making concessions.[31] We should now be less likely to assume than to demonstrate that a state can terminate a crisis by backing down or, even more importantly, that it will believe this avenue is open to it. Furthermore, we can see that a situation will be particularly dangerous if one side thinks the way is open for the adversary to retreat while the latter, in fact, believes that doing so would only invite attack. As Ole Holsti showed, a factor contributing to the outbreak of World War I was that both sides believed that while the adversary had the freedom to retreat, they had no choice but to stand firm.[32]

A third advantage of formalization is particularly relevant to the study of international politics: the need to take all sides into account. Whether I stand firm in a conflict depends in part on whether I think you will back down; whether I try to cheat on an agreement depends in part on how I estimate your abilities to detect my cheating and respond; whether a war occurs depends not only on the incentives of the potential attacker, but also on the incentives of the other side to make concessions rather than be attacked. The results are often counter-intuitive. Although familiarity

---

29. Jervis, "Bargaining and Bargaining Tactics."
30. Jervis, "Cooperation Under the Security Dilemma," *World Politics* 30 (January 1978) pp.167-214.
31. Robert Powell, "Crisis Stability in the Nuclear Age," *American Political Science Review* 83 (March 1989) pp.61-76.
32. Ole Holsti, "The 1914 Case," *American Political Science Review* 59 (June 1965) pp.365-78.

means that we are no longer surprised by the claim that internal weakness can lead to bargaining strength,[33] this is not the case for more recent game-theoretic derivations that indicate that improved detection abilities could lead to more rather than less cheating, or that increasing the penalties for crimes would leave the crime rate unchanged while lowering the intensity of policing.[34] (Of course these claims may not be correct—some difficulties will be noted below.)

A fourth advantage of formalization applies particularly to rational-choice models: This approach takes people seriously, and starts from the assumption that most behavior that seems puzzling, short-sighted or stupid really is designed to meet some goal that we do not yet understand. Rather than explain the behavior as foolish or pathological, we should explore the actor's perspectives. As I noted earlier, this is true of the "soft rational choice" approach of many historians and "traditional" political scientists. Its utility is strikingly revealed by more explicit theorizing. For example, before Schelling, many studies of bargaining assumed that displays of temper and staking one's reputation on carrying out a costly threat were the products of the negotiators' lack of experience, sophistication or self-control. Before Olson, much of the behavior of organizations aimed at supplying private incentives in support of the public good seemed like a diversion from the organizations' main activities, if not a failure to understand what they should be doing. A third, if obscure example, is that for the first 30 or 40 years of this century most experts believed that the southern habit of burning forests was pathological. Eventually, the forest service sent a psychologist to investigate. He dutifully reported that the behavior was an ingrained folk custom. Although he had asked the natives why they did it, he did not give any credence to their recital of the advantages of controlled fires. In fact, these beliefs not only explained their behavior, but were also largely correct.[35]

Costs of Modeling

I have concentrated elsewhere on the disadvantages of models, particularly those involving rational choice, and so will be brief about them

33. Thomas Schelling, *The Strategy of Conflict* (Cambridge, MA: Harvard University Press, 1960).
34. Barry O'Neill, "Why a Good Verification Scheme Can Give Ambiguous Evidence," *International Studies Quarterly*, forthcoming; George Tsebelius, "The Abuse of Probability in Political Analysis: The Robinson Crusoe Fallacy," *American Political Science Review* 83 (June 1989) pp.77-92.
35. Stephen Pyne, *Fire in America: A Cultural History of Wildland and Rural Fire* (Princeton: Princeton University Press, 1982) p.143.

here.[36] First, as I noted earlier, the logic of formalization cannot supply the substance of the argument. To return to the study of conflict, both deterrence and hostility spirals can be presented as formal models, and indeed, both can be presented as rational-choice models. What we need to know are the actor's goals, means-

This is linked to the second criticism of formal models: They may distract us from laborious and time-consuming empirical research. An excessive bedazzlement with parsimonious models and the joy of working out their implications could lead scholars away from a concern with their validity. The dark side of the discipline of economics is that few of its articles analyze much real data, let alone develop new information. Instead, model is pitted against model, without much attention to the real world. The study of conflict can be distorted if scholars pay more attention to puzzles generated by their models and to disputes internal to the formalizations than to the rich and confusing external world.

Similarly, it is easy to get wrapped up in the logic of a model and neglect the fact that the way in which actors think and perceive the world is crucial. This may be happening in the burgeoning literature on reputation.[37] Rather than analyze these intriguing arguments, I want to stress the importance of determining how actors actually establish reputations for behaving in various ways. A reputation, after all, is in the eyes of the beholder. Logic cannot tell us what will impress various observers, although the contributions of branches of cognitive psychology such as attribution theory are extremely helpful. Whether a state is perceived to be tough or not, whether it is thought to have lived up to its pledges and whether other states believe its behavior to be situationally or dispositionally caused are all questions in need of empirical investigation.

First of all, we need to know whether reputation is actually as important as the models would lead us to believe. Some investigations of international politics indicate that it is not.[38] If it is important, do perceivers pay more attention to whether a state has lived up to its commitments or to its general record of behavior, irrespective of the pledges its has made?[39] A related question is whether images of resolve transfer from one area to another. That is, if a state is willing to run high costs to prevail

---

36. See "Realism, Game Theory, and Cooperation," "Rational Deterrence" as well as "Additional Thoughts on Rational Choice," *Political Psychology* 10 (September 1989) pp.511-15.
37. For a summary and bibliography, see Robert Wilson, "Deterrence in Oligopolistic Competition," in *Perspectives on Deterrence* pp.157-90. Also see Jervis, *The Logic of Images*.
38. Glenn Snyder and Paul Diesing, *Conflict Among Nations* (Princeton: Princeton University Press, 1977) pp.498-500.
39. Jervis, *The Logic of Images*.

on one issue, will others infer that it will do so in other kinds of cases? For example, when Ronald Reagan fired the air-traffic controllers, did our adversaries believe that he was more likely to be tough on foreign policy issues?[40] This leads to another question: Does reputation attach to the individual statesman or to his or her country? If Reagan established a reputation for standing firm, will this reputation transfer to an America led by Bush? We also need to know whether reputations are established by making a great effort or by succeeding. For example, did its willingness to fight in Vietnam earn the United States a reputation for being willing to try to protect its allies even though it did not succeed in that case? We also need to know whether a reputation for carrying out threats is gained, preserved and damaged in the same manner as a reputation for giving rewards.[41] Models are likely to make quick and easy assumptions about these crucial questions; they may indeed distract us from them.

Further, I would like to note two difficulties in the use of game theory. First, although the strength of the approach is that it deals with interaction, many problems have no determinant game-theoretic solution. This is especially true of games that are variable-sum and involve many players. One may not be able to draw verifiable expectations from these theories about the outcome or about each actor's behavior.

Second, when game theory—or any theory—yields counter-intuitive propositions about how actors should behave, such propositions may be correct in terms of the actors' best interests, but are not likely to explain how actors in fact do behave unless the actors themselves understand the logic of the theory. For example, imagine that a complex theory showed that in a particular situation an actor should follow tactic A, whereas most people would have thought that tactic B was appropriate. Unless the actor knows this, he or she will follow tactic B, and the theory does not help us explain what the actors do. Similarly, some tactics work only because the adversary makes an error. This is true, for example, of tactics that are designed to provoke the other side. We need, then, to build the actors' beliefs into our models of interactions.

Assumptions, Models and the World

It is both easy and dangerous to build models on the assumption that a general knowledge of what we take to be human nature, combined with

---

40. I am grateful to George Quester for this example.
41. See Jonathan Mercer, "Attribution Error and Threat and Promise Credibility," Unpublished manuscript, (Department of Political Science, Columbia University, 1988).

our understanding of the situation, will tell us what incentives are operating. A fine as well as socially important example of the need to go beyond this is provided by Philip Triesman's work on the poor achievement of black students in college mathematics classes and what can be done to correct this.[42] He started with propositions that seemed almost certainly correct: that the high failure rate among blacks could be explained by lack of high school preparation, motivation or parental support, for example. But he found that none of the propositions were right. Only after prolonged, intensive and detailed study did he find that the operating incentive structure differed from what he had assumed at the outset. In fact, students' beliefs and self-images were the crucial factors. Because these young men and women viewed themselves as strong students, the extra classes could not be touted as remedial and the assignments had to include extremely difficult problems. Because most of the students had succeeded in high school by resisting peer pressure, they had to be introduced to the idea that working with their fellow students could be beneficial. States can also go wrong when they assume that others share their values and perspectives. When Teddy Roosevelt wanted to maintain peace in Cuba, he threatened to intervene if American property was attacked. But he failed to recognize that since each side desired American intervention, the result would be provocation, not deterrence.[43]

In general, there is a danger that scholars will go wrong by assuming that the self-interest which is being maximized is a very narrow one, such as the maximization of wealth or power. Of course, formal models can be based on any incentives, but there does seem to be at least an elective affinity between this approach and the positing of very selfish conceptions of interest. Making such an assumption simplifies the analysis and has some plausibility, but it is interesting that studies of businesses often find performance and profits to be at their highest when the employees are motivated by a sense of duty and the feeling that they are supposed to produce good products, help the corporation and serve customers. In other words, noneconomic incentives may be extremely important; the best capitalist ventures may be those which are permeated by pre-capitalist values. It would be odd indeed for those who have chosen a life of scholarship to base their theories of human behavior on the assumption

42. "A Study of the Mathematics Performance of Black Students at the University of California, Berkeley," Unpublished dissertation in mathematics and mathematics education (University of California, Berkeley, 1985).

43. Allan Millet, *The Politics of Intervention* (Columbus, OH: Ohio State University Press, 1968).

that all people act to maximize power and money. Of course some may: A study of graduate students showed that such behavior was dominant only among economists.[44] Indeed, I do not think it hopelessly idealistic to suggest that most people have a strong sense of duty and responsibility toward others.

Clocks and Clouds

I have left for last the most important and difficult issue, one brought up by the two quotations with which I began. I do not have a good answer, and indeed am not even sure that I can sketch the issues very well beyond the summary question: Does the nature of social phenomena in general and international conflict in particular lend itself to investigation through formal models? As Almond and Genco ask, do politics more closely resemble clocks or clouds (or, rather, in what respects are they cloud-like and in what respects clock-like)? That is to say, workings of clocks are deterministic and can be accounted for by unvarying, unproblematic, universal statements about causes and effects. Cloud-like behavior, on the other hand, involves many more variables, does not display such consistent patterns and is contingent, i.e., depends on the concatenation of many factors. (This is not to deny that the "scientific method" has taught us a great deal about clouds, in part because they may be more clock-like than a great deal of human behavior.)

Many scholars who do historical research are struck by the variability in international conflict: the way that seemingly similar initial conditions lead to very different outcomes; the ways in which threats sometimes achieve their goals and sometimes backfire; the multiple paths by which states' policies evolve that are hard to reconstruct after the fact, let alone predict ahead of time; and the multitude of patterns of interaction among many variables. A number of scholars who were trained in economics but who then turned to the study of international politics have reached the same conclusion.[45]

Of course, complexity *per se* is not a barrier to modeling. Many physical or social science problems cannot be understood (at least not yet) because they involve too many variables and too many hidden interactions. This is true, for example, of the greenhouse effect. But in this case no other approach will yield better results. Indeed, it can be argued that it is the very cloud-like nature of political phenomena that

---

44. Gerald Manwell and Ruth Adams, "Economists Ride Free; Does Anyone Else?" *Journal of Public Economics* 15 (June 1981) pp.295-310.
45. See the essays by Susan Strange and Raymond Vernon in Joseph Kruzel and James Rosenau, eds., *Journey Through World Politics* (Lexington MA: Lexington Books, 1989) pp.429-36 and 437-45.

requires us to use a clock-like approach to study them. It is precisely because politics involves so many variables that interrelate in such complex ways that we will be totally lost without "scientific" analysis. Furthermore, we can construct models that are as complex as the reality we are trying to understand. If the political world were simpler, we could keep all the factors straight in our heads without the assistance of formalizations. When critics are not claiming that models are much too simple, they argue that they are so complicated as to be unusable. Indeed, sometimes both criticisms are made simultaneously, leaving one to wonder how these conflicting objections could ever be reconciled and whether the utility of models is not being denied *a priori*.

The existence of great variability does not show that modeling is inappropriate; if the relations among the variables are themselves tight and invariant, the variability of the behavior or outcome is not cloud-like. To say that the phenomena in which we are interested change is not to say that the laws that generate them change. However, this may well be the case in much of political behavior. Because of changing technology, circumstances and human learning, patterns that hold at one point may not hold at others. The causes of war, for example, may be very different in one historical era than in another. At a certain level of what we mean by causes this is certainly true. Religious differences no longer cause war among "modern" states. We can, of course, say that this is too concrete a level to be useful, and that we are better off building more general arguments, for example, the argument that wars occur when at least one side believes its self-interest will be served by armed conflict. However, the definition of self-interest changes over time as people and collectives change their senses both of "self" and of "interest."

Learning can also be an important source of change. For example, if statesmen come to accept a new version of deterrence theory, they are likely to behave differently; some wars will occur that would not have otherwise and other wars will not be fought that otherwise would have been. Theories of this type can then be self-fulfilling or self-denying, to take only the two simplest possibilities. Even theories that are not as prescriptive as deterrence can change behavior. Wars often occur because statesmen think armed conflict is inevitable in the near future (this is at least part of the explanation for the outbreak of World War I). Any theory that tells decision makers that war is or is not likely can affect what they do.

Indeed, any generalization relevant to conflict, if discovered and believed by statesmen, is likely to influence their behavior as they seek to take advantage of the information they have gained about how others are likely to act. If the statesman changes his behavior, which otherwise would have conformed to the generalization, the latter will no longer hold. It is partly for this reason that Almond and Genco argue that social science laws are likely to have short half-lives.[46]

Arguments about free will and determinism are among the oldest in philosophy and social science, but not the most fruitful. Nevertheless, the subject is hard to avoid entirely. To argue for the great variability of international behavior, as do many of those who develop or draw on detailed case studies, is to imply that states and statesmen have significant freedom of action, hence the need to examine often idiosyncratic decision making. Other scholars consider actors to be more constrained and their behavior to be more regular due to common incentives and the pressing environment in which states exist.[47] Furthermore, formal models have less utility if foreign policies and international outcomes are highly contingent. Wars, of course, are major events, but this does not mean that their causes are major, or even noncontingent. The evidence for this point is notoriously difficult to judge. Would the course of history really have been different if Cleopatra's nose had been a bit shorter? This assertion by Pascal was used by Hans Morgenthau to attack the use of scientific methods in international politics.[48] A representative reply was McGeorge Bundy's evaluation of the role of the North Vietnamese attack on Pleiku, an American base, in February 1965: "Pleikus are streetcars."[49] That is, one will come along if you wait for it, and many different events could substitute for or serve the same function as the one that actually occurred. However, it is far from clear that World War I would have taken place had Archduke Ferdinand's carriage not taken a wrong turn in the streets of Sarajevo. When contingency cannot be dismissed, realist theories that try to deduce the most important aspects of international politics from the structure of the system, Marxist analyses that rely on a different sense of structure and parsimonious models all have grave defects.

Similarly, one may ask whether the outcome would have been different had factors difficult to model been different. To return to the case of Vietnam, even though it seemed clear by February 1965 that Lyndon Johnson would escalate rather than retreat, it is not certain that another president would have behaved in the same way, or that a different decision-making procedure would have yielded the same outcome.

---

46. Almond and Genco, "Clouds, Clocks and the Study of Politics," pp.513-18.
47. I am grateful to Robert Art for conversations on this point.
48. Hans Morgenthau, "International Relations: Quantitative and Qualitative Approaches," in Norman Palmer, ed., *A Design for International Relations Research: Scope, Theory, Methods, and Relevance* (Philadelphia: American Academy of Political and Social Science, 1970) p.78.
49. Quoted in Townsend Hoopes, *The Limits of Intervention* (New York: McKay, 1969) p.30.

According to attempts to model bargaining in the Cuban missile crisis, factors such as skill, chance interventions and coincidences had little impact, and were therefore excluded. The structure of the situation was clear and determined. The United States and the Soviet Union shared the need to avoid a war, although the United States had major bargaining advantages. Although the details of the settlement could have been different, the main outlines were set. Are these claims true? If Robert Kennedy had not thought of accepting the offer Khrushchev had apparently withdrawn, if the president and his closest advisors had not decided to make a private promise to withdraw the Jupiter missiles from Turkey or if Llewellyn Thompson had not persuaded the president that the Soviets would not press for a public trade, the story might have unfolded quite differently.

What is crucial is not only whether the specific events and decisions are unique, but also the dynamic stability of the system, that is, the extent to which the system can be deflected from its path by idiosyncratic events. Even dramatic perturbations will have little long-run impact if they elicit counteracting forces. In this case, modeling can proceed without much concern for such disturbances, even if they cannot be caught in the analysis. Models will still be useful in these cases, especially for outlining the dynamics of the system, but we will not be able to neglect the impact of the events that set the system on a new course.

Conclusions

Decisions affecting war and peace are made by individuals; to say that these people have free will is not to deny that they may feel such powerful constraints that strong and unchanging patterns will emerge. I am skeptical, however, about the extent of the regularity we will find: Individual values, perceptions and calculations are highly variable. How many potential leaders of Germany in the 1930s had values similar to Hitler's that would have led them to risk the destruction of the country in order to try to dominate the world? While my own work has argued that there are important regularities in perception, the exceptions are numerous and trends and propensities are all that can be established.

This is not to claim that politics is completely without patterns. If it were, international life and statesmanship could hardly exist, depending as they do on a degree of regularity and predictability in human affairs. But to focus only on regularities is to pay insufficient attention to the exceptions, which are numerous and important. Both unusually bad policies and instances of creativity and political skill can shape world politics. As noted earlier, we are as interested in why one case fits the common pattern while another does not as we are in what formula catches the average case. Indeed, since statesmen know a great deal about the patterns, they devote much of their energy to seeing that their policies escape the common fate.

To develop a model and test it against evidence, we must develop concepts that can be applied to the range of cases that interest us. This can be problematic when concepts which fit some cases are forcibly conformist Procrustean beds when applied to others. We can reduce all the cases to a manageable number of comparable kinds, but only at a high price, as is illustrated by recent deterrence research. One long-standing difficulty has been accounting for the success or failure of deterrence, especially in what is known as "extended deterrence" cases in which a major power tries to protect a (usually smaller) country against a challenger's threat. Relevant contemporary cases are the U.S. attempts to deter Soviet attacks on Western Europe and the Persian Gulf.

Bruce Russett and Paul Huth have conducted path-breaking research on these questions,[50] in which they coded large numbers of instances of deterrence by their success or failure and by the state of independent variables such as the military balance, links between the deterrer and protege and the history of previous encounters. Lebow and Stein tried to replicate the coding of the cases with startlingly different results.[51] What is relevant here is not the accuracy with which either set of scholars categorized the cases or the necessarily subjective nature of many of the judgments, but rather the fact that many of our standard concepts do not capture the true character of the cases.

We are accustomed to thinking of international relations in terms of deterrence and compellence (the former being the attempt to make the other side refrain from doing something; the latter being the attempt to make the other stop doing what it has been doing or do something different). This notion may catch some periods of the Cold War fairly well—the United States has sought to deter the Soviet Union from invading Western Europe; the Soviet Union has sought to deter the United States from invading Eastern Europe—but it creates two problems. First, to claim that deterrence has worked is to imply that the challenger would have moved had the deterrer not exercised its influence.

---

50. Bruce Russett, "The Calculus of Deterrence," *Journal of Conflict Resolution* VII (June 1963) pp.97-109; Paul Huth and Bruce Russett, "What Makes Deterrence Work? Cases from 1900 to 1980," *World Politics* 36 (July 1984) pp.496-526; Huth and Russett, "Deterrence Failure and Crisis Escalation," *International Studies Quarterly* 32 (March 1988) pp.29-46; Huth, *Extended Deterrence and the Prevention of War* (New Haven: Yale University Press, 1988).

51. Richard Ned Lebow and Janice Gross Stein, "Deterrence: The Elusive Dependent Variable," *World Politics* 42 (April 1990) p.336-369; for a reply see Huth and Russett, "Conceptual and Methodological Issues in the Empirical Testing of Deterrence," *ibid.*

It is one thing to show that the Soviet Union has not invaded Western Europe and quite another to demonstrate that Western deterrence has succeeded. Although this difficulty is well known, it is often ignored.

The second problem is more central here: In many cases, one cannot use the concepts of deterrence and compellence without doing great violence to actual history. Often, there is no straightforward *status quo* that one side is challenging and the other is defending. Rather, both sides (and other nations as well) are in motion, jockeying to protect and expand their interests. For example, who was deterring and who was challenging in the Moroccan crisis of 1905-6? Who was upholding the *status quo* and who was trying to change it?[52] In their *World Politics* article, Huth and Russett classify Germany as the attacker and France as the defender. As Lebow and Stein point out, these designations are reversed in Huth and Russett's later work.[53] I would not argue that they are right in one case and wrong in the other. Rather, the concepts of challenger and defender simply do not fit the example. France was trying to gain control of Morocco and to consolidate her colonial empire. Germany was seeking multiple goals: compensation, recognition of her status as a leading power, limitation of the French resurgence and an end to the new Anglo-French entente. We simply cannot say that one side was challenging and the other side defending.

While these concepts may not be adequate for this particular case, some concepts can and must be used to describe and explain it. But if we use different concepts to fit each small set of cases, then generalizations are beyond reach. Furthermore, it is far from clear that the terms and concepts I use in my sketch of the crisis are adequate. I believe they give a fuller and truer picture than a coding in terms of deterrence versus challenge, although a historian may cringe at my summary. However, there is no visible end to this road. Any discussion must abstract from the events; any account may be impeached on the grounds that the concepts it uses produce not understanding, but distortion. But Rapoport is right: We cannot understand waves by standing at the seashore and watching them, no matter how hard and long we stare.

---

52. It is not entirely correct to equate deterrence with trying to protect the status quo and compellence with seeking to change it. On occasion one side needs to take new actions in order to maintain the status quo, as in the 1968 Soviet intervention in Czechoslovakia, the weak 1980 attempt by the Carter administration to deter the Soviet Union from sending its arms into Poland and the U.S. effort to compel North Vietnam to stop sending soldiers into South Vietnam.

53. Richard Ned Lebow and Janice Gross Stein, "Testing Deterrence Theory: The Problem of Valid and Reliable Data," paper presented at the March 1989 meeting of the International Studies Association.

ALLIANCE THEORY: A NEOREALIST FIRST CUT

By Glenn H. Snyder

One of the most underdeveloped areas in the theory of international relations is alliance theory. Traditional theorists have tended to treat the subject as ancillary to broader topics such as "system structure" or "balance of power."[1] Statistically oriented scholars have been more inclined to focus directly on alliances, but their studies have emphasized correlations between aggregates—between the number of alliance commitments and the frequency of war, for instance—rather than the political processes of alliance making and maintenance.[2] Few attempts have been made to apply theories from related disciplines. The best developed of these efforts—an adaptation of collective goods theory—has been applied primarily to NATO and a particular problem in NATO, burden sharing.[3] Application of N-person game theory is just beginning.[4] There have of course been many studies of particular alliances, especially of NATO, and some of these have theoretical content. One of the most theoretical, and the classic analysis of NATO decision making, is Bill and Ann Fox's *NATO and the Range of American Choice*.[5]

Scholars have been reluctant, however, to attempt comprehensive theories of alliances, *per se*. The first to do so was George Liska, and his *Nations in Alliance*, published in 1962, remains the leading work.[6] Ole Holsti, Terrence Hopmann and John Sullivan published a useful study in a more behavioral vein in 1973.[7] Stephen Walt's recent (1987) book contains valuable theoretical insights, although it is limited empirically

1. Kenneth N. Waltz, *Theory of International Politics* (Reading, MA: Addison-Wesley, 1979); Hans J. Morgenthau, *Politics Among Nations* (New York: Alfred Knopf, 1948).
2. J. David Singer and Melvin Small, "Alliance Aggregation and the Onset of War," in J. David Singer, ed., *Quantitative International Politics: Insights and Evidence* (New York: The Free Press, 1968); Jack S. Levy, "Alliance Formation and War Behavior: an Analysis of the Great Powers, 1495-1975," *Journal of Conflict Resolution* 25 (December 1981) pp.581-613.
3. Mancur Olson and Richard Zeckhauser, "An Economic Theory of Alliances," *Review of Economics and Statistics* 48, no. 3 (1966).
4. E.M.S. Niou, P. Ordeshook and J. Rose, The Balance of Power and Stability in International Systems (New York: Cambridge Univerity Press, 1989).
5. William T. R. Fox and Annette Baker Fox, *NATO and the Range of American Choice* (New York: Columbia Universitty Press, 1962).
6. George Liska, *Nations in Alliance: The Limits of Interdependence* (Baltimore: The Johns Hopkins University Press, 1962).
7. Ole R. Holsti, P. Terence Hopmann and John D. Sullivan, *Unity and Disintegration in International Alliances: Comparative Studies* (New York: John Wiley, 1973).

to alliances in the Middle East.[8] The paucity of such landmark studies over a 25-year span only highlights an overall picture of relative theoretical neglect, considering the central role that alliances have always played in international politics. Certainly the theoretical study of alliances lags well behind the study of crises, wars and other manifestations of conflict between adversaries.

What might explain this neglect? Perhaps the very ubiquity of the phenomenon. As Liska himself put it, "It has always been difficult to say much that is peculiar to alliances on the plane of general analysis." The would-be analyst of alliances is immediately confronted with a difficult problem of delimitation: How are alignments and alliances, properly conceived as informal as well as formal associations, to be distinguished from international politics in general? This task is especially difficult considering another of Liska's aphorisms—that "alliances are against and only derivatively for, someone or something"—which implies that relations with allies and adversaries are inseparable.[9] The analyst, realizing he doesn't really want to attempt a "general theory of international relations" then retreats to something more manageable, such as a study of a particular alliance.

In brash disregard of such common sense, I will suggest here some of the central elements and problems in a theory of alliances and alignments, emphasizing alliance formation and intra-alliance politics as these processes are affected by the structure of the international system. My interest in this subject dates back to my graduate seminars with Bill Fox in the early 1950s. My thinking has also been considerably influenced by the work of a fellow participant in some of those seminars, Kenneth Waltz. Even then, in the brownstones along 117th Street at Columbia University, neorealism could be observed emerging.

Definition and Classification

The first task in any scientific investigation is to define one's subject. Alliances, as I will use the term, are formal associations of states for the use (or non-use) of military force, intended for either the security or the aggrandizement of their members, against specific other states, whether or not these others are explicitly identified. The restriction to military means and security purposes excludes, obviously, such things as voting blocs in international organizations, customs unions, or collaboration on environmental problems. The restriction to states rules out transnational associations of all kinds, including especially ties between governments

---

8.   Stephen M. Walt, *The Origins of Alliances* (Ithaca: Cornell University Press, 1987).
9.   Liska, *op. cit.*, pp.3, 12.

and revolutionary groups in other states. The proviso "specific other states" calls attention to the need for an adversary and differentiates alliances from organizations, such as the League of Nations or the United Nations, which are designed to provide collective security against any aggressor, including members of the organization itself.[10]

Alliances, however, are only the formal subset of a broader and more basic phenomenon, that of "alignment." Alignment amounts to a set of mutual *expectations* between two or more states that they will have each other's support in disputes or wars with particular other states.[11] Such expectations arise chiefly from perceived common interests; they may be strong or weak, depending perhaps on the parties' relative degree of conflict with a common adversary. Formal alliances strengthen existing alignments, or perhaps create new ones, by their solemnity, specificity, legal and normative obligations and (in modern times) their public visibility.[12] However their political reality lies not in the formal contract, but in the expectations they support or create. Alignments may be strengthened or created in many other ways, such as by *ententes*—agreements that settle conflicts between states to such a degree that from then on they expect each other's diplomatic or military support—or by unilateral declarations and actions of various kinds.[13] Of course alignments are continually changing—strengthening, weakening or disappearing—along with changes in states' interests, domestic political configurations, and perceptions of other states' behavior.

After definition the next pre-theoretical task is to develop a typology of alliances and alignments, that is, to identify important variations in the subject.[14] An important distinction is between peacetime alliances and those formed during war—the latter, often called "coalitions", lack many

10. The classic statement of this distinction is Arnold Wolfers' essay "Collective Defense vs. Collective Security," in A. Wolfers, ed., *Alliance Policy in the Cold War* (Baltimore: Johns Hopkins, 1959) pp.49-75.
11. This definition of alignment is similar to Liska's, but differs from the one advanced by George Modelski in his review of Liska's book. Modelkski defines "alignment" as "all types of poltical cooperation," and allieance as "military collaboration.," apparently including in the latter the tacit expectation of such collaboration that I have labelled "alignment." See George Modelski, "The Study of Alliances: A Review," *Journal of Conflict Resolution 7, no.4 (December 1963) pp. 769-76.*
12. Of course this does not mean that formalized alignments are always more solid than informal ones. Prior to World War I, for example, the informal Triple Entente was far more cohesive than Italy's membership in the Triple Alliance.
13. On *ententes*, see Robert E. Kann, "Alliances vs. Ententes," *World Politics* 14 (July 1976) pp.611-21.
14. The best typology currently available is Bruce Russett's. See his "An Empirical Typology of International Military Alliances," *Midwest Journal of Political Science* 15 (May 1971) pp.262-89.

of the political functions, such as deterrence of attack, preclusion and restraint of the ally, that characterize peacetime alliances. Alliances can also be offensive or defensive, *ad hoc* or permanent, bilateral or multilateral, unilateral guarantees or mutual commitments, etc. Non-formal alignments run from "special relationships" to *ententes* to merely good relations; at the boundary between amity and enmity they merge into such hybrids as *detente* or *rapprochement.* A major class of alliance is the mutual defense pact, and I will have this type principally in mind for the remainder of this essay.

Allies, Adversaries and Systems

Alliances are a means to security against adversaries. Therefore they cannot be studied apart from other security policies, nor apart from the enmities and rivalries to which they respond. It is analytically useful to postulate separate alliance and adversary games,[15] despite their entanglement in reality. Each of these games is played on three policy levels: armament, action, and declaration. The armament level in the adversary game is "arms racing"; in the alliance game it is "burden sharing."[16] The action level between adversaries involves simply decisions whether to attack or to resist attack. The alliance game at this level entails decisions to aid or not to aid a victim of attack, or more broadly, whether or not to intervene in an ongoing war. Decisions to act cannot be exclusively identified with either the adversary or alliance game for they are likely to have effects, or to be motivated by goals, in both games. Thus a decision to defend another state that is under attack may be motivated partly to prevent the attacker from gaining power resources (adversary game) and partly to keep the victim's resources available to defend oneself (alliance game).[17]

Declaratory interaction in both games is the use of communication to manipulate others' expectations of one's future behavior. It includes both unilateral declarations and bargaining. Between adversaries, one kind of communication is coercive, intended to intimidate or deter. Another kind is accommodative, signaling concession or capitulation. Accommodative declarations generally occur in the context of negotiation, and the result may be an agreement in which both parties promise to take some action in the future that will implement the agreement.

---

15. I use the word "games" here not in the technical game theory sense but simply to indicate two broad types of strategic interaction.
16. Further discussion of the armaments level is beyond the scope of this essay.
17. I think I first became aware of this seamless quality of adversary and alliance relations when I heard Bill Fox say in the spring of 1953, that "defending an ally for strategic reasons is logically equivalent to preventive war." His seminars were peppered with such striking insights.

Similarly, an alliance agreement is essentially a joint declaration, a mutual promise to act in a specified way in specified future contingencies. Although it is obviously different in many other ways from adversary declarations and bargains, it is similar in that it creates or changes expectations about the parties' future behavior. Various lesser declarations between allies, such as assurances of support on particular issues or warnings of non-support, are analogous to the threats, warnings and commitments that are exchanged between adversaries in a crisis. Of course, actions may also communicate future intentions, changing others' expectations in both alliance and adversary relations.

Alliances should also be placed in the context of system structure and process. Systemic anarchy is one stimulus to ally, although not always a sufficient one. Structural polarity—how military power and potential are distributed among major states—has important effects on the nature of alliances and alliance politics. Alliances are substantially different in multipolar and bipolar systems.[18] The following discussion will highlight some of these differences, focusing on two phases: the *formation* of alliances and their subsequent *management.*

Alliance Formation in a Multipolar System

The central questions concerning alliance formation are: Under what conditions will alliances form? What determines who allies with whom? and What determines how the benefits and costs of the alliance are divided among its members?

It is useful to start with a skeletal model of a multipolar system based on the following assumptions: (a) there are three or more major states, (b) they have approximately equal military power, (c) there are no particular conflicts of interest among these states, (d) they have incomplete information about each others' intentions, and (e) communication is not permitted, that is, alliances cannot form in peacetime. From these assumptions we can deduce that all will feel somewhat insecure, for each perceives that it might be attacked by others even though it has no specific conflicts with them. Indeed, some states may be motivated to attack, if only to reduce their insecurity by acquiring more power resources. However, aggression may be inhibited to some extent by the fear of being attacked from the rear while one is pre-occupied. Each will feel some motivation to come to the defense of any state that is attacked, otherwise the attacker's power resources may be substantially increased. This is the logic of balance-of-power theory. However, each will feel a competing

---

18. Here, by Kenneth Waltz has led the way in his *Theory of International Politics*, especially ch. 8.

incentive to stand aside if aggression occurs in hopes that some other state will stop the aggressor. This is the logic of "passing the buck" or "free riding," as in the theory of collective goods. It is not possible to determine which of these tendencies will prevail in a particular instance, but the balancing tendency will become stronger as an aggressor gains repeated increments of power and will become irresistible, logically, when an aggressor is on the brink of acquiring half of the power resources in the system, for beyond that point it will be able to dominate the entire system.

This is a picture of the "action level." There are no peacetime (pre-action) alliances, since communication is not permitted, although, of course, tacit alliances form when states come to the defense of others. If we revise the model to allow pre-war communication, peacetime alliances may occur in order to reduce the insecurity of anarchy or reduce armament costs. If they do occur, they will tend to create relations of enmity as well as alignment: Even if the initial alliance is not directed at any specific opponent, other states will perceive it as a threat and begin to behave as enemies, perhaps by forming a counter-alliance. Not only will alliances identify friends and foes, they will also create interests consistent with such relations. That is, allied states will acquire strategic interests in preserving their alliance and in protecting their allies' power resources, and in preventing their designated opponent from increasing its power resources. They will also have acquired an interest in maintaining their reputation for loyalty to their allies and their reputation for resolve *vis-à-vis* their adversaries.

In short, alliances in this imaginary system focus the otherwise diffuse insecurity of anarchy on specific other states and largely eliminate it *vis-à-vis* still others, and they buttress these new relationships by a new set of interests. This point is worth making not just as a preliminary theoretical exercise, but because these structurally induced incentives and interests will be present and will affect alliance behavior in real systems, even though such behavior may appear to be a function entirely of non-structural conflicts and affinities.

We can now increase the realism of the model by relaxing two more assumptions to permit (a) particular (non-structural) conflicts and affinities (specific territorial disputes, for example, or ideological attractions and repulsions) and (b) marginal inequalities of military strength. Conflicts and common interests generate a pattern of alignment that exists prior to, and independently of, formal alliances. That is, states will have some expectation of being supported in war or crises by states with whom they share interests and values, and of being opposed by states with whom they have conflicts. These expectations will generate "strategic interests" in defending states that are expected to be supportive and in blocking the accumulation of power resources by putative opponents.

Strength inequalities will also influence expectations and interests. Thus, two weaker states will feel naturally aligned against a stronger state that threatens them both, while two strong states with a weaker state between them will tend to be rivals and protective of the weaker state against each other.[19] The alignment pattern will be clearest, of course, when the effects of strength differences and conflicting or common interests are mutually reinforcing rather than opposing.

Introducing these variables has two general effects relative to the initial model of pure anarchy: It increases incentives to ally and it increases the predictability of who allies with whom. However, these effects may not be sufficient to determine alliance partners if some states have several alliance options of similar desirability. Partners are actually chosen by a process of bargaining and the exigencies of bargaining may override the conflict-affinity-strength pattern to produce alliance line-ups that are contrary to it.[20]

When formal alliances are superimposed on this prior pattern, their effect is to modify the expectations of mutual support and opposition that are inherent in the tacit alignments. Alliances generally strengthen alignments by introducing elements of precision, obligation and reciprocity. The interests and expectations that underlie tacit alignments are inherently uncertain; verbal statement of what the parties intend to do in specific circumstances strengthens mutual expectations at least for those circumstances, even though expectations of support may be weakened for contingencies not included. Expectations are further buttressed normatively by the legal and moral obligation entailed in the alliance contract. Finally, the alignment is strengthened by a non-normative sense of reciprocity—that is, by the mutual recognition that the partner's support depends, at least in part, on the fulfillment of one's own commitment to him.

Besides formal alliances, other kinds of behavior may be superimposed on the alignment pattern and thus change it. This includes verbal utterances of many kinds—diplomatic notes, official statements, etc.— as well as physical acts, such as movements of forces.

In summary, the pattern of conflict, common interest and capabilities (pattern of alignment) lie "between" structural anarchy and formal

---

19. Space limitations forbid any further detailed discussion of strength differences.
20. Thus an apparently natural Anglo-German alliance failed to materialize in 1901, largely because Germany demanded too high a price in British commitments. The somewhat unnatural Anglo-French Entente followed in 1904.

alliance. Although anarchy alone generates some motivation to act to defend others and to form alliances, the motivation is weak. The alignment pattern adds further incentives to aid or ally with others, and greater predictability of who will aid or ally with whom. Formal alliances and other supportive behaviors generally strengthen and clarify incentives and expectations of mutual aid. The independent effect of alliances will be greatest when conflicts, common interests and power inequalities in the system are moderate, or when they are contradictory in their alignment implications.

The Values of Alliance

What exactly do states gain from allying and what determines how the gains are allocated? The gain is the surplus of benefits over costs. The primary benefit of alliance is obviously security, but many non-security values may also accrue. Security benefits in a mutual defense alliance include chiefly a reduced probability of being attacked (deterrence), greater strength in case of attack (defense) and prevention of the ally's alliance with one's adversary (preclusion). The principal costs are the increased risk of war and reduced freedom of action that are entailed in the commitment to the partner.[21]

The size of these benefits and costs for both parties will be determined largely by three general factors in their security situations: (1) their alliance "need," (2) the extent to which the prospective partner meets that need, and (3) the actual terms of the alliance contract. Alliance need is chiefly a function of the ratio of a state's capabilities to those of its most likely antagonist(s), and its degree of conflict with, or perceived threat from, that opponent. The greater the shortfall between its own military strength and that of its opponent and the deeper its conflict with the adversary (hence the greater the likelihood of its being attacked), the greater its alliance need and the greater the deterrent and defense benefits it will gain from any alliance that satisfies that need. However, different prospective partners will satisfy the need to different degrees, depending

---

21. The restraint function of alliances is emphasized by Paul Schroeder in "Alliances, 1815-1945: Weapons of Power and Tools of Management," in Klaus Knorr, ed., *Historical Dimensions of National Security Problems* (Lawrence, KS: University Press of Kansas, 1976) pp.227-63. Robert L. Rothstein suggests that formal alliance establishes a "right" to be consulted. See his *Alliances and Small Powers* (New York: Columbia University Press, 1968) p.49.

on their capabilities and perceived reliability. Obviously, an ally whose military strength is too weak to fill up the capabilities deficit will provide little security benefit. On the other hand, a very strong ally may provide surplus security and be able to dominate the alliance.[22] Further, the value of the alliance must be discounted by the likelihood that the partner will not fulfill his commitment.

The costs of alliance will turn on similar factors as they affect the ally. The weaker the ally *vis-à-vis* his adversary, the more one will have to contribute to his defense. The deeper his conflict with his adversary, the more likely he will be attacked or the greater the chance that, counting on one's support, he will precipitate a crisis or war himself. The costs of alliance will be minimized when the allies have the same adversary (or when their different adversaries are allied) because they will then have a strategic interest in defending each other even without alliance.

Benefits and costs also include effects on states other than the adversary. Alliance with a state that is closely aligned to another by interest brings along the other as a tacit member. For instance, when Bismarck made his alliance with Austria in 1879, he counted England as a "sleeping partner" because of the convergence of British and Austrian interests in the Balkans. Conversely, alliance may entail a cost in alienating an ally's enemy.

Alliance values, like all security values, are future-oriented. In estimating them, the parties must take into account not only the general benefits and costs just mentioned but also specific events and effects that the alliance might precipitate over time and across the entire system. Thus the value of the alliance must be discounted by the probability that it will trigger a counter-alliance, provoke the adversary to greater hostility, or increase the hostility of some other state that is friendly to the adversary. Its value should be appreciated by the likelihood that it will make the adversary more amenable in settling disputes, or that it will attract additional alliance members.

Negotiating the Alliance Contract

The alliance values just discussed are those that are inherent in the parties' security positions, that is, in their need for alliance, without reference to the terms of the alliance contract. However, the actual benefit

---

22. However, the distribution of payoffs in an alliance is not directly a function of the relative strengths of the allies as suggested in much of the psychological-sociological literature on coalition theory. It turns on the parties' strengths relative to their adversaries rather than relative to each other; this is what bears on their comparative dependence on the alliance and on their capacity to bargain for payoff shares. See Theodore Caplow, *Two Against One: Coalitions in Triads* (Englewood Cliffs, NJ: Prentice-Hall, 1968).

to individual alliance members will depend on some combination of their inherent values and the contract terms. By its specific commitments, the contract delimits and distributes the inherent values that accrue to the members from their security positions and may also introduce non-security values. The terms, of course, are a product of bargaining, and they may favor one party or another, depending on the parties' relative bargaining power. Here there is an important link between inherent valuations and contract terms. The parties' comparative inherent valuations (crudely, their comparative need for alliance) is one of two important determinants of relative bargaining power. The other determinant is the comparative attractiveness of other alliances available to the parties. Thus, *ceteris paribus*, the party that values the alliance least or has the better alternatives will be able to demand and get terms advantageous to itself. It might, for example, be able to get a stronger and broader commitment from the partner than it has to give, or it might be able to extort side-payments extraneous to the mutual security commitments, such as a free hand in some colonial area. But if the party with the lesser need (value) for the alliance also has the less attractive alternatives, the contract terms will be fairer. In general, we may hypothesize that if one state gets a greater inherent value from the alliance because of a greater security need, the terms of the contract will favor its partner, thus tending to equalize payoffs, but that this tendency will be either weakened or strengthened by asymmetries in alternatives. However, both of these tendencies may be overcome or inhibited by the salience of, or normative preference for, equal terms.[23]

Alliance Management in a Multipolar System

After an alliance has formed, the partners face a variety of management tasks: coordinating foreign policies (especially toward the adversary), coordinating military plans, allocating preparedness burdens and collaboration during adversary crises, for example. On some of these issues they may see eye-to-eye and on these their joint activity is equivalent to joint problem solving. On other issues they will be in conflict. For these, the word management is a bit antiseptic; it might better be labeled "intra-alliance politics" or "bargaining"—the prosecution and resolution of conflict while maximizing the realization of common interests.

The principal common interest in any alliance is holding it together; the principal source of conflict is the stance to be taken toward the

---

23. J. G. Cross, "Some Theoretic Characteristics of Economic and Political Coalitions," *Journal of Conflict Resolution* 11, no.2 (June 1967) pp.184-95.

adversary or adversaries. The first gives rise to fears of the ally's defection and perhaps realignment; the second generates worries about being dragged into a war over the ally's interests that one does not share. Following Michael Mandelbaum, I call these twin anxieties "abandonment" and "entrapment."[24] Together they constitute the "alliance security dilemma" since reducing one tends to increase the other. Thus, the risk of abandonment can be reduced by strengthening one's commitment to, hence value to, the ally, but this increases the risk of entrapment for two reasons: (1) the ally is emboldened to stand firmer and take more risks *vis-à-vis* his opponent, and (2) one becomes more firmly committed to the ally. The danger of entrapment can be reduced by weakening one's general commitment or by refusing support to the ally on a particular issue, but this increases the danger of abandonment by reducing the alliance's value to the ally. The cost of abandonment (as distinct from its risk) varies with a state's dependence on the alliance, largely a function of its strength and its degree of conflict with its adversary. The cost of entrapment varies with the extent of shared interests with the ally; it is highest when the parties have different opponents or have different interests at stake *vis-à-vis* the same opponent. Outright abandonment of allies has not occurred frequently in history, but the structure of a multipolar system, combined with the congenital worst-case thinking of statesmen, generates persistent fears that it might occur.[25]

Balancing between abandonment and entrapment fears is, strictly speaking, not so much a dilemma as a trade-off; the problem is to optimize between them. It is, however, only a part (though a large part) of the overall alliance bargaining problem in which the partners seek to optimize across a broader range of values. Post-formation alliance management might be conceived as a continuous bargaining process in which the members seek to maximize their alliance benefits while minimizing their risks and costs. The greater bargaining leverage will accrue to the party that is least dependent on the alliance. Relative dependence is essentially a function of the parties' comparative need for alliance (as defined above) along with the comparative attractiveness of their alliance alternatives, viewed from a post-formation perspective.

---

24. Michael Mandelbaum, *The Nuclear Revolution: International Politics Before and After Hiroshima* (New York: Cambridge University Press, 1981) pp.151-52.
25. For a fuller discussion of abandonment and entrapment, see my "The Security Dilemma in Alliance Politics," *World Politics* 36, no. 4 (July 1984) pp.461-96.

Less dependent allies will enjoy a preponderance of influence over their partners' policies and the general policies of the alliance. They will be least affected by Kenneth Waltz's axiom that "flexibility of alignment" makes for "rigidity of strategy".[26] Because they can tolerate the risk of alliance dissolution better than their partners, they need not so carefully tailor their policies to suit the partners' wishes.[27]

However, the "balance of dependence" (and hence, relative bargaining power) may shift over time as a consequence of changes in individual members' security environments and their perceptions and evaluations of such changes. For example, a state's intra-alliance leverage may increase because of a reduction in the degree of threat from an opponent or an increase in the attractiveness of its alliance alternatives, or because of a change in its domestic political configuration that reduces the value it places on the alliance. Such changes, and other members' perceptions of them, may be exploited to increase alliance benefits or reduce costs and risks. Successive revisions of the Triple Alliance in Italy's favor, possible because of a reduction in Italian dependence and an increase in German-Austrian dependence, exemplify this. Decreased dependence may yield implicit benefits, as when a state feels less compelled to support its ally in a crisis, or less inhibited in accommodating the ally's opponent, or the ally feels more compulsion to support the state. However, such advantages must not be exploited too vigorously, lest the ally's valuation of the alliance be degraded to the point where his alternatives appear more attractive and he begins to consider realignment.

As in the abandonment-entrapment trade-off, the broader alliance management problem for an individual state is to optimize net benefits in the context of a changing balance of dependence. This may be accomplished partly in formal renegotiations of the alliance's terms. Such renegotiations generally occur when alliances come up for renewal, but may occur at other times as well; the terms of the Austro-German alliance and the Franco-Russian alliance for instance, were strengthened in 1909 and 1912, respectively. Theoretically, such events may be considered iterations of the original "play" when the alliance was formed, but with somewhat different preferences, relative power and other background conditions. Between such formal iterations, or in their absence,

---

26. Waltz, *op. cit*, p.169.
27. For this reason, states will tend to choose their allies in the first place with an eye to the post-formation balance of dependence and influence. Thus Bismarck chose to ally with Austria rather than Russia in 1879 partly because he could "ride" Austria, whereas with Russia he would be the "horse" to Russia's rider. Raymond J. Sontag, *European Diplomatic History, 1871-1932* (New York: Appleton-Century-Crofts, 1933) p.19.

the size and allocation of benefits, costs and risks will continuously change as background conditions change.

However, this still is not the whole story. Alliance management must take account of relations with adversaries as well as allies; that is, it must consider the close interplay between alliance and adversary "games." This involves a host of dilemmas. In the adversary game, conciliating an opponent may be seen as preferable to firmly resisting him, but it may also be perceived by the ally as a move toward realignment and cause the ally to defect. Supporting an ally too vigorously in a crisis may provoke the opponent to some dangerous reaction.[28] On the other hand, restraining an ally may weaken one's deterrence of the adversary. A tough stance toward the opponent risks entrapment by emboldening the ally. Adversaries face a "prisoner's dilemma" when they see mutual advantage in collaborating to restrain their respective allies who are in conflict, but also fear losing their allies as a result.[29] Some of these dilemmas can be at least alleviated by reassuring or warning the party, whether ally or adversary, which has overheard the message directed toward the other. But again, these dilemmas are really trade-offs wherein the problem is to optimize among competing goals *vis-à-vis* both adversaries and allies.

One of the curiosities of international security theory is that we have no theory of bargaining between allies remotely comparable to the rich theory about bargaining between adversaries, as developed by Schelling and others.[30] Yet there are many parallels and analogies between the two which might be exploited theoretically. Both alliance and adversary bargaining involve an interplay of common and conflicting interests. Typically, in both realms coercive bargaining employs threats to destroy the common interest in order to get one's way on issues in conflict, while accommodative bargaining sacrifices interests in conflict in order to realize a common interest. The ultimate common interest in adversary bargaining is the avoidance of war; in alliance bargaining it is preservation of the alliance. Thus, the coercive alliance analogue to deterrence is restraint of the ally. Deterrence is accomplished by threatening war; restraint is accomplished by threatening non-support and implicitly, alliance break-up. In each case the threat must be credible to be effective;

---

28. A good example is David Lloyd-George's Mansion House speech during the Morocco crisis of 1911 between France and Germany. The speech triggered a dangerous sub-crisis between Germany and England.

29. Britain and Germany successfully surmounted this dilemma when they restrained Russia and Austria during the Balkan Wars of 1912-13, but they failed to do so during the crisis of July 1914.

30. Thomas C. Schelling, *The Strategy of Conflict* (Cambridge: Harvard University Press, 1960).

in adversary relations credibility is undermined by the cost of war to the threatener; in the alliance game it is weakened by the extent to which the threatener needs the alliance or has an interest in defending the ally even without an alliance.

A theory of alliance bargaining tactics might profitably borrow from the detailed menus of tactics that are available in the literature on crises and coercive bargaining between adversaries. Such borrowing must be limited by the recognition that alliance bargaining may be more accommodative than coercive—that is, more oriented toward the realization of common interests than the prosecution of conflict.

Tactics employed primarily in either the alliance game or the adversary game will have side-effects in the other game, effects which may be either counterproductive or supportive. When the objective in both games is coercive, the side-effects will be reciprocally undermining. Thus, a strong explicit commitment toward an opponent maximizes deterrence but minimizes capacity to restrain the ally. Restraining the ally—more generally, maximizing bargaining leverage over the ally—counsels keeping one's commitment ambiguous but ambiguous commitments tend to weaken deterrence. Similarly, tactics which promote the common interest in one game will tend to undermine the common interest in the other. Hence, when adversaries compromise their disputes in order to reduce tension, the solidarity of their alliances is weakened, and when allies tighten their bonds, tension with their adversaries rises.

On other hand, when the objective is coercive in one game and accommodative in the other, the side-effects across games will be mutually reinforcing. Thus, standing firm *vis-à-vis* the opponent in order to preserve one's resolve reputation also shores up one's loyalty reputation with the ally and reduces the likelihood that the ally will defect. Conciliation of the adversary facilitates restraint of the ally.

It should not be forgotten that the fundamental focus of analysis is, or ought to be, alignment rather than alliance. In other words, the center of attention should be the expectations of states regarding the likelihood and degree of support from others, whether these expectations derive from perceived interests or from treaties or some other form of behavior. Although formal alliances may have their special management problems, the broader and more fundamental problem in a multipolar system is that of managing alignment. There is a vast area of political interaction lying between the relatively static interests and conflicts in the system and the formation and management of formal alliances. In this area much turns on nuances—friendly gestures, concessions, symbolic demonstrations, and so on—well short of alliance or even *entente*. The broad alignment management problem for any state is to optimize across the twin goals of security and independence. Thus, if a threat increases in one quarter, a state may reestablish (some) security by moving toward another state, although with some cost in lost diplomatic freedom or perhaps in tangible concessions. Conversely, if an enemy threat declines, a state may feel safe in putting distance between itself and a friend, at some risk of alienating the friend. There are many other possible situations and trade-offs.[31] When the armament and action levels of behavior are thrown into the equation, the calculus becomes considerably more complex, since since armaments costs or war costs can substitute for the dependence costs of alignments.

Alliance Formation in a Bipolar System

Alliance formation is a much simpler process in a bipolar than a multipolar system. Who allies with whom is much less a matter of choice and more a matter of systemic determination; at least this is so in the core sector of the system (i.e., Europe) where the principal security interests of the superpowers lie. The superpowers, of course, have no incentive to ally with each other since there is no third party strong enough to threaten them both. In their own interest, they will throw their protective arms around the lesser states that are in closest geographical proximity, whether the latter want protection or not. Such protection will be formalized as "alliance" but in reality it will amount to a unilateral guarantee. The superpowers will extend their guarantees to small states outside the core sector that will accept them, but many of these states will remain without such guarantees, mostly because they do not feel sufficiently threatened by either superpower to need protection by the other, and they feel confident that if attacked by one they will be defended by the other even without a formal alliance. In general, alliances in a bipolar system will have less independent effect on relations than alliances in a multipolar system because interests and expectations, and hence alignments, are substantially established by the structure of the system.

Allowing for differences in detail due to "unit level" and geographical differences—notably the Soviets' need to impose their "protection" by force compared to the voluntary acquiescence of American allies—this seems a fair picture of the structural forces behind the formation of NATO, the Warsaw Pact and other alliances of the United States and the Soviet Union. Unlike in the usual multipolar system, these alliances did not take shape against a backdrop of crosscutting patterns of conflict, common interest and capabilities that left a state uncertain about who its natural

---

31. For an excellent discussion of some of them, with historical illustrations, see Robert Jervis, "Systems Theories and Diplomatic History," in Lauren, *op. cit.*, pp.212-45.

allies and enemies were. For non-communist states there was one clear common enemy (since the Sino-Soviet bloc was perceived to be a monolith into the 1960s) although the degree of threat perceived in that enemy varied. It was also clear who among them must bear the principal burden of resisting that enemy. These two givens, along with the U. S. willingness to take up the burden, established a clear alignment between the United States and most non-Communist states.[32] The alignment was formalized for states who felt particularly threatened or regarding whom the United States felt it was particularly important to make known its own intentions for deterrent purposes.

There was bargaining during the formation of these alliances but it was of a quite different sort than had typically occurred in multipolar alliance making. The high degree of common interest inherent in facing a common opponent, along with the absence of alliance alternatives, meant that the interaction approached a "game of pure coordination" rather than the "mixed motive" game that typically characterized alliance bargaining in a multipolar system. The interaction was less a bargaining than a problem-solving process—finding the solution to a common security problem, rather than exercising leverage to get the most for oneself. If what the United States proposed was generally accepted, U.S. proposals usually took some account of its partners' concerns, at little or no cost to itself. Some of the non-European states (as well as the traditional European neutrals) chose to be nonaligned, but this stance was somewhat hypocritical since the nonaligned knew they could count on U. S. protection in any case.

Alliance Management in a Bipolar System

The alliance management problem is easier in bipolar than in multipolar alliances, at least in alliances of the superpowers, basically because the structure of the system provides little opportunity or incentive for defection. The two superpowers have no common enemy strong enough to motivate them to ally, and their allies either have no incentive to realign with the opposite superpower, or if they do have an incentive, they will be prevented from acting upon it by their own patron. Since the danger of abandonment is low, the alliance security dilemma is weak. The fear of entrapment is present for both the superpowers and their clients, but

---

32. In the case of NATO, domestic factors may account for the fact that the United States' willingness to provide protection of Europe lagged a little behind the Europeans realization of this need for it. On the other hand, quick the U.S. response to European requests (despite the massive inertia of tradition) suggests the dominance of systemic constraints over internal ones.

the distancing measures they may take to reduce this risk do not significantly increase the danger of alliance collapse.

Although weak, the alliance security dilemma is not absent. It is complicated in U.S. alliances, especially in NATO, by the coexistence of two sorts of commitments: the general commitment to mutual defense, and the implicit U.S. commitment to use nuclear weapons in that defense. The lesser partners worry about abandonment and entrapment at both levels, the superpowers only on the first level. For example, at the first level the European allies may fear U.S. abandonment either by a relapse into isolationism or the establishment of a "condominium" with the Soviet Union. Their entrapment worries center on the possibility that a U.S.-Soviet fracas in the Third World might spill over into Europe. American leaders have expressed concern about European neutralism and about a general rush to the Soviet bandwagon if the United States should flinch in fulfilling its alliance commitments.[33] The United States' primary entrapment concern is being dragged into war or crisis by a client, though usually a Third World client rather than a European one.

The nuclear commitment is not, of course, explicitly stated in alliance contracts, but it is inherent in U.S. declarations, armaments and deployments, in alliance military planning, and in the allies' expectations. European anxieties about abandonment and entrapment are somewhat more intense at the level of the nuclear commitment. Nuclear abandonment is equivalent to a drastic decline in the credibility of the U.S. deterrent; nuclear entrapment is a limited nuclear war fought on European territory.

The Europeans tend to oscillate between these opposite worries at both levels of U.S. commitment but in response to somewhat different stimuli in each case. At the general level, the primary stimuli are the degree of perceived Soviet threat to Europe and the state of relations between the superpowers. When the threat is perceived to be high, the dominant European worry is that of U.S. abandonment, but this concern will be eased if the United States shares this perception and takes a firm stance. When the threat is seen as low, Europeans will have moderate fears of abandonment if U.S.-Soviet tension is also low (as in the *détente* period of the early 1970s); their concern shifts to that of entrapment—being crushed between the two giants—if U.S.-Soviet tension is high while Soviet-West European relations are relaxed. These tension differentials with the Soviets will also affect European concerns at the nuclear level, but here two additional factors are important: the perceived credibility and effectiveness of the U.S. nuclear deterrent and the prevailing U.S.

---

33. Walt, *op. cit.*, p.20.

military doctrine. Thus European fears of nuclear abandonment sharply intensified with the Soviets' attainment of nuclear parity. Their anxiety about nuclear entrapment increases when the United States apparently tries to mitigate its own vulnerability by planning and preparing to fight a limited nuclear war in Europe.

Bipolar structure accounts for another phenomenon not present in a multipolar system—the capacity of allies to take quite different stances toward a common adversary. Thus, in the early 1980s, the West European allies in NATO could practice *détente* with the Soviets while the United States conducted a renewed Cold War. In the multipolar age, such a fundamental policy split would have fractured any alliance; nowadays it is only an irritation. The reason, of course, is that the Europeans can count on the durability of the American interest in the defense of Europe on structural grounds—regardless of irritations. From this point of view, European detente is simply a free ride on the U.S. guarantee. However, some European commentators see *détente* also as a hedge against weakness of the American nuclear guarrantee. In other words, general bipolar structure permits divided *détente*, while the possible failure of nuclear deterrence generates a security motive for European *détente*. It is as if some of the uncertainty about allied support that is inherent in multipolarity still survives in the nuclear dimension of bipolarity—in both cases a logical response to the uncertainty is to maintain ties to the adversary.

Structural logic says that the U.S. and its West European allies have little bargaining leverage over each other. The Europeans are dependent, but this weakness is offset by the known U.S. strategic interest in their defense—a kind of indirect dependence. Thus neither can credibly make the ultimate threat of withdrawal. Of course there are lesser sources of leverage, varying in effectiveness across issues. While the United States does not fully dominate NATO, it virtually does so in the realm of nuclear strategy, where it controls most of the weapons and supposedly the expertise concerning their use. It has been able and willing on occasion to use economic clout to control its allies, as in the Suez Crisis of 1956. But both of these influence bases are declining as the credibility of the nuclear deterrent wanes and as the alliance shifts toward a conventional strategy, and as European economic power grows.

It is abundantly clear that the European allies will not do the United States' bidding when it is not in their own interest, but it is also clear that they have little positive influence over U.S. policy—when the United States does not wish to be influenced.[34] The general truth seems to be that the allies get along very well on a wide range of issues where their interests closely coincide—where there is nothing to bargain about—and that on other issues, the word that most accurately describes their behavior is not domination or even bargaining, but unilateralism. Both the relative absence of conflict and the unwillingness to bend when conflict does occur can be largely explained in structural terms. The Europeans enjoy the "freedom of the irresponsible"[35]—confident that the United States will not withdraw its ultimate protection, they are free to indulge their own preferences or make ego-bolstering "Euro-gestures." Conversely, the United States has the "freedom of the powerful"—free of worry about its' allies defecting (on grounds either of probability or of cost) it can safely take unilateral initiatives which the Europeans deplore.

But structure only constrains, it does not fully determine behavior. It puts the United States and its partners on either end of a very long leash, but when their policies diverge they feel a "sharp tug of mutual dependence," as Josef Joffe has aptly put it.[36]The tug comes late because over a wide range of policy divergence, the specter of alliance collapse does not arise; beyond that range, however, it becomes at least uncertain whether the temptations of isolation or appeasement might not overcome structural compulsion. The "tug" comes more quickly in a multipolar system because alliance collapse is a far more imminent possibility. Allies must be far more wary of provoking each other because they know the other has realignment options; conversely, their own options can facilitate restraint of the ally.

Recent events in Europe suggest that we may be moving toward a multipolar world, with the weakening of one superpower, the Soviet Union, and the rise of another state, Germany, to near-superpower status. If this occurs, NATO and the Warsaw Pact may collapse or be radically transformed. What seems more likely for the near term is that bipolar and

---

34. This is consistent with the Foxes' findings in their study of NATO decision making. "To identify any instance in which American diplomatic behavior changed as a result of NATO consultations or followed advice given by others in the secret meetings of the North Atlantic Council would be difficult," they wrote. "This government has mainly 'consulted' in NATO in order to summon up diplomatic support for its own already elaborated policy... And support will not be given if its effect clearly runs counter to what another member views as its interest...." Fox and Fox, *op. cit.*, p.283.
35. Waltz, *op. cit.*, p.185.
36. Josef Joffe, *The Limited Partnership: Europe, the U. S. and the Burdens of Alliance* (Cambridge: Ballinger, 1987) p.42.

multipolar tendencies will coexist and compete. Thus, the current bipolar alliances will persist formally, reflecting what remains of the structural rivalry between the United States and the Soviet Union, while the multipolar tendency will appear in greater scope for informal realignment and increased ambiguity about the souce of greatest threat.

Alliances Outside Europe

The global structure of power is less determining of alliance formation and alliance behavior outside Europe. As Stephen Walt shows in his study of alliances in the Middle East, regional states are much more concerned about threats from local rivals than about threats from a superpower. When they do ally with a superpower, it is to get aid against a local enemy, rarely against the opposite superpower. Ideological affinity is frequently important in regional states' selection of a superpower patron. On the other hand, alignments shift fairly easily, often depending on which of the behemoths is willing to offer the most largesse. The reasons these small states are indifferent to the global balance, Walt explains, are that they are so weak they are unable to affect that balance in any case, that neither superpower is seen as a serious threat, and that even if one were a threat, they could be confident of being protected by the other.[37] The relative importance of global structure and regional conflicts varies among regions, however. The global balance is somewhat more determining of relationships in South Asia than in the Middle East, and more determining still in East Asia, but nowhere is it as central as it is in Europe.[38]

These structural differences generate different alliance political processes in less central regions; on the whole one finds greater flexibility, more options and closer similarity to the multipolar model outside of Europe. Thus it is possible for clients of the superpowers to use the threat of realignment to extort more support—hardly an option available to the European allies. Conversely, the superpowers can try to break up their rival's alliances with some hope of success. Outside Europe, the alliance security dilemma affects the superpowers more than their clients. It is the superpowers who are most subject to both entrap-

---

37. See Walt, *op. cit.*, especially chs. 5 and 6.
38. For a discussion of these regional variations, see Raju J. C. Thomas, *The Great Power Triangle and Asian Security*, especially pp.8-11.

ment and abandonment, the entrapment concern being obviously the most worrisome. The smaller allies are hardly likely to be entrapped by their patron's initiative, and, if abandoned, they can simply shift patrons.[39]

There has been a general trend away from formal alliances in the Third World in favor of other kinds of military and political collaboration, such as military aid and arms sales. Third World states are reluctant to accept outright alliance with a great power because it carries overtones of colonial domination. The great powers prefer to strengthen their clients by arms transfers rather than by alliance because the latter carries some risk of direct confrontation with their nuclear opponent. The clients prefer arms to alliance because their freedom of political action is preserved. The extent to which military aid programs strengthen or establish alignments—that is, strengthen expectations of future mutual support—is a matter of some debate. In one view, the alignment is usually already established by mutual interest and aid programs merely strengthen the client without tightening political bonds. If the mutual interest does not exist, the donor cannot exact alignment as the price of aid because he cannot credibly threaten to withdraw aid, while the recipient can threaten to shift donors.[40] A more familiar view is that aid and sales programs can significantly affect the recipient's alignment by increasing both his dependence and his expectations of more direct support.[41]

This essay has been a "first cut"—it has necessarily omitted several subjects that should be included in a comprehensive theory of alliances. Among them are the effects of domestic and bureaucratic politics, the interplay between alliances and armaments, alliance behavior during war, and the causes of alliance dissolution. Relevant theories that were barely mentioned include balance of power, collective goods, N-person games and sociological coalition theory. They will provide material for second and subsequent "cuts."

---

39. There is a small but excellent literature on the foreign policies, including the alliance policies, of small states. See especially, Robert L. Rothstein, *Alliances and Small Powers* (New York: Columbia University Press, 1968); Annette Baker Fox, *The Power of Small States* (Chicago: The University of Chicago Press, 1959); Robert O. Keohane, "The Big Influence of Small Allies," *Foreign Policy*, no. 2 (Spring 1971) pp. 161-82; and Michael Handel, *Weak States in the International System* (London: Cass, 1981).
40. Stephen M. Walt, "Alliance Formation and the Balance of World Power," *International Security* 9, no. 4 (Spring 1985) pp.27-30.
41. Robert E. Osgood, *Alliances and American Foreign Policy* (Baltimore: Johns Hopkins, 1968) pp.91-99.

SOVIET FOREIGN POLICY AND WORLD POLITICS

by William Zimmerman

This essay examines the links between the study of Soviet foreign policy and theory building in world politics. It is intentionally an idiosyncratic and indeed almost autobiographical account. I hope to accomplish three things in the process. The first is to impart some sense of how one research practitioner has worked at the interface between world politics and Soviet foreign policy. The second is to provide some indication of the evolution of Soviet studies over the last quarter century. Third, I seek to persuade the reader that trafficking at the intersection of world politics and Soviet foreign policy is advantageous to each area of inquiry. An attention to the literature on world politics enhances the likelihood that the study of Soviet foreign policy will produce results of interest to persons not especially interested in the Soviet Union *per se*. Moreover, Soviet foreign policy constitutes an important testing ground for hypotheses pertaining to the behavior of states.

To accomplish these tasks I focus on four areas of inquiry of interest to students of world politics, drawing upon Soviet materials. The areas are: the comparison of various approaches to world politics, the comparison of international systems, mass and elite foreign policy attitudes and civil-military relations including the societal determinants of military performance.

Each of these represents an area where William T.R. Fox either worked or encouraged the work of others. Thus, with respect to the comparison of approaches to world politics, Fox chaired Kenneth Waltz's thesis that became *Man, the State and War*, a classic study of the alternative explanations by political philosophers for the causes of war in the international system. In the case of the comparison of actual and putative international systems, he was similarly supportive of Morton Kaplan's *System and Process in International Politics*. Likewise, he sponsored Gabriel Almond's seminal study of the foreign policy attitudes of elites and attentive mass publics, *The American People and Foreign Policy* (as well as, it should be noted, Robert Dahl's *Congress and Foreign Policy*). Finally, Fox himself had an enduring research interest in civil-military relations and, as director of Columbia University's Institute of War and Peace Studies, encouraged a host of studies by others within the broad domain of civil-military relations.

Each of the four domains also represent instances in which I have devoted considerable effort to utilizing Soviet materials to illuminate theoretically interesting propositions. The four also illustrate a progression in Western Soviet studies that reflects the evolution of our perceptions of the Soviet Union. To put too simple a gloss on that evolution, I would characterize it as a movement away from the attempt to ascertain whether and in what ways the Soviet Union is unique, and toward a view of the Soviet Union as a more or less ordinary state both in its international behavior and in domestic relations between state and society. That evolution in Western thinking, moreover, has been both a product of and a guide to research on the Soviet Union. It has moved our research agenda increasingly in the direction of middle-range theorizing comparable to the research questions asked in world politics or in the study of American foreign policy.

Soviet Perspectives on International Relations

Thus, in the mid-1960s, I began the research that ultimately resulted in *Soviet Perspectives on International Relations*[1] in an intellectual climate in which there was a strong and well-founded presumption of the distinctiveness of Soviet foreign policy. The radical transformation of Russian society brought about by the Bolshevik seizure of power in 1917 and Stalin's subsequent "revolution from above" resulted in a novel political system which in turn gave a unique cast to Soviet foreign policy goals and to the outlook of the Soviet leadership. Unlike most great powers, the Soviet Union was perceived to be seeking to transform and supplant the contemporary international system. It was, moreover, thought to be ruled by leaders sharing a novel outlook on international events that the label "Bolshevik" aptly described.

Beginning with Marshall Shulman's *Stalin's Foreign Policy Reappraised*[2] and Jan Triska and David Finley's "multiple symmetry model" of Soviet-American relations,[3] however, a more reactive interpretation of Soviet foreign policy began to evolve.

I, in turn, found that changes in the international environment—most notably the advent of the atomic era and the onset of the Sino-Soviet dispute—and Soviet perceptions of these changes had major consequences for Soviet goals and the Soviet assessment of the international system.

---

1. William Zimmerman, *Soviet Perspectives on International Relations* (Princeton: Princeton University Press, 1969).
2. Marshall Shulman, *Stalin's Foreign Policy Reappraised* (Cambridge, MA: Harvard University Press, 1963).
3. In "Soviet-American Relations: A Multiple Symmetry Model," Triska and Finley argued that both the United States and the Soviet Union respond *in kind* to the foreign policy innovations of the other. *The Journal of Conflict Resolution* IX (March 1965) pp.37-53.

These changes in Soviet perception extend over a decade beginning with Malenkov's statement in 1954 that nuclear war would be a catastrophe for all civilization and culminating in the Soviet statement to the Chinese in 1963 that the atomic bomb does not observe the class principle.

These changes in perception had profound implications for Soviet interactions with the other actors in the international system. Persons thinking in the Marxist-Leninist tradition took as axiomatic the inevitability of the revolution and the desirability of the transformation of the existing international order. Those thinking in the Leninist-Stalinist tradition assumed that world war was functional for global revolutionary advance—that World War I had resulted in the Bolshevik seizure of power in Russia and that World War II had resulted in the formation of the Soviet bloc.

But the possibility of nuclear war called these core assumptions into question. Most important, Soviet international-relations commentary, both among scholars and among the leadership, came increasingly to recognize that nuclear war might put an end to history. If it was an open question as to whether there would be a future, so too was it an open matter as to the direction global events might take. If the future was not inevitable, then neither was a particular future, even a communist one.

In addition, coming to grips with the possibility of nuclear war placed Soviet decision makers in what I have characterized as the "revisionists' dilemma." In other words, how does one accomplish the radical transformation of an existing order in which one has a stake? There were two reasons in Marxist thought as to why the proletariat would lead the revolution. First, Marx believed that with modernization and the development of capitalism's general crisis, the proletariat would grow in size. More importantly, the members of the proletariat were capable of revolutionary consciousness because, lacking any stake in society, they had no ideology and thus could see capitalism for what it was. In the well-known phrase from *The Communist Manifesto*, the workers of the world would unite because they had "nothing to lose but their chains." Late nineteenth-century German socialists encountered this dilemma when they found that they had a stake in the preservation of the German social and economic order which they were committed to overthrow. Under Eduard Bernstein, they ultimately opted for instrumental goals and democracy rather than retaining an increasingly costly revolutionary purity.

The potential consequences of nuclear war posed the same dilemma for Soviet aspirations to transform the existing international order. As *World Marxist Review* editorialized in the aftermath of the Cuban missile crisis, "Gone are the days when the working men rising in struggle against capitalism had indeed nothing to lose but their chains. Through selfless, heroic struggle, the masses have won immense material, political and cultural gains, gains that are embodied in the socialist world system."[4] When it comes to revolutionary transformation, nothing fails like success.

The perception of the consequences of nuclear war challenged the inevitability of the desirable transformation of the international system. Whatever else Soviet elites may or may not have believed traditionally, they held the view that relations among socialist states would be better than those among capitalist states or between capitalist and socialist states. The Sino-Soviet dispute challenged the desirability of what had been thought to be inevitable: In a socialist international order, conflict might be even greater than among capitalist states or between capitalist and socialist states in the existing international order.

The ability of Soviet observers of the international scene to absorb the implications of the development of thermonuclear weapons and long-range delivery vehicle systems, the inferences they drew as a consequence of the Sino-Soviet split, as well as changes in the nature of the Soviet political system led me to several conclusions about how we should theorize about the links between world politics and Soviet foreign policy. These conclusions subsequently influenced my approach to the study of Soviet foreign policy after the publication of *Soviet Perspectives*.

Comparing Regional Systems

First, it no longer made sense to think seriously about the emergence of a world system dominated by the Soviet Union and composed primarily of communist states, which had seemed at least a plausible alternative to the contemporary international system as recently as the early 1960s.[5] By the beginning of the 1970s it had become clear that a communist alternative to the contemporary international order could no longer be seen as a shot on the board. Communist states in general revealed neither the boundary-maintaining nor conflict-containing qualities that would have been necessary for the emergence of an "international relations of a new type," an alternative communist system that would supplant the current international system. What did seem appropriate, however, was to treat the Soviet Union and its East European allies (i.e., those communist states whose interactions were separable behaviorally from rela-

---

4. "The Policy of Peaceful Coexistence Proves its Worth," *World Marxist Review* (December 1962) p.6.
5. George Modelski, *The Communist International System* (Princeton: Princeton University Press for the Center of International National Studies, Woodrow Wilson School of Public and International Affairs, Research Monograph No.9, 1960).

tions with both noncommunist and other communist states) as constituting a regional system that might be compared with other regional systems.

This approach permitted the systematic comparison of Soviet and American foreign policy behavior in relatively similar settings and with a minimum of extraneous confounding variables.[6] Moreover, it made it possible to explore some interesting propositions about the behavior of great powers and small powers in a hierarchical regional system, that is, a system composed of a single great power—the regional hegemon—and a number of relatively small states.

One set of questions pertained to the behavior of the regional hegemon with respect to the maintenance of the "boundaries" of the regional system. (System boundaries here may be defined geographically, by marked discontinuities in international transactions or by identifying norms, especially those pertaining to conflict management and resolution, specific to a group of states.) In this important domain of superpower international behavior, it turned out that long before the Gorbachev era with its putative new thinking, one could get rather considerable purchase on Soviet behavior by focusing on general patterns of regional hegemon behavior rather than by emphasizing that which was distinctively novel about Soviet foreign policy. Thus, an initial proposition that had some *prima facie* attractiveness in describing the behavior of both regional hegemons was that they pursue policies intended to maintain or increase the barriers which separate the regional system from the outside world. This proposition seemed to account for behavior such as the colorful Soviet utterances concerning the involvement of the United Nations in Eastern Europe in the aftermath of the Soviet occupation of Czechoslovakia (Western "pigs were told to keep their snouts of the socialist garden") and the long-time Soviet position that relations among members of the East European system should be based on proletarian internationalism (i.e., should include the unilateral Soviet right to intervene to preserve socialism) and not peaceful coexistence, which was a norm governing relations between states with different social systems.

Some reflection, however, reveals that the proposition failed to account for several important considerations that affect hegemonic behavior. Regional hegemons are not merely great powers; following the distinction made by William T.R. Fox in 1944, they are world powers. As such, they are engaged in multiple games, only one of which is the

---

6. For a recent extensive effort in this respect, see the articles in Jan Triska, ed., *Dominant Powers and Subordinate States* (Durham, NC: Duke University Press, 1986).

regional system game. The zeal, therefore, with which they pursue boundary-maintaining policies in a region may be tempered by an awareness that their influence outside the region depends somewhat on the perceptions of relations within the regional system held by actors outside that system. Likewise, superpower decision makers may conclude that the achievement of any influence in a region dominated by another great power is purchased in part by tolerating the erosion of the superpower's own regional system boundaries. Beyond that, the regional hegemon's decision makers are often disposed to view the regional system as a potential resource to be mobilized against an extra-regional rival with the result that the lesser states in the regional system will emphasize the limited domain of that system. The United States sought to involve Latin American states in the Korean war and was generally rebuffed. So too Soviet efforts to include the Mongolian People's Republic in the Warsaw Treaty Organization (WTO) and to station East European military units along the Ussuri against the People's Republic of China (PRC) during the nadir of Soviet-Chinese relations were rebuffed by the Romanians who stressed that the WTO was a *European* organization.

When in 1972 I first examined Soviet and U.S. behavior *vis à vis* the East European and U.S. regional systems, it was important to emphasize that there were differences between the behaviors of the regional hegemons that stemmed primarily from the nature of the Soviet system. There was compelling evidence that Soviet decision makers had been and remained more intense in their determination to maintain system boundaries than were U.S. leaders.

At the onset of the 1980s, however, it had already become evident from Soviet behavior that "in some instances the Soviet Union might at the margin trade off reduced intra-regional system cohesion for gains elsewhere."[7] Therefore, by the early 1980s, one could already generate plausible hypotheses about possible Soviet attitudes toward Eastern Europe that were driven by assumptions about the cross pressure a superpower experiences in its roles as a world and regional power. These differed from those that emphasized the distinctiveness of Soviet behavior *vis à vis* its regional allies as a consequence of the nature of the Soviet political system. At this writing they also appear to have anticipated Soviet behavior better than did the latter.

Indeed, while in some domains the claim of novelty in the putatively "new thinking" of Gorbachev's early tenure as General Secretary was

---

7.   William Zimmerman, "Soviet-East European Relations and the Changing International System," in Morris Bernstein, Zvi Gitelman and William Zimmerman, eds., *East-West Relations and the Future of Eastern Europe* (London: Allen and Unwin, 1981) p.96.

tenuous or dubious, there can be no mistaking the novelty of Gorbachev's assertion in his speech on the 70th anniversary of the October Revolution in 1987 that peaceful coexistence, with its implied commitment to military non-intervention, should be the basis of Soviet relations with its East European allies. Such a statement by no means precluded the possibility that in practice the Soviet Union would under certain circumstances resort to military force to prevent changes from transpiring in Eastern Europe. It does suggest that the worries small European communist states have about Soviet behavior in the 1990s are more characteristic of any acutely asymmetrical power relationship than of one that stems from specific attributes of the Soviet Union as a regional hegemon. Being located between Germany and Russia is a lousy place for a state whose elites seek to behave independently in the international system, but that is a proposition whose validity does not depend on the nature of the Soviet political system.

Implications for Dependency Theory

The Soviet-East Europe hierarchical regional system can be used to assess the explanatory power of dependency theory as well. Dependency theory shares with much of the traditional literature on Soviet foreign policy the assumption that the nature of the domestic system of the hegemonic state explains that state's relations with other, lesser states. Where the two differ is that one sees in the American socioeconomic system—capitalism—the explanation for the observed dependency relationships, whereas the other focuses on the Soviet political system—socialism—for an explanation.

The only way, after all, that hypotheses linking the nature of the socioeconomic and/or political systems of states and the character of relations between those states can be verified or falsified is by comparing relations between states that have capitalist socioeconomic systems and those that do not. Consider the proposition that "everyone dies under capitalism." It turns out, of course, that everyone dies under feudalism and socialism as well. This being the case, there might well still be a sense in which capitalism is a cause of death but most persons would find searching for other, more proximate, causes a more fruitful pastime.[8]

What I did, therefore, was to compare international systems by applying four concepts central to dependency theory that have been used in analyzing U.S.-Latin American relations—inequality, penetration, dependency and exploitation—in the Soviet-East European context. Doing so did not lend credence to the dependency theorists' focus on the causal

---

8.   I am indebted to David Abernathy for this example.

role of capitalism. To the extent that conditions dependency theorists have ascribed to relationships between developed and less-developed capitalist states are actually observed, preliminary findings indicated they were found at least as often in the Soviet-East European regional system as in asymmetrically configured systems of capitalist states. At the same time, my findings also constituted evidence that the credibility of the argument that there was something distinctive and distinctively opprobrious about interstate relations among asymmetrically powerful socialist states had diminished substantially since Stalin's time.

There was, to be sure, some evidence to suggest that (between 1957 and 1972 in any event) interstate inequality as measured by GNP among the WTO members had actually increased—thus indicating, ironically, that it might be that under socialism the rich states get richer and the poor, poorer. The East European states are also more dependent on trade with the Soviet Union than the larger Latin American states are with the United States, exacerbating the level of inequality.

On the other hand, it is noteworthy how trade-oriented the East European states remain, despite the strong traditional Soviet impetus to autarky, and how much the Soviet Union has found itself encouraging East European states to decrease their trade dependence on the Soviet Union. Moreover, however one operationalizes the notion of political, socioeconomic and cultural penetration, it is clear that Soviet penetration of East European states has diminished substantially since the late 1940s.

Finally, it is important to appreciate how complicated and controversial is the issue as to whether the Soviet Union has exploited Eastern Europe economically since Stalin's time. The answer may be said to be one of the following: Either Eastern Europe has exploited the Soviet Union economically, an action the Soviet Union has tolerated for the political peace it buys within the WTO, or after 1956 the Soviet Union has marginally exploited Eastern Europe.

Neither answer serves as evidence for the proposition that there is something distinctive about the level of exploitation in Soviet-East European relations, a claim that could have been advanced about the years prior to 1956. As Paul Marer has shown, after World War II the Soviet Union took out of Eastern Europe about what the United States put in to rebuilding Western Europe.[9]

---

9. "Soviet Economic Policy in Eastern Europe," in *Reorientation and Commercial Relations of the Economies of Eastern Europe*, Joint Economic Commission, U.S. Cpmgress, 2d. session (Washington, DC: Government Publications Office, 1974) p.144.

Elite and Mass Attitudes Toward Foreign Policy

The second conclusion linking world politics and Soviet foreign policy to which I came was that given the perceived implications of the thermonuclear era, further efforts to assess Soviet perspectives on the international system would require a much greater level of specificity. This was partly because it was clear that using the terms "Bolshevik" and "Soviet" interchangeably to depict Soviet thinking about contemporary international relations was just plain wrong. One was not likely to improve analytical clarity by invoking hypotheses about the "Bolshevik" thinking of persons who, long before "new thinking" became *de rigueur*, had explicitly rejected the proposition that the workers had nothing to lose but their chains. There were other vividly un-Bolshevik utterances in the early 1960s as well, including the dramatic declaration by the Communist Party of the Soviet Union (CPSU) in its polemics with the Chinese that the atomic bomb did not observe the class principle, authoritative charges that another putatively socialist state was pursuing a Cold War policy against the Soviet Union and open questioning Clausewitz's dictum that war is a continuation of politics.

In addition, the open-ended quality of the Soviet reading of international relations combined with the general political decompression epitomized by the 20th Congress of the CPSU to produce a noticeably more diverse political dialogue within the political leadership, and even more so among analysts specializing in international relations. Documenting that diversity and taking steps to develop criteria for predicting which elements among elites and either the attentive or mass public would be more disposed to particular attitudes became an important task.

An example of the documentation of elite diversity was the paper assessing the Soviet lessons of Vietnam that I published with Robert Axelrod in 1981.[10] It came at a time when there had been a resurgence in the West of views emphasizing the homogeneity of Soviet elite perspectives and the unchanging, purposive nature of Soviet goals. We concluded that the notion of monolithic Soviet preferences was unsustainable. Rather, we found—as had others in the early and mid-1970s— that in speaking of Soviet goals, it was necessary to specify the particular individual, institutional or media source as well as the context.

There was a clear tension in Soviet commentary among those who ranked peace as a priority and who showed only token obeisance to the support of the national liberation movements, and those who attached

---

10. William Zimmeramn and Robert Axelrod, "The 'Lessons' of Vietnam and Soviet Foreign Policy," *World Politics* 34 (October 1981) pp.1-24.

great weight to supporting national liberation movements but were considerably more cavalier in their protestations in favor of peace.

The Soviet commentary we examined was also divided as to whether increasing U.S. weakness was a favorable or unfavorable development. In several instances, the proposition was advanced that the weaker the United States became, the more prone it would be to lash out violently and to engage in aggressive acts. Other statements reached the opposite conclusion that as the United States became weaker, it would become more reasonable and pliant.

Similarly, it turned out that one could not speak about *the* Soviet view of the role of force in world politics. We encountered utterances that were quite in keeping with conventional Soviet and with indeed Bolshevik utterances. We found, for instance, claims that superior military force for (their) good guys was conducive to peace and that the imperialists were rethinking the role of force in international politics in light of the changed global distribution of power.

However, we also encountered assertions, prefiguring observations that have become commonplace in the Gorbachev period, that one lesson of Vietnam was that the role of force had lost some of its value for everyone including, by implication, Moscow.

A criterion that has proved an important discriminator of mass and attentive public attitudes in the Soviet Union is that of age. This is certainly important for developing broad notions about the evolution of the Soviet system and probably for Soviet foreign policy in particular. We now have data from three major surveys which bear on Soviet foreign policy attitudes. The results are mixed with respect to the relevance of inter-generational differences for foreign policy attitudes. The data from the Soviet Interview Project (SIP), which in 1983 interviewed almost 3000 Soviet emigres to the United States, most of whom arrived in 1979-80, are unambiguous about the link between age and foreign policy attitudes.[11] Deborah Yarsike and I found, for example, a negative and almost straight-line relation between the age of former Soviet citizens and their assessment of the relative power of the United States and the Soviet Union. The younger the Soviets, the less likely they were to say that the United States was more powerful than the Soviet Union. They

---

11. On SIP generally, see James Millar, ed., *Politics, Work and Daily Life in the USSR* (Cambridege: Cambridge University Press, 1987).

were also more likely to assert that the Soviet Union was more likely to win a war between the two. Two Moscow telephone surveys, in May 1988 and January 1989, were considerably less clear-cut in identifying inter-generational differences that bear directly on foreign policy.[12]

All three, however, are unambiguous in showing that support for traditional Soviet institutions decreases with the age of the Soviet citizen, and conversely that the younger Soviets are, the more likely they are to support attitudes one would associate with *perestroika* and *demokratizat-siia*.

Another major potential dimension differentiating Soviet society with respect to foreign policy attitudes involves the supporters and opponents of political and economic reform. It turns out that those who support the decentralization and marketization of industrial and agricultural strategies are less likely to support an activist foreign policy in the Third World and more likely to support reductions in military expenditures, a key element in the Soviet Union's overall disposable surplus for foreign policy.

By comparison, the answer to the question as to whether there is an important attitudinal link between support for political democratization and support for a more benign foreign policy turns substantially on each respondent's notion of democracy. It is, of course, another matter—but should be stressed—that attitudes notwithstanding, increased political participation increases the number and intensity of domestic claims on Soviet resources and thus likely will result in a decrease in the disposable surplus available for foreign policy. If one interprets support for democratization as support for authentic political participation, then support for democratization and for a more benign foreign policy are linked at both the level of mass and of attentive publics.

If, however, one's concept of democracy is grounded in liberal notions such as the marketplace for ideas or the legal priority of individual rights over those of society, then the answer is different. With such a definition

---

12. Both Moscow surverys were done by the Instite for Sociological Research, the first for the *New York Times*/CBS news poll and the second in conjunction with a Martilla and Kiley study of four cities in the United States. Zimmerman and Yarsike, "Intergenerational Change in Soviet Foreign Policy, " unpublished paper, 1987, and "Mass Publics and Soviet Foreign Policy in Zimmerman, ed., *The Changing Soviet Union and Wester Security Policy*, in draft.

in mind, one would conclude that in the Soviet Union, support for political democratization has practically no implications for foreign-policy attitudes. Those who support political democratization in this sense are no less or more likely to support an activist foreign policy than others, and they are at most only marginally more likely to differ from others in attitudes toward military expenditures.[13] Consequently, there are no easy and automatic answers to questions about the links between domestic cleavages and foreign policy attitudes. We will make, however, little headway in anticipating Soviet behavior unless we treat these links as matters to be discovered empirically rather than assumed *a priori*.

Civil-Military Relations

A fourth area of research that encourages a view of the Soviet Union as an increasingly normal state with performance attributes relevant for foreign policy comparable to other states is civil-military relations. Data from the Soviet Interview Project along with interviews of more than a thousand male former Soviet citizens, almost all of whom were of military service age in the early or mid-1970s, testify to a trend extending from World War II at least through 1980 (the last year for which we have data) and, in all probability, continuing today, judging by Soviet news accounts in 1988-90. The more recent the birth date of those interviewed, and hence the year in which they would have been called to service, the higher the proportion of those reporting that they attempted to avoid military service. As the years when terror was used as an instrument of social control recede into the past, it has become less and less plausible to regard the Soviet Union as a political system distinctive in its capacity to mobilize its citizenry for foreign and security policy goals.

Instead, service avoidance has become a major problem in a state where virtually universal military service was long thought to be the norm. As one Soviet military commentator observed wryly in 1988, in place of the old Soviet adage that "the army is a school for life," young people today assert that "the army...is, of course, a school, but it is better to graduate from it as an external [correspondent] student."[14] Small wonder Gorbachev has sought to achieve a new and more truly authentic political participation.

---

13. These findings are based on the Soviet Interview Project data. The 1988 Moscow survey responses support the findings drawn from the SIP data regarding the link between attitudes favoring political participation and foreign policy attitudes. Unfortunately, no questions were asked that addressed economic decentralization or the liberal notions of democracy. Zimmerman, "Economic Reform, Democratization and Foreign Policy Attitudes in the Soviet Union," in Seweryn Bialer and Robert Jervis, eds., *East-West Relations in the 1990s* (Durham, NC: Duke University Press, 1990).
14. *Krasnaia Zvezda* 9 April 1988, translated in *FBIS-SOV-88-077*, p.68.

Data from the same surveys, moreover, reveal that the notion that the Soviet Union is uniquely advantaged in its competition with Western states is suspect in another important respect. There has been a widespread tendency to view the Soviet military as performing better than the civilian economy. Certainly, the military sector is relatively advantaged in the allocation of high-quality materiel and resources that are a critical component of military performance. Moreover, it has often been maintained that the Soviet Union has a comparative advantage over Western political systems in the use of military power and in providing states with arms and other military aid. By extension, a plausible hypothesis would be that performance levels in the military were higher than in the notoriously inefficient Soviet civilian sector.

However plausible *a priori*, this was not what we were told by our informants. Michael Berbaum and I found that our respondents in the aggregate saw no difference in the level of performance in the civilian and military domains, though the mix of variables affecting performance differed between them.[15] What this serves to do for the broader study of Soviet foreign policy is to intensify our doubts about the validity of thinking about the Soviet Union as a political system able to perform at a distinctive level at least in the military security domain. For while we do not have comparable data for American military performance, a finding that peacetime Soviet military performance levels are the same as performance levels in the Soviet civilian sector runs counter to the image of a distinctive Soviet political system with a comparative advantage in a competitive East-West relationship.

Conclusion

This has been an account of the evolution of theory building at the intersection of world politics and Soviet foreign policy. That evolution has been in keeping with the movement of the Soviet Union in the direction of becoming a more or less "normal" state. It has been partly a process of ruling out some long-standing concepts about the Soviet Union. In several instances this has been as much a function of change in the Soviet Union as it has of change in our thinking. The results of research presented in this paper testify that considerable demobilization

---

15. "Equal But Not Separate: A Comparison of Soviet Military and Civilian Performance," paper presented at the 1987 annual meeting of the American Political Science Association. We achieved this result by asking them to "think about the *best* possible way [the unit] could have performed. That would be 100 percent. Overall, during your stay with that unit, what percentage would you give it for the performance of its mission?" Our informants were all former Soviet citizens living in the United States. Almost all of those who served in the 1970s.

has occurred in the Soviet Union rather than disproving hypotheses about mobilization systems and their behavior in world politics. Similarly, the evolution of Soviet perspectives on international politics in the late 1950s and early 1960s constituted fundamental departures from traditional Bolshevik-Stalinist modes of thinking.

This evolution of theory has altered our research agendas. Increasingly, the research questions we will want to address in the study of Soviet foreign policy are those asked in the general study of foreign policy rather than in the specific study of the Soviet Union. As if to emphasize this point, Gorbachev and his advisors—many of whom (Gennadi Gerasimov, Boris Piadishev, Fedor Burlatskii, Evgeny Primakov *et al.*) were the young turks of international relations in the early 1960s—are fond of speaking of common global problems. A truly comparative foreign policy, in which all states are involved and may be constructively discussed as members of a truly international political system, may be on the horizon. We can see the prospect of asking parallel questions about Soviet and American foreign policy and of joint collaboration by, for instance, Soviet and American students of the foreign policies of the two states. Not only is Soviet foreign policy becoming more akin to the foreign policy of a "normal" state, it is now seriously possible to imagine "normal" social science being done about an increasingly normal, while militarily very powerful, Soviet Union. In such a pursuit, it will inevitably be profitable to compare Soviet foreign policy and that of other "normal" states, both for the light such comparisons shed on the behavior of the Soviet Union and the other states in question and for the broader insights into world politics theory that may result.

TOWARD A THEORY OF
INTERNATIONAL REGIMES

Mark W. Zacher

The road to my present theoretical explorations into the nature and bases of mutual interests and their importance in regime formation has been a long one. Most of my work since graduate school at Columbia University in the 1960s has been concerned with international collaboration, and like that of many others interested in the same field in the 1960s, it has focused on the United Nations. I became particularly involved in the possibilities for and limits on international organizations. The resulting studies in the field of conflict management tried to project a very realistic picture of where the United Nations and regional organizations could fit into the control of international wars. They were based on the perspective that there is no generally held consensus on the legitimate and illegitimate use of force (outside of territorial revisionism at a regional level). For the most part collaboration in conflict management was viewed as a coincidence of interest among groupings that were products of particular configurations.

In the mid-1970s my research began to focus on international economic regulations and regimes since their varied strength and nature provide fruitful grounds for the study of how and why states collaborate. I attempted to develop a formal theory of economic collaboration, like the theory of collective security in *International Conflicts and Collective Security, 1946-1977* (1979), but did not succeed. Hence, studies of the politics of both marine pollution control and commodity market regulation adopted an eclectic approach to the analysis of actor policies and regulatory outcomes. The analysis drew on various explanatory literatures, but did not employ a particular theoretical framework.

Further reflection on the last two studies uncovered conclusions not highlighted in my earlier works to the extent that they should have been. First, a moderately strong regime for marine pollution control is likely to develop because state and commercial interests favor universal regulatory arrangements that prevent unilateral interventions in international shipping. Shipping and oil companies, as well as governments, want to minimize the costs of pollution control, but above all they want to be certain about the costs they will incur. In addition, national shipping companies resist surcharges not imposed on firms in other states to avoid being at a competitive disadvantage. In *Pollution, Politics and International Law* it was phrased as follows:

> Considering the complexity and diversity of the industries' operations across numerous boundaries, unilateral action that would create a variety of national standards is anathema... For maritime interests, uniformity has been the battle cry in a struggle to retain free access to all the world's oceans and to prevent the imposition of uneven costs.[1]

As the study makes clear, there are many conflicts of interest and issues of cost distribution in marine pollution regulation. At the same time, there is a common interest among almost all actors to develop a universal regime and to avoid a patchwork of national regulations.

In the study of commodity market regulation, on the other hand, it became clear that there is likely always to be a rather weak international regime because states seldom share mutual economic interests. In certain restrictive conditions when price instability is due to variations in supply, it is possible that regulation to promote price stability could bring quite modest joint gains for exporting and importing countries. But, generally, regulation depends on producers finding it in their political interest to transfer resources to consumers through international price and supply agreements. As is evident from the historical record, these circumstances do not often exist. The international commodity trade regime has been, and probably always will be, very weak because export prices and market shares affect relative gains and losses among states. As the book notes:

> The prices of commodities and the earnings of exporting nations are at the heart of the international competition for wealth. These issues do not relate merely to the facilitation of exchange relations; in this they differ from many other international economic issue areas. Given that rules concerning commodity prices and earnings in large part define the terms of competition, it is difficult to develop a set of rules that all parties will view as beneficial—any scheme is likely to produce economic winners and losers. In fact, if the creation of ICAs (International Commodity Agreements) depended solely on states' judgments of their economic impacts, it is probable that none would have been created.[2]

A synthesis emerged from the studies of the marine pollution and commodity trade regimes that had a strong effect on subsequent research: When a common set of rules (or a regime) can facilitate the flow of international commerce, without significantly disrupting the distribution of economic gains and losses among the most powerful states, strong regimes are likely to emerge. If, on the other hand, international regulations have an important influence on the competitive positions of major

---

1.   Mark W. Zacher and R. Michael M'Gonigle, *Pollution, Politics and International Law: Tankers At Sea* (Berkeley, CA: University of California Press, 1979) p.261.
2.   Jack Finlayson and Mark Zacher, *Managing International Markets: Developing Countries and the Commodity Trade Regime* (New York: Columbia University Press, 1988) p.292.

states and coalitions, then strong regimes are not likely to develop. In other terms, strong regimes will tend to develop in areas where regulations augment international commercial transactions by creating greater certainty of costs and reducing the impediments to such exchanges. Conversely, when areas concern the central terms of competition among states, very weak regimes are likely. Some conflicts of interest always accompany the development of regimes that facilitate the flow of commerce, but common interests are often significant enough to override the losses that some states incur.

These conclusions initally led to speculation about the circumstances under which regulation would facilitate the flow of commerce—and then more broadly to investigations of the conditions under which regulation would promote states' mutual realization of economic welfare and security. At this point I began to work on a project concerning the evolution of the international regimes for shipping, air transport, telecommunications and postal services with Brent Sutton, a researcher with a strong background in economics. In exploring how regulation might promote joint economic gains for all or most states, particular attention was directed to economic theory. And in seeking to determine how regimes might enhance autonomy or security for all states, it was logical to turn to international relations theory. Each body of literature offered important explicit or implicit insights.

A great deal of the literature on economic regulation focuses on governments' conceptions of "the public interest," the capture of regulatory agencies and processes by organizations or groups of voters and the self-serving strategies of bureaucrats. The literature presupposes a hierarchical political structure where governments are able to provide certain types of regulation to their constituents in exchange for political longevity and other benefits. These writings are obviously not particularly relevant to international regulation because they presuppose the existence of a government.[3] Furthermore the above literature does not generally deal with conditions where mutual interests are likely to exist.

The economics theory of market imperfections and failures does concern mutual interest. Neoclassical economic theory states that regula-

---

3. B.M. Mitnick, "Theories of Regulatory Origin," in B.M. Mitnick, ed., *The Political Economy of Regulation* (New York: Columbia University Press, 1980); R.G. Noll, "The Economics and Politics of Regulation," *Virginia Law Review* 57 (1971) pp.1016-1032.

tion can increase efficiency or the community welfare pie (and hence the probability that all will gain) if it corrects market imperfections and failures. In so doing it provides a conception of the public interest applicable at the national and international levels. Market imperfections are violations of the assumptions of the neoclassical economic model; market failures are situations where the characteristics of the economic good prevent the market from achieving efficient outcomes.[4]

The second step in exploring common interests entailed looking at general international relations theory and asking what insights it offers concerning those conditions where there may be mutual interests in regulation. On the whole, the dominant schools of classical realism and neorealism address collaboration with respect to the obstacles that are posed by state goals (power or security) or the dominant strategy in realizing them—namely, increasing or avoiding losses in one's relative power position.[5]

However, neorealism, with its stress on the preeminence of security among state goals, offers some *implicit* insights. Security means basically an absence of foreign control over the state and its society (i.e., autonomy) and an absence of any fear that such control might be imposed. The most serious infringement on security is foreign military conquest and rule, but there are lesser incursions on security and state autonomy. Foreign control over parts of the economy can constitute significant infringements, and the more important that part is to the operation of the overall economy and the welfare of the population, the greater the incursion on state autonomy. Therefore, one could posit that all states have a concern to maintain state control over certain important sectors of their economies and societies, and would support international regimes that would facilitate such control. While this is a logical argument based on states' primary goal of security, neorealists have not explicitly pushed their theoretical explorations in this direction. Also,

4.   F. M. Bator, "The Anatomy of Market Failures," *Quarterly Journal of Economics* 72 (August 1958) pp.351-79; Robin Boadway, *Public Sector Economics* (Cambridge, MA: Winthrop, 1979); Carl Dahlman, "The Problem of Externality," *Journal of Law and Economics* 12 (1979) pp.141-62; Harold Demsetz, "The Cost of Transacting," *Quarterly Journal of Economics* 82 (1968) pp.33-53; and Richard A. Posner, "Natural Monopoly and Its Regulation," *Stanford Law Review* 21 (February 1969) pp.548-649.

5.   Kenneth W. Waltz, *Theory of International Politics* (Reading, MA: Addison-Wesley, 1979); Robert O. Keohane, ed., *Neorealism and Its Critics* (New York: Columbia University Press, 1987).

they are, in any case, very dubious about the prospects for the development of strong regimes because of their distributional consequences.[6]

Another relevant body of theory is associated with the "international society" school developed largely by Martin Wight and Hedley Bull.[7] Like neorealists, they believe that states' central concern is the preservation of their own independence, but they believe explicitly that states' commitment to their sovereign existence does provide a bedrock for the development of some general regimes.

If there is one central implication of both neorealism and the international society school for the analysis of mutual interests underlying international economic collaboration, it is that one should seek to identify those domestic economic sectors that states are committed to keep out of the control of foreigners and then to determine whether international interactions in these sectors might undermine state control. If such actions strongly affect state control, then there are mutual interests in international regimes in preventing foreign incursions on that control.

The theoretical exploration of the origin of mutual interests is found both in the focus of traditional international theory on states' concern for their autonomy and in the views of neoclassical economic theory on market imperfections and failures. This endeavor does not represent a complete break from what has been done by political scientists in the past. In fact, a number of scholars have focused on the same economic characteristics, while tending to focus on just one characteristic.[8] Robert Keohane, in fact, highlighted the importance of market imperfections and failures as bases for collaboration in *After Hegemony*, but he examined only uncertainty and transaction costs. As Keohane made clear in the book, a theoretical concern with common interests in international regulation does not mean that one is ignoring other conflicts of interest or power relationships. In fact, these factors always come into play in the creation and reform of international regimes. It is, however, valuable at times to highlight mutual interests—especially since they have generally not been given adequate attention in studies with a clear theoretical focus. Both the limitations and strengths of "functional" approaches that highlight common interests are discussed in the final section of the article.

---

6. Joseph Grieco, "Anarchy and the Limits of Cooperation: A Realist Critique of the Newest Liberal Institutionalism," *International Organization* (Summer 1988) pp.485-507.
7. Hedley Bull, *The Anarchical Society: A Study of Order In World Politics* (New York: Columbia University Press, 1977); Hedley Bull, "The Grotian Concept of International Society," in Herbert Butterfield and Martin Wight, eds., *Diplomatic Investigations* (London: Allen and Unwin, 1967) pp. 51-73.
8. Uncertainty of costs and high transactions costs are treated in Robert O. Keohane, *After Hegemony: Cooperation and Discord in The World Political Economy* (Princeton, NJ: Princeton University Press, 1984), especially ch.6.

Mutual Interests and International Regimes: Theoretical Explorations

The presentation of this theory of international regimes begins with a discussion of assumptions and posits probable outcomes if certain conditions exist. Two sections then present general hypotheses concerning conditions where there is likely to be a mutuality of interests among most states, one, in terms of the protection of their security and autonomy and two, in terms of the promotion of their economic welfare. The third section outlines five broad policy sectors found in most international economic issue areas—namely, jurisdictional competences, prices and market shares, market access, accidental and intentional damage, and labor welfare standards. Projections of the extent of mutual—and different—interests form the basis for hypotheses concerning the likelihood of strong regimes in each of the five sectors. (See Figure 1).

The central assumptions of this theory of collaboration are, as noted above, drawn at least in part from neorealist thought. States are the dominant actors in the international system and are self-interested. While security or independence from external control is accepted as the preeminent goal of states, economic welfare is viewed as an important goal in and of itself. States might at times trade-off some degree of autonomy for gains in economic welfare.

The possibility of such trade-offs points toward a liberal theory of international relations. This theory does not posit that the system is completely anarchical. Rather, it accepts that states have erected some modest international norms and institutions for the mutual realization of domestic control and economic welfare. That these norms and institutions break down at times does not mean that they are without significance. Regulations that appear to legitimize discretionary behavior often are not signs of anarchy, but signs that states respect each others' right to maintain internal control.

Regimes to Enhance Autonomy

If the preeminent objective of states is to achieve a high degree of autonomy, there are likely to be situations in which shared interests in security regimes overcome both their own acquisitive instincts and their security dilemmas. Although there is no body of international relations theory that identifies such situations, two examples have emerged from the study of international transportation and communications regimes:

1) When states can be attacked from geographical areas adjacent to their territories, they are likely to support the jurisdiction of the littoral state over a broad range of activities (especially those with a potential

Figure 1

PROJECTIONS OF REGIME STRENGTH IN FIVE POLICY SECTORS

Policy Sector	Issue-Area Characteristics Mutual Interests	Probability of Regime Creation/Strength
Jurisdictional Competencies	Adjacent geographical areas from which states can be attacked. Uncertainty of costs, high transaction costs, impediments to factor mobility, externalities, scarce common property resources, public goods.	Very high: mutual benefits from a clear, unified set of rules on access and legislative authority are considerable. Distributional consequences pose obstacles at times, especially when market failures exist.
Accidental and Intentional Damage	Uncertainty of costs, high transaction costs, impediments to factor mobility, externalities, scarce common property resources, public goods.	Very high mutual benefits from making costs more certain and lowering costs are considerable. Distributional implications are minor for most states on most issues— but can be high when market failures exist
Market Access	Impediments to factor mobility, high transaction costs.	Moderate; high in the case of technical barriers, moderate or less in the case of non-technical barriers. Joint gains can be considerable but losses for some and effects on relative power can constitute serious obstacles.
Prices	An industry that has wide implications for the economy and that states are committed to control. Natural monopoly, collusion. Externality, public good.	Low overall; central to international competition. Where states committed to control of an industry or a natural monopoly exists, joint gains from regulation can override conflicting interests.
Labor Welfare	None	Very Low; almost no possibilities for all to benefit.

military purpose) in that zone. Examples are the regimes for inland waters, territorial seas and airspace.

2) When an industry has widespread effects on the economic welfare or autonomy of states, they are likely to agree on international rights and obligations that facilitate state control of that industry. These could encompass agreements on price setting and the sharing of international markets which assure states both control over international linkages and produce significant revenue to finance state enterprises. A good example is the regime that has controlled prices and market shares for international telecommunications for over a century.

Regimes to Enhance Economic Welfare

Neoclassical theory posits that regulation can increase efficiency or global output if it corrects market imperfections and failures. Imperfections constitute violations of the assumptions of the neoclassical model, and failures constitute situations where a good's characteristics prevent the market from achieving efficient outcomes. Neoclassical assumptions include the possession of perfect information, zero transaction costs, atomistic markets, perfect factor mobility and utility maximization by actors.

The market imperfections that flow from these assumptions are uncertainty of costs and commercial opportunities, high transaction costs, impediments to factor mobility (e.g., tariffs), collusive arrangements among producers and natural monopolies.

Natural monopolies require some explanation. They exist where there are increasing economies of scale and goods can be produced at the cheapest price by a single entity (for example, some infrastructure industries such as telecommunications). In such situations open and unlimited competition results in a single firm dominating and exploiting a monopoly position if it is not regulated. Regulation in such circumstances can actually take the form of prescribing and proscribing rules for either a monopoly firm or a number of firms whose activities are coordinated so that, in a sense, they act as one.

Market failures are characteristic of goods that undermine the efficient operation of markets; efficiency in such situations can only be achieved through governmental or intergovernmental regulation.

Market failures occur in three forms. First, there are externalities or sideeffects of activities that impose harm or bestow benefits on third parties. A second form is scarce common property resources or resources that belong to all actors such that unfettered exploitation reduces long-run total output. A third form is that of public goods, goods that once produced provide benefits for all and from which no one can be excluded. There is a tendency toward the underproduction of such goods since actors try to have a "free ride" in the hope that others will pay for their production.

The literature on economics does not claim that regulation will take place in such circumstances—just that regulation can increase efficiency or actors' overall economic welfare. In fact, economists recognize that some actors have nothing to lose or gain when efficiency is increased, which in itself can prevent regulatory accords. Political science scholars would be even more insistent about the problematic character of regimes forming under such conditions since they realize that states have other and even more important values than economic welfare. For example, if the gains derived from efficiency increased the vulnerability of certain states to sanctions by other states, the former would be predisposed against the creation of a regulatory regime. The lack of an international government makes the probability of global agreements to regulate market failures much less likely than agreements at the national level.

The Probability of Regimes in Different Policy Sectors

After concluding that international regimes are more likely to form if certain security-related characteristics or market imperfections and failures exist, the next step in the development of a theory was to ask if there are any situations or policy sectors where there is a high probability that these factors indeed exist and have produced relatively strong regimes. Analyses of patterns of regulation in international economic issues led to a five-fold classification of policy sectors: jurisdictional competences, prices and market shares, market access, accidental and intentional damage, and labor standards. In each of these it is possible to generalize about the probable existence of areas where regulation will enhance autonomy and economic welfare.

Jurisdictional Competences

Jurisdictional issues concern the rights of states to legislate and to have enforcement powers in other geographical areas. Jurisdictional regimes have major impacts on international commerce because goods and services are constantly moving from one geographical area to another.

All states, if possible, prefer to have some legal control over a range of activities in areas adjacent to their territory. This mutuality of interests forms the basis of strong regimes on these matters. Evidence of this tendency lies in international public law for inland waters and territorial seas, airspace, and to a lesser extent, radio waves in surrounding airspace.

There are a number of situations exhibiting market imperfections and failures where strong incentives are created for jurisdictional regimes. Economic actors want clear jurisdictional regimes established so that they know whose rules and what rules they have to obey in various stages of an exchange. They want a high degree of certainty of costs and commercial opportunities. In a sense one could say that just as nature abhors a vacuum, businessmen abhor uncertainty as to the costs they have to assume. To quote Louis Henkin, "Both general law and particular agreements avoid the need for negotiating anew in every new instance; both create justified expectation and warrant confidence as to how others will behave."[9]

Another situation that states dislike is high transaction costs that result from the need to make separate jurisdictional agreements with a large number of other states.[10] Bilateral or limited multilateral agreements with other states achieve certainty of costs, but the price of achieving certainty by this route is very high. The probability of reaching accords with all of the 160 states in the world is problematic to say the least. A global jurisdictional regime minimizes transaction costs and is certainly the least expensive route to a high degree of cost certainty.

The potential reduction of impediments to the exchange of goods and services provides still another incentive for international regulation. Only a regime that constrains every state from interfering with the international movement of goods and services is likely to provide this. The regimes for international ocean and air space that allow the same access to all vessels and planes are good examples.

The central jurisdictional reality of the international system, namely state sovereignty, poses particularly difficult problems to the regulation of market failures at the international level. It is usually necessary to alter the discretionary power of states in order to eliminate or greatly reduce the inefficiencies that result from externalities, scarce common property resources and public goods. For example, if activities in certain states are having harmful effects in other states (i.e., a negative externality, such as air pollution), it may be desirable to circumscribe the ability of states to undertake activities in their own territories without the approval of other countries. In the case of common property resources that are being seriously depleted (e.g., fish or minerals in the oceans), it may be desirable to establish international bodies with binding power to allocate resources among states. In the modern language of the Law of

---

9.   Louis Henkin, *How Nations Behave* (New York:Columbia University Press, 1968) p.29.
10. This point is stressed by Keohane in *After Hegemony*, chapter 6. It should be noted that this argument is applicable particularly to liberal capitalist states—and is basically not applicable to highly mercantilist states seeking power over other states (e.g., Nazi Germany).

the Sea there may be strong incentives to move from a free-access (freedom of the seas) to a common-heritage regime.[11]

The major problem with public goods is that they are underproduced because states hope that others will pay for them and then they will be able to free ride at no cost. Hypothetically, states could agree that international political organs have jurisdiction over the provision of such goods and that all countries are obligated to contribute as these political bodies dictate. There have not been major strides in this direction, but there could be in the future in a major area like the protection of the ozone layer.

In conclusion, strong jurisdictional regimes serve to correct certain market imperfections, for example, cost uncertainty, high transaction costs and impediments to factor mobility, although the distributional consequences of such regimes pose major obstacles to agreement. However, there are likely to be very strong commercial incentives to resolve such distributional issues. Of course, if the largest gainers from a potential regime are also the most powerful states in the system, the chances of regime creation are enhanced.

Some jurisdictional regimes are likely to develop in order to correct market failures such as externalities, scarce common property resources and public goods, but here the potential regimes' limitations on state autonomy and the distributional consequences are apt to pose very serious hurdles. The incentives for mutual gain exist, but the political obstacles are overpowering in most cases.

Prices

The policy sectors of prices and market access are often difficult to separate in international regulatory politics since the regulation of the former often concerns the latter. On the other hand, market access does arise in many contexts where price setting is not on the table. In the case of prices there are generally no possibilities for mutual gain since producers and consumers have contrary interests over prices—in the case of producers alone there can be conflicts of interest over both prices and market shares. Occasionally, mutual interests exist in a particular price stability. However, market imperfection that can exist in such circumstances is natural monopolies or increasing economies of scale. These have, in fact, formed bases for relatively strong regimes in international telecommunications and shipping, although there are indications

---

11. E.D. Brown, "Freedom of the High Seas versus the Common Heritage of Mankind: Fundamental Principles and Conflict," *San Diego Law Review* (1983) pp:521-60; R.P. Anand, *Origin and Development Of The Law Of The Sea:History of International Law Revisited* (The Hague: Martinus Nijhoff, 1983).

of some weakening because of changing economic conditions. Outside of this circumstance, there are no bases for capturing mutual economic gains in the area of price regulation.

The situations where regulation of prices is beneficial to autonomy are quite limited. They could arise if states regarded control of an industry, more particularly its international dimensions, as crucial to their ability to influence important domestic developments. Examples of these situations are the telecommunications and postal industries. Support for international price regulation as well as regulation of market shares in such circumstances facilitate control over the domestic industry. International regulation of prices could also be a way for states to insure high revenues from an industry in order to assure its financial self-sufficiency. Overall the chances for intergovernmental regulation of prices on the basis of mutuality of interests do not seem very good, but there are some restrictive circumstances where they could occur.

Market Access

A dominant issue in the global economy is market access. There is one market imperfection that exists in this area known to almost all observers of the international scene—namely, impediments to factor mobility. Many international relations scholars may not think of such impediments as market imperfections, but they certainly know what liberal economists have been preaching over the years—that almost everyone in the world can be better off in the long run if states adopt a free trade regime. Adam Smith and his apostles have propounded that total global welfare will be maximized, and the possibility that all consumers will realize larger gains will be enhanced if the lowest-cost producers can sell their wares worldwide, free of any impediments or protectionism.

Two types of barriers, technical and non-technical, affect market access. Technical barriers rule out exchanges or make them very costly largely because of differences in standards among states. Non-technical barriers rule out or control the volume of exchanges through the imposition of restrictions imposed by the importing states. States are much more likely to agree to regimes for technical barriers (e.g., interconnection standards between telecommunications networks) because they make exchanges possible; states can still impose non-technical barriers to limit imports if they so choose. While there will thus be stronger regimes for technical barriers, there are likely to be some important ones for non-technical barriers as well. However, in the latter case there will often be strong political incentives for some states to erect barriers to protect domestic producers. In addition, the projected effects of regimes on power relationships will play an important role.

Accidental and Intentional Damage

Market imperfections loom large in the policy sector of accidental and intentional damage—particularly as regards uncertainty of costs, high transaction costs and impediments to factor mobility. Obviously the possibility of accidental or intentional damage to goods and services in transit and the chance that losses will not be compensated pose serious problems of cost uncertainty and act as deterrents to international commercial exchanges. If traders are worried that goods will not arrive at their destination and shipping firms are concerned that their vessels will not arrive—and both are not assured that losses would be compensated, they certainly will shy away from a great deal of international business.

Another market imperfection relevant to the creation of damage-control regimes is high transaction costs. States could negotiate on a bilateral or limited multilateral basis with other states to set prevention and liability standards as well as to provide for the prosecution of accused violators, but to negotiate a large set of agreements is an unwieldy, drawn-out and costly process. Transaction costs are much lower if states erect a single global regime. There is also a very real possibility that if states enter into a variety of agreements to control the crime and accident problem, they will create barriers to the movement of carriers as well as goods and services. For example, if states regulated ships as well as liability and insurance standards on a bilateral basis or among small groups of countries, they would soon find that they had created standards that were at cross-purposes and prevented their vessels from entering each others' ports. Problems already arise along these lines with regard to states' interpretations of international conventions, and the problem would be magnified a hundred fold if most states were not party to or *de facto* adherents to global conventions.

In the case of the damage-control problem there can also be market failures that create incentives for regime creation. From a global perspective, externalities such as air and marine pollution create incentives for regulatory arrangements since both benefits and costs must be internalized in order to realize economic efficiency. However, in the case of many externalities, one group of states is responsible for most of the damage, and another group bears most of the damage. Obviously they are unlikely to have mutual interests in regulation.

While the small number of strong damage-control regimes created to correct market failures are apt to rest significantly on the sanctioning power of certain states, those created to correct market imperfections, such as uncertainty, usually also rest to some extent on imposition. There is seldom a regime where at least a few states do not see themselves as absolute losers, or where some states do not perceive that they would gain more if they could stay outside of the regime. One of the the most serious sources of opposition to damage-control regimes is the perception by some states that their firms will gain a competitive advantage if they do not have to comply, while companies in other states are forced to comply. These potential dissidents have to be made to comply in order to prevent defection by the supporters. It has certainly been the case with maritime safety conventions that some shipping states would not have accepted them if the major trading states had not threatened to deprive them of access to their ports. At the same time it should be stressed that some gains were realized by virtually all states as a result of the greater certainty of costs promoted by the conventions.

Labor Welfare Standards

The fifth policy sector is labor welfare standards. There are in fact, few, if any, opportunities for mutual gain with regard to economic welfare standards themselves. Labor costs are central to the competitive standing of national industries involved in struggles for markets and profits, and hence they are central to the terms of competition among states. In addition, the legislation of labor standards is such a central aspect of state social policy that external constraints on a state's autonomy in this realm would be equated with a serious incursion on that autonomy. It is not just that there would be no possible gains in state independence; there would be important infringements.

In going over the various market imperfections and failures there are none that seem very prominent in the realm of labor welfare standards. A case might be made that international regulation would promote some greater certainty of costs, but the gains would be extremely marginal.

As is clear from the discussions of the five policy sectors, strong regimes are most likely to exist with regard to jurisdictional competences and accidental and intentional damage. States' mutual interests in promoting certainty of costs, lower transaction costs and greater factor mobility (and occasionally enhanced autonomy) are likely to override conflicts of interests over specific regulatory outcomes. Market failures often exist with regard to jurisdictional and damage-control issues, but in these circumstances the distributional implications of particular regime proposals are likely to pose serious obstacles to the creation of strong regimes. States can enhance joint access to markets by promoting factor mobility, but the implications of accords for states' relative power and wealth are much larger than in the previous two sectors.

The history of trade-barrier regimes indicates that market-access regimes are apt to vary considerably in strength. The price-policy sector is not generally susceptible to strong regimes because price levels are so central to international economic competition. However, in certain circumstances such as the commitment of states to complete control over national segments of an international industry and the existence of increasing economies of scale in an industry, common interests can be strong enough to sustain strong regimes. Finally, as noted, there are almost no common interests in economic labor standards to sustain regimes. The above projections reflect the patterns of regime strength that have evolved in the international transport and communications industries. They should exist in other economic-issue areas as well.

Some Reflections on the Theory

A number of questions have arisen about aspects of this and similar theoretical enterprises. Some question the state-centric approach that leaves out consideration of transnational actors and domestic politics and, second, the ranking of states' preferences for autonomy and economic welfare. A much larger and more complex issue concerns the shortcomings and strengths of functional theories of collaboration.

The underlying substantive concern of the theory and the study of transport and communications regimes is not the creation of a particular regime, nor even the particular characteristics of that regime. Rather it is the pattern of regimes that form over time under certain circumstances. Transnational actors and domestic politics may affect the timing and particular characteristics of a regime; but in the present world, states are still the dominant international actors, and their preferences and power relations shape evolutionary patterns of collaboration. The integration of domestic political systems into a study of the evolution of general patterns of international collaboration should examine how their general economic characteristics and the linkages among their elites impinge on the occurrence and form of regimes, along the lines of the work by Robert Cox.[12] The theoretical thrust of this article is clearly more applicable to liberal capitalist states, although it is not without some relevance to other types of states.

Although the goals of states change over time, it seems difficult to deny that autonomy or security takes precedence over economic welfare. While some states cannot do a lot to assure their security, this does not negate its importance. The caveat that economic welfare is important enough that states are willing to trade-off limited amounts of autonomy

---

12. Robert W. Cox, "On Thinking about Future World Order," *World Politics* 28 (January 1976) pp.175-96; "The Crisis of World Order and the Problem of International Organization in the 1980s," *International Journal* 35 (Spring 1980) pp.370-395; "Social Forces, States and World Orders: Beyond International Relations Theory," *Millenium* 10 (1981) pp.126-155; *Power and Production*, vol. 1; *Production, Power, and the World: Social Forces In The Making of History* (New York: Columbia University Press, 1987).

does admittedly deserve a more thorough treatment, but that will unfortunately have to be postponed until future research endeavors. The task of understanding states' changing perceptions of and strategies toward that tradeoff is, in fact, one of the most important in the field of international political economy.

As a prelude to addressing criticisms of functional theories such as this one, it is important to repeat what this theory seeks to do and what it does not do. Most importantly, it identifies those characteristics of international issues that tend to generate mutual interests. Common interests are probably more important to the politics of international collaboration than has been conveyed by most of the literature, which implicitly stresses structural impediments, conflicting interests and the power of opposed coalitions. It is also probably the case that differences in payoffs from many economic regimes are not nearly as great an impediment as some realists imply. In part, their impact on security is often not very strong or is very difficult to determine in the long run. In many international economic issues, states are more likely to be concerned with short-term economic gains and losses than with long-term impact on international vulnerability.

These comments are relevant to the discussion of functional theories of regimes in a recent article by Haggard and Simmons. Functional theories are generally viewed as those that posit that under certain circumstances regimes can provide benefits for all or most states; in different terminology, regimes perform services or functions for the community of states. Haggard and Simmons have noted that such theories are subject to a number of interrelated criticisms. First, functional theories "are better at specifying when regimes will be demanded rather than suggesting how or when they will get supplied."[13] They also tend to be "teleological." They assume that because there is a possibility to increase joint gain, collaboration will occur or has occurred.[14] Functional approaches also fail to prove that regimes are instituted for the reasons specified. According to Haggard and Simmons, "The proper test of a functional theory is not the mere existence of a regime, but the demonstration that actors' behavior was motivated by benefits provided uniquely, or at least more efficiently, through the regime, or by reputation concerns connected to the existence of rules."[15] Finally, functional theories tend to ignore the distributional consequences of particular

---

13.   Haggard and Simmons, "Theories of International Regimes," p.506.
14.   *Ibid.*, p.507.
15.   *Ibid.,* p.508.

regimes and the fact that they "are certainly more likely to reflect the interests of the powerful than the interests of the weak."[16]

These are valid criticisms of any theoretical analysis that seeks to provide both a complete explanation of when and why regimes are formed and a thorough proof that actions were taken for stated reasons. However, one can have more modest goals concerning explanation and proof. In fact, when looking at broad trends over time, it may be virtually impossible to overcome completely the shortcomings noted above. With respect to the first criticism that functional approaches are better at analyzing why regimes are demanded than how and when they are created, one can retort that the ability to identify when most states are likely to see regulation resulting in absolute gains is not an insignificant accomplishment. That one cannot predict exactly when and how regimes will be formed under such conditions is a shortcoming, but it does not negate the value of the approach. Also, in employing a functional approach one can seek to supplement it by analyzing both factors that cause conflicts of interest and the power of opposing coalitions.

A central problem in any functional analysis, as noted by Haggard and Simmons, is the matter of evidence. The evidence can be of two interrelated types. First, there is evidence that states support regulation to realize certain goals. It can include information that certain problems (e.g., market imperfections) existed and that the certain regulations are desirable in order to ameliorate unfavorable conditions. One can also turn to statements of the parties involved and see published studies of experts. It would be desirable to have good records of statements by government officials who participated in international deliberations, but unfortunately they often do not exist.

Second, the other type of supportive information is that which indicates that all or most states gain from regulatory regimes. Widespread support for and compliance with regulations and an absence of any signs that coercion was necessary in order to secure their backing are good indications of common benefits. (Of course, this is not sufficient proof since lack of opposition may be attributable to fear of the consequences of opposition, resignation to the inevitable or ideological hegemony.)

With regard to patterns of support it is particularly important to observe where political rivals backed a regime since their mutual support would provide a strong indication of mutual gains for most states. In a related vein, good evidence of common interests in a regime would be found if its basic features did not change significantly over time despite changes in alliances and the distribution of power. As noted above, it

---

16.   *Ibid.,* p.508.

would be desirable to obtain statements of government participants and information on decision-making in many states, but these are difficult to obtain—especially in international economics. However, the types of evidence to which it is possible to turn provide reasonable substantiation of functional explanatory analyses.

The final shortcomings of functional explanations relate to their failure to recognize the distributional consequences of regimes and the negative and positive sanctions that are employed in securing their acceptance.[17]

No student of international regimes could challenge the fact that some potentially mutually beneficial regimes are rejected because of their distributional consequences or that some are adopted in part or largely because of distributional implications and the power of certain states. However, there are quite a few areas in which regimes have been established because almost all states achieved some gains. Those who gain less than others accept the regime because they do benefit, and because the larger gains of others are not seen as threatening to them. Also, in some cases it is very difficult to project the relative gains of regimes and their implications for interstate vulnerabilities. The theoretical orientation here is liberal in the sense that it posits that states will only reject a regime from which they achieve some gains if they can clearly see that serious vulnerabilities will result. Of course, for realists almost all disparities in relative gains constitute an effective barrier to collaboration.

Another important rebuttal to the above criticism of functional theories is that most regimes are not based on the need for the most powerful backers to apply sanctions against a large group of weaker states because most states will achieve some benefits. Many regimes disadvantage a few states, and various sanctions are applied against them by the majority to secure their compliance. But in most regimes it is only a few states that have to have strong sanctions applied against them to get them to toe the line. All regimes rest on some sanctioning, but it has not been stressed enough that a very large number rest significantly on benefits that result for the great majority of states. The international legal scholar Ian Brownlie has written that most international treaties are "freely concluded" and based on "expectation of reciprocity," and that "the dictated treaty" is best viewed as "the exception" and not the rule.[18]

The stress on the bases of mutual interests in this theory is not meant to put blinders on students of international regimes with respect to

---

17. The realist concern for relative gains is highlighted in Grieco, *op. cit.*
18. Ian Brownlie, "The Roles of International Law," *Zin en Tegenzin In International Report* (Deventer: Kluwer, 1986) p.19.

conflicting interests and power relationships; it is just meant to encourage scholars to look systematically at the sources and importance of common interests in international politics. Even realist theorists recognize that many commonalities of interest exist among states, although they think that distributional issues will impede collaboration on most issues—and certainly those that impinge on security. At the same time, they should be interested in the nature and sources of common interests and in those circumstances when they might lead to regime formation. Therefore, it should be of importance to both realists and liberals of various stripes that progress is made in furthering our theoretical and empirical understanding of mutual interests among states.

LIMITS AND POSSIBILITIE
WEAK THEORY:
INTERPRETING NORTH-SOl

by Robert L. Rothstein

The Theoretical Debate: Paradise for Skeptics?

I owe much to Bill Fox, more than I can properly express, and nothing gives me more pleasure than editing and contributing to a collection dedicated to his memory. He inspired all who were lucky enough to work closely with him not only by his scholarly achievements and scholarly judgments, but also by his generosity of spirit, his unfailing willingness to help others and his wisdom about matters both professional and personal.

I owe also to Bill an abiding concern with the problems of the weak in international relations. When I was looking for a dissertation topic and suggested that I was interested particularly in the years between World War I and World War II, Bill made a passing comment on the behavior of some of the military regimes in the "successor states" of the Austro-Hungarian Empire that set me thinking: Would it be useful to look at the international relations of the period from the perspective of the European small states? That research led to my first book and subsequently to several books on the role of the developing countries in the international system. In the circumstances, it seems appropriate to focus my contribution to this collection on one of the great episodes of interaction between the weak and the strong, the effort to establish a New International Economic Order (NIEO) in the 1970s. It is especially poignant for me to do so because at my last meeting with Bill at an International Studies Association Convention three years ago he asked me whether a rethinking of the NIEO debate was now pertinent and whether I thought a neorealist or modified neorealist perspective was the proper approach. My answer to the latter question has been published elsewhere but I shall attempt a preliminary response to the first question in this paper.[1]

In the spirit of this volume, however, I want to make a few brief comments on the evolution of the theoretical debate in international relations since my years as a graduate student with Bill in the early 1960s. It is not my intention obviously to recapitulate a massive, complex, and

---

1. For my criticisms of Stephen Krasner's "modified" neorealist approach to North-South, see "Epitaph for a Monument to a Failed Protest? A North-South Retrospective," *International Organization* 42, no..4 (Autumn 1988) pp.725-47.

inconclusive debate that has gone on for more than three decades but rather to discuss some aspects of the debate that have affected perceptions and interpretations of the North-South arena. Subsequently, the perspective will be reversed: What do events in North-South relations suggest about the adequacy or value of different approaches to theory?

There is in some scholarly circles something akin to radical skepticism about the possibility of developing genuinely scientific theories about international relations or even a discipline that represents more than a "limited convergence of scholarly interests."[2] Disappointment with the results of so many determined efforts to theorize is understandable. The indictment is formidable, if familiar. The cumulative development of consensual knowledge has been limited, central concepts such as the state, power, the national interest, interdependence, autonomy and dependence remain "essentially contested concepts" (indeed, we have an essentially contested discipline), there is limited and uncertain agreement about the questions that we should be asking and the methods we should be using to get some answers to whatever questions we do ask, different values, beliefs, and perceptions undermine any attempt to establish a consensus (except among the "like-minded," a group which frequently seems to be an artifact of where one went to graduate school), and shifts in theory or at least theoretical vocabulary seem more a response to fashion or to unanticipated external developments than to progress in theoretical understanding.[3] Moreover, there is something inherently suspect about any discipline that so frequently seems to rely on borrowed goods from other disciplines for theoretical progress, although, as we shall see, there are also some benefits from borrowing in terms of new insights and perspectives.

Ferguson and Mansbach reach the sobering conclusion that the discipline should forego the quest for theory and seek instead, as with the humanities, insight and wisdom.[4] The constant reappearance of the same grand themes in the theoretical debate—power versus justice, the weak versus the strong, autonomy versus dependence, etc.—suggests that we cannot resolve the central questions that confront the discipline in different periods and that even approximations of answers are more a reflection of the temper of the times than increased understanding. Put differently, the real world temptations that seem to influence most scholars of international relations—the temptations to be, or to catch the

---

2. See Yale H. Ferguson and Richard W. Mansbach, _The Elusive Quest: Theory and International Politics_ (Columbia, SC: University of South Carolina Press, 1988) p.24.
3. For the criticisms, _ibid._, especially ch.1. The phrase about "essentially contested concepts" was, I think, first used by W. B. Gallie.
4. _Ibid._, pp.37-38

ear of, the practitioner—are bound to fail, by this reckoning, if they rest on the hope of providing advice drawn from grounded theory.

There is, however, something inherently unsatisfying, perhaps even misleading, about these arguments. In the first place, the argument that the discipline ought to concentrate on providing insight and wisdom is not itself without ambiguities. The point, of course, is not that there is something wrong with the provision of such advice (should it be possible), but rather that it is as hard to derive and identify as advice based on more scholarly achievements. Such advice may be even more time-bound and reflect biased normative preferences than whatever passes as "theoretical" advice in any period—theory which presumably will at least seek to meet or to attain some higher epistemological standard.

In the second place, and perhaps more importantly, while Ferguson and Mansbach are acute and sophisticated critics of what the discipline's theoretical endeavors have produced and while they may indeed be correct in asserting that "linear theoretical growth is impossible," they may be attacking only one kind of scientific theory and sharply underestimating the value of the theoretical enterprise even if it does not produce wholly adequate explanations of international events.[5] That is, theory is more than just an explanation of empirical events or an explanation of the truth of certain descriptions or an "explanatory shell" to enclose whatever we seek to theorize about; it is or may be all of these things, but it also can or may produce other, ancillary benefits for the discipline. The quest for theory may help to establish priorities in a discipline that might otherwise become even more chaotic, it may guide research toward the discovery of common patterns (and uncommon anomalies), and it may help in discriminating between what we know and what we do not know. The failure to achieve any or all of these aims does not mean that the quest is useless, for it is the quest itself that gives shape to the discipline. Moreover, it is in all likelihood the quest for theory in an extraordinarily complex environment that may attract and keep our most creative minds within the discipline. And to focus primarily on the provision of insight and wisdom—presumably on problems of policy choice—may compel too narrow a focus on experience, which may rapidly be dated and may deflect attention from the problems of change.

The gap between what various theorists promised or anticipated and what they have produced is perhaps largely a function of excessive ambition, of a failure to acknowledge the limitations intrinsic to theorizing about a multi-level discipline operating in a rapidly changing context. There is also a sense in which Kurt Lewin's famous assertion that

---

5.   For the quoted phrase see Ferguson and Mansbach, *op. cit., p.4.*

"nothing is so practical as a good theory," which was widely accepted in the discipline, may have done more harm than good as it tended to focus attention on a particular kind of "good" theory and divert attention from some important connections between theory and practice. The point in the present context is that international relations does not have good theories but has, at best, "weak" theories that may be time-bound and value-bound, that provide only tentative and partial explanations of international events, and that necessitate the use of very fallible human judgment in application. Consequently, the key question is not about the utility of good theory, which is indisputable, but about the limited utility of weak theory, which is very disputable.

There is a fine line between defining theory too loosely (for example, as any body of propositions about political relations between states) and defining it too narrowly in terms of some set of formal criteria.[6] What we seem to be doing with weak theory or theories is provide a common framework to discuss certain events or issues, a framework that sets out some working definitions of key terms, that specifies a particular set of questions that require analysis, and that it is hoped will facilitate the transformation of a web of partial explanations of events or issues into more general, plausible, and always provisional, answers to the questions asked. While the ultimate hope remains the creation of genuine explanations of international political phenomena (what else?) the quest itself will continue to suffer from all of the afflictions that a variety of critics have specified. Still, increased understanding may be a preface to improvements in theorizing and there may at least be progress of a sort from successful debunking of superficial explanations. In addition, even if contested concepts remain contested, there is some virtue in being clear about what is being contested (about where the ambiguities lie). It is also important to be clear about the need to specify how concepts are being used and defined in particular cases. None of this guarantees good theory but it may well be argued that producing weak theory that is constantly questioned and evaluated is preferable to bad theory that is used from habit or inertia, without thought.

How can one set the debate on the NIEO within the context of a discussion about both the limits and possibilities of weak theory? Clearly none of the available theoretical approaches answered all of the questions we might have about the NIEO: All the theories explained some events or outcomes reasonably well but also failed to explain other events or outcomes that were equally consequential. In addition, values and nor-

---

6.   The definition in parentheses is from John C. Garnett, *Commonsense and the Theory of International Politics* (Albany: State University of New York Press, 1984) p.4.

mative predispositions tended to affect theoretical perspectives and may indeed have carried more weight in some circumstances and for some countries than calculations of interests. This tended to structure the debate in terms of classic themes: the rich versus the poor, the strong versus the weak. Finally, the axis of the theoretical debate has shifted sharply in the last decade, not because of theoretical progress or the resolution of the problems that generated the debate in the first place, but rather because of exogenous factors (slower growth, the decline of the OPEC threat, the arrival of conservative administrations in various countries, etc.). In short, much of the debate seems to provide a sad confirmation of the Ferguson-Mansbach indictment.

Yet more needs to be said. Without a clash of theoretical perspectives, how could or would North-South have been interpreted? The answer obviously is uncertain, but one surmises that some combination of sunken intellectual capital, historical allusions, intuitions, short-run calculations of interests and superficial "theorizing" would have structured the debate. Would this have led to wise and insightful policy? In the circumstances, the theoretical debate had at least some negative virtues. While failure to agree on a common, albeit weak theoretical approach no doubt has its costs—conceptually, aesthetically and practically—it also had the virtue of challenging oversimplification. That is, each approach was reasonably effective in illustrating deficiencies in the other approaches. More important, the quest for explanation tended to focus the debate on the correct questions: in effect, questions about questions. What were we trying to explain in North-South—a transient (cyclical) phenomenon reflecting the unusual circumstances of the time, or a more permanent phenomenon reflecting structural changes in the international order? Why did the challenge of the South largely fail? None of these questions could be answered definitively, certainly not by the available approaches, but the attempt to answer them was crucial for the discipline itself. Minimally, it generated more sophisticated *provisional* answers than a focus on practical wisdom—which is certainly valuable and important but also even more limited and precarious than the insights that may emerge from the theoretical quest. The inadequacy of certain explanations, the need for further research and the values and interests that were at stake became clearer even without "strong" theory.

Two issues, analytically separable but also partially linked, came to dominate the North-South debate. The first concerned the perennial and apparently insoluble issue of change: Both sides to the debate, as well as the different theoretical approaches, perceived different kinds and degrees of change at work and thus had very different interpretations of what policy prescriptions made sense. The revival of neorealism, which had significant theoretical and practical implications, was particularly significant in this regard because of its tendency to emphasize continuity over change. By contrast, alternative approaches tended to see much more change than continuity. However, it is unclear whether they were seeing the right kind of change or whether they had the structural principles capable of clarifying a world of multiple chessboards, great risk and uncertainty and what were rising levels of both "complex interdependence" and "complex dependence" for much of the Third World. If not, the retreat to the structural simplicities of neorealism, "modified" at the margin by the perceived benefits of cooperation within regimes, was probably inevitable. In any case, we shall attempt to look at the issue of change in North-South from a perspective that differs from either the neorealists or their critics.

The second issue concerned the relationship between domestic and external policy. The rise of "low" politics to "high" politics and the breakdown of the foreign policy consensus during and after the Vietnam War obviously began to undermine classic realism's emphasis on the primacy of foreign policy. Neorealism once again challenged the extent to which domestic factors were likely to be consequential, despite the fact that the external realm itself was largely a function of beliefs, perceptions and attitudes of internal decision makers and thus in some important ways a subjective phenomenon. In any event, there are presumably large elements of co-determination between the two realms and the key question becomes how to analyze realms that are both separate and linked. This is especially true in North-South, where the effects of the external structure are powerful but where internal conditions in the South also have a strong effect on the nature of responses to external pressures.

Paradoxes of Power: A Structural Challenge by the Weak

North-South, by which we have come to mean the multilateral part of the relationship between the developing and the developed countries, has been extensively described and analyzed but it remains theoretically underdetermined. No single approach seems adequately to capture what transpired in North-South either during the period when it was near the top of the international agenda nor during its subsequent phase in the 1980s as something of a residual backwater, an arena of concern because of deteriorating performance but not of central interest as a challenge to the prevailing system. We shall in this section ask why it became so important in the 1970s and how analysts perceived it.

North-South was not a very salient dimension of activity in the 1950s and 1960s largely because the developing countries seemed to be doing well politically and economically. Their elites were still reasonably optimistic about the future, control of the agenda of the United Nations system was still rudimentary and the Nonaligned Movement—the major group forum—was not greatly concerned with economics and tended to focus mainly on anti–colonial rhetoric. The international environment itself was relatively benign and concerned with such matters as rising aid and trade. From the East-West perspective, the developing countries largely provided an arena for political and ideological conflict, a substitute in some ways for direct conflict between opposed alliance systems.

A number of developments combined in the 1970s to make the North-South conflict a "relationship of major tension." These included the impact of the OPEC oil shock, widespread perceptions of emerging resource shortages, the rise of interdependence and the attendant shift in perceptions about relative dependencies, growing fears among many Third World elites about stability, prosperity and autonomy, and perhaps even a partial shift in moral sensibilities in some developed countries as a result of Vietnam and the failure of conventional growth strategies to reduce poverty and income inequalities in many Third World countries. Of course all of these developments were variously interpreted, not only in terms of causation but also in terms of policy responses. In addition, the consequences of slower growth, the costs of adjusting to stagflation, and a certain resentment against excessive Third World demands also generated a backlash against major concessions (especially in regard to restructuring the international order primarily to benefit developing countries) and against the easy assumption that there was a long-term harmony of interests between North and South. In short, the challenge of the South occurred in a complex and ambiguous framework, a framework in which there were both new strengths and new weaknesses. The odds on the challenge succeeding—however one defined success— were not good, but many Third World elites thought they were probably as good as they were going to get, especially if they could hang together and if the disarray of the developed countries continued.

The countries of the South, as well as their supporters in the United Nations system, sought to increase their bargaining leverage by unifying, in effect, by mobilizing in an attempt to increase their collective assets. Indeed, some analysts have argued that increased institutionalization of the South during this period was actually its greatest achievement. In retrospect, however, the argument seems overstated as institutionalization did not lead to more than marginal substantive gains and it did not facilitate greater gains in the 1980s. Mobilization was facilitated by the South's control of certain crucial assets (especially oil), by the hope that

OPEC would use its power to support Third World demands (even demands that might be costly for some key OPEC states), and by fear that previous gains in power and wealth could easily be lost. Mobilization did lead to some gains, if largely in terms of increased discussion of the problems and perspectives of the South. But the counter–mobilization of the North, the unwillingness of the richest and most conservative states in the South to risk much for their allies, a poor choice of bargaining strategies by the leadership of the South (who were not powerful enough to prevent defections or to provide a coherent vision of the future), and the absence of policy proposals that were well-grounded technically and that were politically feasible, meant that greater gains were not possible. With insufficient political and economic power, the South desperately needed a strategy of persuasion that rested on consensual knowledge and a clear sense of the other side's needs; instead, they pursued a strategy based on confrontation, rhetorical power and one-sided demands.[7]

Realists and neorealists have maintained that the South's efforts to create a strong coalition—a coalition based on shared interests and not shared sentiments and rhetoric—were bound to fail because of insufficient power and insufficient shared interests both within and between coalitions. And of course the conditions necessary to create a strong coalition, especially among the weak, are difficult to establish. At least three sets of conditions had to come together and reinforce each other in order to achieve substantive unity. First, the internal strength of the coalition had to reflect more than psychological and ideological affinities: Interests also had to overlap sufficiently to overcome political and economic conflicts and the difficulties of sacrificing short-run gains for presumably greater long-run benefits. Second, the structure of the system—the distribution of power and influence, the ability of the powerful to establish unified positions, the state of the world economy— had to be relatively favorable in terms of responding to the needs of the weak. Finally, perceptions of who was likely to benefit or lose from future trends had to facilitate the creation of a political and psychological climate favorable to the idea of mutually beneficial reform. Since North-South was a dynamic arena of interaction, these conditions shifted in complex ways in different periods.

The power of the South was to some extent artificial because it did not rest on a strong enough base of shared interests, which meant that group positions were always unstable. The power that it could muster was largely procedural or residual in the sense of the transitory disarray of

---

7. On consensual knowledge and its potential effects on North-South, see my article "Consensual Knowledge and International Collaboration," *International Organization* 38, no.4 (Autumn 1984) pp.733-62.

the opposition. In a world still dominated by traditional calculations of power and interest by the most powerful developed countries, the elements of power that the South did have could produce some small gains that perhaps could not have been achieved by individual states acting alone. These gains, however, fell far short of what the South and its leaders felt was appropriate, desirable or justified. The South *felt* more powerful because of beliefs about the new importance of "resource power," because of an unusual degree of procedural power in international institutions, and because of rather oversimplified assumptions about the aggregate economic and political power of the group in an interdependent world. But this subjective and procedural power was also undermined by subjective fears about increasing marginalization, by an unwillingness to accept the degree to which domestic failures were also linked to mistaken domestic policies, and as a result, by a confused and inappropriate bargaining strategy that mixed together reform and revolution and paid insufficient attention to the needs of the developed countries.

"Good" theory presumably would have explained why weak countries could decide to launch a frontal assault on international regimes that provided at least some of them with substantial benefits, why the assault was turned back, and what policy prescriptions followed. Weak theory obviously cannot answer such complex questions. More critically, because North-South was so strongly affected by the normative and ideological biases of most analysts and because interpretations of events and trends was largely subjective, even the limited benefits of weak theory (or theorizing) were frequently lost. There was no common framework of analysis, there was no common definition of terms, there was no agreement on the questions that needed to be asked (apart from why the other side, whoever that might be, was responsible for failure), and, inevitably, no web of partial answers to weave into a plausible pattern. Indeed, as I have already suggested, perhaps the only benefit of contention among weak theories was that premature consensus on one "proper" explanation was avoided and debate on critical questions continued.

Clearly, in contexts dominated by great complexity, unclear interests, conflicting values and rapid and unsettling patterns of change, even the potential benefits of weak theory may be lost. By the same token, however, it is far from clear how we can achieve wisdom and insight in such circumstances without some concern for the kind of questions raised in the quest for theory. Can this quest improve our understanding of change and of the links between domestic and external policy, even if that quest thus far has not done much more than make us aware of the need to continue to ask questions and to doubt the adequacy of received wisdom?

Social Change in a North-South Context

Change, both domestically and internationally, thrust the North-South arena into prominence. Other changes subsequently reduced the salience of direct North-South conflict and we can be sure that yet another round of change will once again have a significant impact on perceptions of what can or should be done within a North-South setting. Virtually all analyses of North-South mention the importance of change and some of these analyses include sophisticated discussions of particular patterns of change. However, while describing and suggesting responses to change has become something of a cottage industry, attempts to explain why it is happening, whether it will persist, and how important it is likely to be are, absent a theory of change, virtually impossible. In such circumstances, some key questions about change can obviously be answered only after the fact (for example, about persistence and importance) and the "why" question cannot be answered at all. Interpretations of change are thus heavily affected by subjective judgments about whether it is "good" or "bad" or whether one or another kind of response is necessary or unnecessary. The uncertainties are so great that the temptation to argue against the need for a policy response is understandable, except that the risks of not responding may be as great as the risks of responding. Perhaps one might say that there is no difficulty, up to a point, in discussing changes, but we are at sea in turbulent waters in trying to discuss the idea of change itself.

There are so many different kinds of change, so many different causes, and so much intermingling between change and continuity that bemoaning the absence of "good" theory or asserting the need to wait its arrival seems pointless.[8] In addition, in international relations one needs also to consider the differential impact of change, which has important policy consequences. Thus change not only affects each state differently but also frequently affects international and domestic systems differently, with a more diffuse effect in the former and a more direct and immediate

---

8.   The point about the intermingling of change and continuity is important because so many analyses of change seek to understand change in terms of sharp dichotomies: continuous versus discontinuous, qualitative versus quantitative, tangible versus intangible, etc. This is misleading because elements of both components of these dichotomies are always present.

effect in the latter.[9] Differential impacts mean that it is inordinately difficult to synchronize common policy responses and that the impact of learning (perceiving change and then devising a response) will be diluted because different lessons will be learned, different goals will seem sensible and different aspects of change will seem important to various actors. In North-South, for example, change that may seem massive for the South, or parts of it, may seem insignificant to rich, relatively insulated developed countries. This leads to sharp disagreements about appropriate responses and the perception in the South that the North is selfish and unfeeling. The difficulties of devising common policies are compounded in international relations when change can come from massive events (war, depression, etc.), from incremental and cumulative steps (the division of labor, environmental deterioration), or some combination of the two.

We obviously cannot "solve" the problem of change, which is to say we cannot define what is changing in what time period, when "more or less" becomes a difference in kind or what is "meaningful" and what is "superficial."[10] Are we then left only with a conventional plea for more research (even if we know that it is unlikely to greatly diminish obstacles to understanding) and an assertion about the need at least to be aware of the difficulties of saying anything very useful about change? Perhaps some progress is possible if we move away from the apparently insoluble problem of trying to define change and instead focus on how it is perceived and what practical consequences we need to be concerned about. These are hardly easy questions to answer but the attempt to answer them may provide a useful, if partial, framework for understanding or thinking about some aspects of change. Responses to change, because of the uncertainties, are inherently risky. Thus it is important to try to understand the nature of the risks (in effect, the different kinds and levels of risk), the differential impact of change on different actors, and the kinds of policy responses that might lower the risks and spread the

---

9. Some structural realists seem to disagree, insisting that change occurs primarily at the unit level. But changes at the latter level can change the systemic level which, in turn, can lead to changes in state actors or decision makers—for example, changes in the international division of labor or even in normative changes, such as the pressures for democratization, which flow in both directions.

10. In a broad sense, one can devise a definition of change that at least focuses on what one is seeking to talk about. I prefer a definition that focuses not only on an alteration in the way individuals or groups behave because of perceived structural changes but also an alteration that reflects a new definition of the situation and thus learning or relearning. For a similar argument, see Gerald Zaltman and Robert Duncan, *Strategies for Planned Change* (New York: John Wiley and Sons, 1977) pp.9-10.

costs of responding more equitably. For example, we need to distinguish between technical and policy risks as they affect different levels of the policy–making process, we need to understand who is likely to benefit or lose from different responses, and we need to consider policy characteristics that make risk more manageable. In the latter sense, prudent responses ought to focus on policies that are reversible, that allow some degree of divisibility (which is not always possible for "big" projects), that facilitate feedback and adaptive learning, and that do not require very large initial commitments of scarce resources.[11] But we need also to consider how complexity may undermine the ability to devise such policies, whether prudent policies may also be inadequate policies (especially to weaker and poorer actors), and whether the provision of consensual knowledge might be a useful means of reducing both political and technical risks.[12]

In what follows I shall seek to provide some insights into these issues by focusing on the South as an international social protest movement that seeks to respond to change and redirect it in presumably beneficial ways. It is hoped that this discussion of one set of perceptions and one set of responses to the problems of change will help to clarify the comments in the preceding paragraph and perhaps thereby add to our understanding of the questions we need to ask about change.

The Third World as an International Social Protest Movement

In retrospect, the 1960s seem to be an "Age of Innocence," although the roots of later problems may also be discerned. Growth rates were buoyant, Keynesian techniques seemed to be working, the path to development seemed clear if gaps in savings, investment and foreign exchange could be diminished, developing country elites were relatively optimistic about political and economic prospects, and Western analysts and officials tended to assume that economic development would lead inevitably to political development. In short, the liberal economic order established at Bretton Woods was producing, and seemed likely to continue to produce, unprecedented prosperity which would, at worst, "trickle down" to the Third World. Decolonization did not seem premature. No one thought very much about the problem of change since change seemed to be continuous, manageable and easily facilitated by rising levels of trade and aid.

---

11. For a similar argument, see Gerald Zaltman and Robert Duncan, *Strategies for Planned Change* (New York: John Wiley and Sons, 1977) pp.9-10.
12. I discuss the potential benefits of consensual knowledge (and how it might be produced) in "Adaptations to Change: Reform and Resistance in International Regimes," prepared for the International Studies Association conference (London: March 1989).

This rather benign vision began to crumble well before the OPEC oil shock and the "limits to growth" debate transformed perceptions of the future. Growth rates in the Third World remained impressive in the aggregate but the benefits of growth both within and between countries were asymmetrical: The number living near or below the poverty line was increasing, the problems of development and nation building in the Third World were proving more intractable than prevailing theories and assumptions implied, aid fatigue seemed to be escalating in the Western world, and the United States found that it could not continue within a fixed exchange rate system and forced a change in the rules of the game. When the OPEC phenomenon seemed to imply a new era of "resource power" (a judgment reinforced by fears of reasonably imminent resource scarcities), when pressures to acquire greater resources to deal with rising domestic problems began to increase in the Third World, and when the developed countries seemed weak, indecisive and increasingly dependent on Third World resources, the temptation in the Third World to launch a challenge to the existing international order was overwhelming. The challenge sought to create a new structure favorable to Third World needs and to act as if the changes that had occurred or were occurring had already shifted the configuration of power in international relations.

The attempt to understand these trends, as well as the debate about the implications of interdependence, had to be set within some conceptual framework. Given the lack of theory, the quest for meaning and interpretation went on largely in terms of a shifting combination of casual empiricism, extrapolations from presumably relevant historical analogies, largely intuitive judgments about the direction and importance of different trends, and felt perceptions of the interests involved in either change or continuity. The North, not surprisingly, saw primarily cyclical changes that could be dealt with by correct domestic policies and minor reforms of existing international regimes. The South saw the need for massive structural change, the need for prior agreement on new principles and norms before compromises on specific programs or policies could be struck, and the need for central management of the world economy to insure that the developing countries would gain not just opportunities (which would benefit only the most advanced developing countries) but widely shared benefits. Underlying these disagreements was a more profound disagreement about whether we were witnessing the "beginning of the end" for the Bretton Woods system or merely an adjustment crisis that would or could be dealt with in a few years. In retrospect, perhaps both sides were wrong as the North clearly misperceived or underestimated the severity of the changes that were occurring and the South saw the wrong kind of changes occurring which were, in contrast to the more optimistic assumptions of many Southern or pro-Southern analysts, fundamentally unfavorable to the South. We shall for the moment withhold comment on these changes and instead focus on the South as a social movement that thought, or hoped, or wanted to act as if, the changes were largely beneficial and that was opposed by a stronger coalition that believed time was on its side and the old regime could be patched together. (We shall not consider the North as a reactive social movement because the minimal changes perceived did not seem to require greater mobilization of collective resources and national, not collective, responses were still considered adequate to meet the challenges of the day.)

Most analyses of North-South have focused on the conflict between two large coalitions and the disparities in power, interest and ideology that have seemed to determine particular negotiating outcomes. This analytical perspective, while certainly useful and valid, has had, however, one important consequence: an emphasis on relatively short-run calculations of power and interest and a de-emphasis on the more long-run, unclear and uncertain patterns of internal and external change that have created the grounds for conflict. To get at the issue of change we need to move beyond analyses of the weaknesses and strengths of a coalition of the poor—a coalition that mingled together interest, sentiment and rhetoric—and instead think about the South as an international social movement responding to change and seeking to control or redirect it in a manner favorable to the members of the movement. This is a small and tentative step toward a sociology of North-South, which may be useful in an interdependent world where socioeconomic changes are increasingly affecting political choices.[13]

Social movements usually arise because of discontent, fueled by a sense of relative deprivation about what is just, expected or perceived as possible, or because of changes that seem to create new resources for a group. Both conditions held for the developing countries in the Group of 77 during the 1970s. Social movements can be considered as collective attempts to bring about change in the existing order or to resist such changes: in effect, exogenous changes create discontent, which leads to the creation of a social movement, which in turn leads to more change.[14] The creation of a social movement, which can be costly and time-con-

---

13. There are also other important differences between a coalition focus and a social movement focus; the latter focus is broader in that the central concern is not merely the power and interests of a group but also the role of third parties, the impact of the media and the public, and the ability to affect the agenda under discussion.
14. See especially Robert H. Lauer, "Introduction: Social Movements and Social," pp.xiii-xiv, in Lauer, ed., *Social Movements and Social Change* (Carbondale, IL: Southern Illinois University Press, 1976).

suming, is obviously not the only possible response to unpalatable change. Thus organized collective action is likely only if several conditions hold: large numbers of similarly situated individuals, groups or states must feel similarly deprived and discontented; they must be able to communicate and be in regular contact with each other (a process greatly facilitated for the South by the U.N. system), the social system must have clear power differentials that suggest the potential need for collaborative action, and there must be some evidence that collective action can create the desired kind of change.[15] As should be clear, these conditions were largely met by the developing countries, if through an effort to revive, empower and institutionalize the already existing Group of 77 and, to a lesser extent, the Nonaligned Movement. Any social movement must mobilize the resources of its members and organize effectively to mount a challenge against the opposition. Mobilized groups may, however, remain largely rhetorical in function; that is, they are likely to initiate collective action only if they feel the relative power balance has shifted or is likely to shift in their favor, if the balance between costs and gains is likely to be favorable, and if the target group seems vulnerable or seems likely to launch some kind of threatening action.[16] These are important points in that they make clear the contingent and uncertain nature of social action. Nevertheless, it needs also to be emphasized that the necessary calculations are essentially subjective and thus more likely to be affected by degrees of confidence in the likelihood of success and confidence is as much a function of other characteristics of social movements as it is of rational calculations of power and interest. This is especially true of the Third World in the 1970s, which was virtually euphoric, not to say naive, about the possibilities of changing the international order.

The other factors that affect the likelihood of initiating action and achieving some degree of success include group solidarity, the nature of the group's ideology, and the group's leadership. And of course the choice of strategies is also consequential. Solidarity ("consciousness of kind") was reasonably strong for the Group of 77, especially during the mid-1970s, but was always under threat because of divergent interests, pressing internal needs, political disputes and the delaying tactics of the developed countries which focused on passive resistance and partial offers that were designed to fragment unity. Centrifugal tendencies were to some extent contained by a strong ideology that specified discontents,

---

15. See *ibid.*, p. xvii for a good discussion of these issues. Obviously the OPEC "shock" seemed to suggest genuine possibilities of change through collective action.
16. See Ted Robert Gurr, "On the Political Consequences of Scarcity and Economic Decline," *International Studies Quarterly* 29, no. 1 (March 1985) p.62.

prescribed solutions, and justified particular kinds of (biased) changes. The ideology was also accepted uncritically by many members of the group, if primarily because its content (assumptions about exploitation and inequality, a single–factor explanation for all difficulties and a belief that external changes would solve domestic problems) was broad and uncritical.[17] However, because the Group of 77 was a loose and decentralized coalition, the leadership could not do much to contain fissiparous tendencies, it could not provide gains to buy off dissent or defection, and it was always in danger of being outflanked and out-promised by more radical leaders. The result was that the "action programs" that the coalition produced were a confused amalgam that sought to provide something for all members of the group, that simply added up demands, that did not pay much attention to questions of technical or political feasibility, and that was always ambiguous about whether only revolutionary changes would suffice or whether the group would accept better terms for integrating with the existing international order.

The question of whether the Third World's demands were truly revolutionary has always been somewhat misleading. While some members of the group (and many Third World intellectuals) certainly aspired to revolutionary change, most countries needed gains too quickly. The discipline and control necessary to achieve revolutionary gains were not present, many ruling elites in fact feared massive change, and there was always substantial doubt about the real power the group possessed. Thus a social movement (or a coalition) of the weak can rarely be truly revolutionary, rhetoric apart. This point, however, was at least partially obscured by the nature of the Third World as a social movement. Too many promises had to be made to too many states to prevent defections, needs were so pressing that only massive change seemed likely to be able to deal with them, euphoria over OPEC was dangerously high, and the leadership tended to follow rather than lead.

One result of this was that the movement's strategy was inappropriate. Rather than focusing on a strategy of persuasion that rested on mutual interests, the search for consensual knowledge and technically sound proposals and a clear sense of what the opposition could see as in its interests, the focus was on a strategy of confrontation and a demand for the acceptance of biased and controversial principles. The ensuing stalemate represented a victory for the developed countries' strategy of delay. In short, the strategy seemed to be revolutionary (or potentially

---

17. On the influence of ideology on social movements, see Rudolf Heberle, "Social Movements: Types and Functions," *The International Encyclopedia of the Social Sciences* (New York: The Macmillan Company, 1968) pp.440-42.

revolutionary) and the fact that real goals for most members of the movement were moderate and integrative, or became so over time, was not widely perceived. Goals and strategies did not converge but the unwieldy nature of the movement made it difficult to make the necessary adjustments. Consequently, cooperation with other groups was difficult, the legitimacy of the movement was challenged, and its unity was always suspect.[18] Since a weak social movement clearly requires third party support and major efforts to increase solidarity and cohesion in order to achieve even part of its goals, the strategy chosen was almost perverse.[19] In effect, the South had to act as if it was stronger, more unified and more radical than it actually was in order to maintain itself even as a weak social movement. It was a movement that could never establish a stable equilibrium.

Social movements of course rarely achieve all of their goals and indeed frequently generate unanticipated or contradictory outcomes or changes. This happened in this case also as the developed countries increasingly resorted to small group negotiations and as support for neoclassical market approaches grew much stronger (even in parts of the Third World). Still, although the Third World did not achieve any of its major goals as a coalition pursuing specific interests, as a social movement the Third World was marginally more successful in pursuing specific interests and seeking to have its issues placed much higher on the agenda, some of its ideas incorporated in the mainstream (debt as a development issue, linkages between issues and groups, the need for increased financial transfers, etc.), and achieving a limited effect on public opinion and public discussion. One point here is that standards of success, which were always inherently ambiguous in North-South, are also different in part for coalitions and social movements—they are longer term and more diffuse in the latter case. It should also be noted that in the broader sense of dealing successfully with the problems that generated the South's challenge, neither side was successful.

The literature on social movements is of course largely drawn from the domestic arena. The implicit analogy between such domestic movements and an international movement such as the South thus has to be used with great caution. The differences are obvious and important: the members of the international movement in this case are states, not individuals, and thus already coalitions of interests; the target of mobi-

---

18. On the latter points, see the discussion in Lauer, "Introduction," p. xx.
19. On the need for third party support, see Michael Lipsky, "Protest as a Political Resource," *American Political Science Review* LXII, no.4 (December 1968) pp.1145-46, and William A. Gamson, *The Strategy of Social Protest* (Homewood, IL: The Dorsey Press, 1975) p.112. Gamson especially emphasizes the dangers of pursuing goals that are too broad and that seem to threaten to displace opposing elites or groups.

lized action is a structure of authority that is weaker and more diffuse; the goals of the movement are likely to be more amorphous or even contradictory; the leadership is likely to be weaker and perhaps more ideological; and standards of success are more ambiguous and longer range. Given the differences and the difficulties, the minimal gains achieved were probably all that could be expected and at least arguably more than were available by national action although, by the same token, perhaps marginally less than might have been available with different leadership and more favorable environmental changes. In any case, focusing on the South as a social movement does have the virtue of moving analytical attention away from narrow questions of power and interest, where the South can rarely win, to broader questions of change and responses to change where patterns of winners and losers may be more complex.

Even the South's small gains seem to have been dissipated in the 1980s. Part of the reason for this obviously has to do with the difficult conditions in the world economy (and the U.S. economy) during this period. But I want to argue in the concluding section, if in a very brief form, that another part of the reason is that the Third World misperceived the kinds of changes that were occurring in the 1970s. The problem of the powerless can come not only from an inability to amass enough resources to achieve desired goals, but also from misperceptions abou: the kinds of change that are in fact occurring and the kinds of responses that are entailed.

Conclusion

The very weak theories or approaches that structured the discussion of North-South relations were not very helpful in understanding the problem of change. Each side tended to see only the kinds of change that it wanted to see. Each side also tended to focus on very salient and very immediate kinds of change that seemed to require governmental action, but paid scant attention to how change was creating problems for the other side, to how long-run patterns of continuous change were affecting the international division of labor, and to how domestic and international changes were increasingly linked. This encapsulation of perceptions of change was dangerous not only because it led to important misperceptions, but also because the failure to see the different risks of change for different actors or the asymmetrical impact of different changes was costly. It meant especially that common policy responses to reduce risks or to protect or compensate large losers from change were difficult to negotiate. Indeed, perhaps any effective response to change must rest on some shared perceptions or interpretations of the implications of the changes that are occurring.

The environment of the 1980s has been dominated by the weakening of the Bretton Woods system; declining faith in Keynesian solutions and the possibility of a "New Deal" for the Third World; energy, food and population pressures in much of the Third World; a "lost decade" for development as the Third World has fallen further behind the North because of a variety of factors (low spending on scientific and technological activities, closed markets to protect inefficient domestic producers, increased arms expenditures, etc.); debt burdens that have lowered already low standards of living; and a growing perception in the North that growth in the South may be threatening and that a long-run harmony of interests can no longer be taken for granted.[20] In addition, a growing trend toward structural dualism in many Third World countries seems to be creating societies in which income and wealth is even more inequitably distributed and in which the rich elite is more focused on external ties than on improving the lot of its less fortunate brethren. This suggests rising unemployment, massive welfare problems, declining agricultural productivity, and as a result, persistent domestic turmoil which will, in turn, deter or inhibit potentially beneficial linkages with the developed countries. Some developing countries will surely avoid or overcome many of these problems but many, perhaps the majority, will not. Consequently, the international economic system is likely to become an international caste system with many poor countries locked into poverty and lacking the ability to rise by their own efforts to a higher economic level.[21]

The developing countries hoped to diminish many of these problems through a variety of international programs: higher commodity prices, increased exports of manufactures, a substantial increase in resource flows (aid, loans, trade credits) and other programs. However, the likelihood of achieving any of these gains has been undermined by a number of structural changes, mostly overlooked or ignored in the 1970s, that are making the prospects for the Third World even grimmer in the 1990s. I will merely list some of these changes, since detailed discussion is impossible in this article.

One key adverse trend, which was already discerned in the 1960s, is that the primary products economy has become less closely linked to the

---

20. See on the latter issue Michael Beenstock, *The World Economy in Transition* (London: George Allen and Unwin, 1984) p.12ff.
21. See on the caste versus class system, Robert L. Rothstein, *The Third World and U.S. Foreign Policy* (Boulder, CO: Westview, 1981) ch.5.

industrial economy.[22] The amount of raw materials necessary for a given unit of economic output has been steadily declining and alternative markets for raw materials in the Third World itself have not increased enough to compensate. Also, declining investment in raw materials production probably means shortages, higher prices and continued price and revenue fluctuations in the future. Exporters of raw materials are thus likely to face increasing difficulties, not the least in being able to earn enough foreign exchange to import capital goods—a factor which will also affect exports from the developed world.

Another such trend concerns decreased linkages between manufacturing production and manufacturing employment.[23] As labor costs become less important as a factor in competition, Third World exporters who have relied on advantages in labor costs will face increasing difficulties, especially as it will be very costly to replace workers with machines or to shift into high-technology products. Competition in exporting low-level manufactured goods is likely to increase (thus depressing their terms of trade) and it will be very difficult for additional NICs (newly-industrializing countries) to emerge. Competition from the United States as it seeks to reduce its trade deficit by increasing manufactured exports (or substituting for manufactured imports) may also become important.[24] "Export substitution" may also be very difficult for the Third World because services may become technology-intensive and because many services are difficult to export. And, of course, shifting to more advanced manufacturing exports may require skills in short supply in most of the Third World and may generate even stronger protectionist responses from the North.

Finally, the dominance of the "symbol" economy (capital movements, exchange rates, credit flows) will create substantial problems for Third World countries who are short of capital, information and power to compete effectively in this arena.[25] The debt crisis exacerbates these difficulties, especially as various plans to deal with it flounder and as the debtors continue to export more capital than they receive (for example, a net deficit over $31 billion in 1988). As the risks, uncertainties and volatility in this part of the world economy continue, it will be difficult for the Third World to acquire sufficient resources to adjust to the other problems already noted or to plan effectively for the future.

---

22. Peter F. Drucker, "The Changed World Economy," *Foreign Affairs* 64, no.4 (Spring 1986) pp.771-75.
23. *Ibid.*, pp.775-80.
24. See Lester C. Thurow, "The Post-Industrial Era is Over," *New York Times*, 10 Aug 1989.
25. Drucker, *op. cit.*, pp.782-87.

There are yet other developments whose implications are unclear for the Third World. For example, will the move toward the market in many Third World countries increase growth rates and provide greater flexibility in dealing with the problems noted above, or will it exacerbate these problems by increasing domestic inequities, dependence on unstable foreign markets and political and social instabilities? Or, if the transition to relatively more democratic governments in some parts of the Third World continues, will it lead to declining economic performance as demands for consumption expenditures increase? Or will it help governments (at least over the long run) deal with some of their problems because citizens are willing to bear some short-run losses in growth in exchange for increased political participation? The uncertainties are vast, but the way in which they are resolved will obviously have profound implications for the ability of the Third World to begin to deal with its problems.

These structural changes were not widely perceived in the 1970s, in part because so much attention was focused on the OPEC shock (and its aftershock in 1979) and in part because the changes themselves tended to be continuous and incremental (up to a point of salience) and affect different countries in different ways. In practical terms, however, the changes were also actually or potentially negative in terms of Third World interests. This also implies that the strategies pursued by both North and South were at least partially inappropriate and required adjustment, although we cannot pursue here the question of what the appropriate strategies should have been. Discussion of the Third World as an international social movement hardly solves the problem of change or guarantees that the right changes will be seen. Still, in contrast to other approaches or even to the quest for wisdom, this approach does direct our attention usefully: It may diminish the effects of oversimplification, and it may suggest which questions we may really want to answer (even provisionally) and which may be an artifact of fashion or ideology.

I shall conclude with a brief comment about one issue that may illustrate some aspects of this argument. Focusing on change, the patterns it creates and the responses it evokes tends inevitably to lead to an attempt to understand the linkages and feedback between the domestic and international systems. This is a discussion that is as yet at the pre-theoretical, empirical mapping stage, but unless we begin to seek a proper conceptual framework, the questions that we ask about the choices that confront us are likely to be inadequate or misleading.

North-South issues have tended to differ from North-North or East-West issues in a number of ways. For the most part, North-South issues have had to struggle to get on Northern domestic agendas, most of the internal conflict goes on within different bureaucracies, the outcome of the internal bargaining process is usually an incremental compromise, and the President and other top leaders are not usually heavily involved or willing to risk much political capital to push for new initiatives.[26] Moreover, if a North-South issue does become politically salient and the top leaders decide to expend some of their political capital, the outcome is not entirely predictable. Public, media or congressional involvement could in some cases lead to policies that are narrower, more nationalistic and less effective. In short, the Third World's desire to see its issues rise higher on the political agenda may not always be wise.

Putnam has developed an interesting two-level model of the relationship between domestic and external systems that is quite valuable. He argues quite rightly that what is politic at one level may be quite impolitic at the other, thus suggesting the need to expand the bargaining process to link issues and open up new opportunities for agreement.[27] There are, however, many practical and conceptual difficulties in developing such linkages and establishing viable trade-offs between different issues and different time periods.[28] In addition, in North-South a two-level model is not entirely adequate because both North and South, but especially the latter, are also playing at a third level: influence within each coalition. Putnam's model could also be usefully extended by including some discussion of the effects of recent economic performance and differential expectations about future gains from any agreement. Thus, some Northern countries have not been enthusiastic about boosting trade with the South because they believe most of the benefits will go to Japan and West Germany and some countries in the South have resisted agreements that seem likely to benefit only the NICs.

Finally, the model of the external level in Putnam's game could also be expanded. We have linked incremental systems at the three levels, which has meant that except in crisis, the most that can be expected are limited initiatives, a bias toward domestic solutions to interdependent problems, and a short-run focus on managing events rather than seeking to deal with problems. Since it is unlikely that incrementalism will be superseded by a superior policy–making process, we need to begin rethinking what can be accomplished incrementally, how incremental systems can be revised (as systems of adaptation), and how to avoid

---

26. Robert D. Putnam, "Diplomacy and Domestic Politics: The Logic of Two-Level Games," *International Organization* 42, no. 3 (Summer 1988) pp.427-60, is interesting on the relationship between degrees of domestic conflict and the likelihood of creating transnational coalitions.
27. *Ibid.*, p.434.
28. See, for example, my "Regime-creation by a Coalition of the Weak," *International Studies Quarterly* 28, no. 4 (Fall 1984) p.324.

deterioration into a "garbage can" model of policy making. In any event, while we are a long way from adequately conceptualizing the relationship between different levels of policy making, the effort of thinking about the issue in theoretical and pre-theoretical terms may provide the only hope of avoiding some of the worst aspects of incremental political systems.

LAW AND POLITICS IN INTERNATIONAL RELATIONS: STATE AND HUMAN VALUES[1]

by Louis Henkin

Bill Fox took international law seriously. For him, any theory of international relations has to take account of centuries of human activity and the expenditure of immeasurable treasure devoted to establishing international norms and building institutions to apply them. Above all, a theory of international relations must take account of the uses of law in regulating those relations and of the profound influence of law on how nations behave.[2]

Students of law as well as students of politics are taught to distinguish law from politics. Law is normative and obligatory, and failure to abide by legal obligations invites legal remedies and responses; politics suggests freedom of choice, diplomacy, bargaining, accommodation. In fact, however, the distinction between law and politics is only a half-truth. In a larger, deeper sense, law *is* politics. Law is made by political actors, not by lawyers, through political procedures, for political ends. The law that emerges is the result of political forces as are the influences of law on state behavior.

In the second half of the twentieth century, international law, like international politics, has been reshaped by the nuclear arms race, the ebb and flow of ideological conflict between the superpowers, the proliferation of new states and the needs of an increasingly interdependent, but free-market international economy. The approaching end of the century finds significant movement towards the control of armaments, reflecting and promoting in turn a significant thaw in superpower relations; the newer nations are "maturing" in the system; less promisingly, the international economy is in straits, if not in crisis. These developments will churn up political forces that will bring change in international law.

---

1. I dedicate this essay to the memory of a friend and colleague of more than 25 years for whom I had deep affection and high regard. In these pages I address one of the themes developed in the "General Course" at the Hague Academy of International Law, summer 1989, to be published in the *Recueil des Cours* of the Academy under the title "International Law: Politics, Values, Functions."
2. See Henkin, *How Nations Behave*, 2nd ed. (New York: Columbia University Press, 1979), *passim*.

No doubt, the end of the century will inspire survey and appraisal of the evolution of international law and its future direction. In these pages I address one remarkable development of the past half century, namely the movement in the international system—movement that has been neither steady, linear, nor without resistance and regression—from "state values" to "human values." Bill Fox was particularly interested in this development, for he was deeply committed to human values[3] and was highly sensitive to the tensions and turbulence in the international political system.

The Values of the State System

As national law promotes state interests, international law serves the purposes and advances the values of "international society" and the interstate political system. Those purposes and values are nowhere articulated and, in general, can only be inferred from a long history of political actions and occasional statements and declarations. At particular, decisive, "constitutional" moments, the purposes and values of the system may be more explicitly expressed, if only rhetorically. A notable, modern example occurred when the U.N. Charter re-laid the foundations of the international system after World War II. Even the Charter, however, did not begin from the bottom, did not articulate the underlying assumptions and values of the political system and of international law. The Charter declares the purposes of the United Nations Organization and of the Charter itself (including the law it contains), and promises additional law that would serve values of peace, justice, social progress and human rights. It expresses the determination of "We the peoples of the United Nations" to promote respect for treaties and international law. But it says little about that law and its values generally.

International law shares some of the same purposes and values embodied in virtually every legal system. Like national law, international law promotes order. In an international system without a government commanding a monopoly of force, order begins with international peace. Even in earlier times, when war was not unlawful (and indeed created a legal regime of its own), peace was the norm; law sought to help maintain peace by determining rights and duties and helping to resolve disputes. In our time, when the costs of the use of force have become prohibitive, international law prohibits the threat or use of force.[4]

---

3. See, for example, W. T. R. Fox, "Human Freedoms in a World of States," 75, *Proceedings of the American Society of International Law* 72 (1981).
4. United Nations Charter, Article 2(4).

Peace is a requisite for international order but it is not sufficient. Law seeks to promote wider, deeper order, to provide confidence in relationships and to build reliable expectations. Like national law, international law sometimes claims also to promote justice; but justice is not defined, and when it is, the definition is often derivative, declaring as just that which realizes other values.

Some of the values that international law promotes are implied in, or determined by, the fundamental character of the system as a system of independent states. Traditionally—and to this day—the system has been devoted to promoting what I call "state values," the hallmarks of a liberal state system.

State Values: The Liberal State System

With due caution against the danger of analogy from domestic society and domestic law, it is instructive to look at kindred domestic ideology in order to understand the traditional international system. Political philosophers have identified one form of political society as "the liberal state." The international system is a "liberal state system."

Recall the succinct, famous articulation of the theory of a liberal state in the American Declaration of Independence:

> We hold these truths to be self-evident, that all men are created equal, that they are endowed by their Creator with certain unalienable Rights, that among these are Life, Liberty and the pursuit of Happiness. That to secure these rights, Governments are instituted among Men, deriving their just powers from the consent of the governed.

Substituting "states" for "men" in that declaration would produce a fairly accurate description of the ideology of the traditional international political system, largely the system we have today:

> All states are [created] equal. They are endowed [by their Creator] with certain [unalienable] *inherent* rights. Among these are [life] *existence*, [liberty] *independence/autonomy*, and the pursuit of [happiness] *national interest*. To secure these rights [governments] *law* is instituted among *states*, deriving *its* [just powers] *legitimate authority* from the consent of the [governed] states.

Like men in the liberal state, states in the international system are equal in status and rights, as well as in responsibility. Like the liberal state, the state system is "individualistic." Indeed, the international system has apotheosized state individualism, as subsumed in that dangerous, much-abused term "sovereignty." Sovereignty implies state liberty, autonomy and the political independence necessary to make decisions without external control or limitation, except those to which the state has consented.[5] Sovereignty also includes "privacy," impermeability and the right to maintain a hermetic, monolithic posture *vis-à-vis* the rest of the world. State autonomy and impermeability protect the state's right to pursue its own national interest, maintain its own values, and determine the condition of its own society and the life and destiny of its inhabitants.

The autonomy and impermeability of states are protected and promoted by law prohibiting the use or threat of force against the state's political independence and territorial integrity, and by norms against intervention generally.[6] International law helps ensure that other states do not pierce "the veil" of its statehood, do not penetrate its territory, its society, or its political-legal system. In principle, international relations are relations between states as entities, not within states; international law operates only externally *on* a state, not within a state, unless the state willingly incorporates international law into its legal system.[7]

A liberal state does not have its own agenda, its own vision of "the Good"; its purpose is to help its citizens realize *their* agenda, their vision of the Good. Like the liberal state, the international system—since it became secular—does not have its own vision of the Good, but is designed to further each state's realization of its own notion of the Good, its own value system. Therefore, when the international system has "worked," the system and its law have tolerated, and indeed sought to secure, liberal as well as authoritarian states, republics as well as monarchies, theocracies as well as secular states and capitalist as well as socialist states.

In the liberal state, law is made by the authority of the people and with the consent of the governed, but liberal states have had to accept representative government and majority rule. However, in the international system of equal states, law is made by the states themselves, not by a representative legislature. It is made not by a majority but only by unanimity, by consent of all the states.[8] Customary law results from

---

5. International law is a limitation on state autonomy, but its norms are limitations to which the state has consented.
6. See, for example, Declaration on the Inadmissibility of Intervention in the Domestic Affairs of States, U.N.G.A. Res. 2131 (1965).
7. In terms of a traditional debate, international law permits a state to be "dualist," to treat its domestic legal system as independent of international law. See, for example, Fitzmaurice, "The General Principles of International Law Considered from the Standpoint of the Rule of Law," 92 *Recueil des Cours* 50, 70-85 (1957); Starke, "Monism and Dualism in the Theory of International Law," 1936 *British Yearbook of International Law*, no.66.
8. The principle of unanimity does not prevent those who agree from making law for themselves, and they may in time persuade dissenters or abstainers to join. They will, however, not be able to make general law if important states are not included. For a major contemporary example, the system cannot create law prohibiting the use or possession of nuclear weapons if the principal nuclear powers do not agree. A few "haven" states can carve a major loophole in an anti-hijacking or anti-drug-smuggling agreement.

voluntary state participation or acquiescence and a state that dissents from an emerging principle of customary law is not bound by it. (This is called the "persistent objector" principle.) Even more clearly, law made by treaty requires direct consent: No state is bound by an agreement unless it has voluntarily adhered to it.

Law, making by consent reflects the liberal international system's commitment to state autonomy. Inevitably the requirement of state consent favors *laissez-faire*, non-regulation, or at most the "lowest common denominator" of acceptable regulation. This is not merely the result of rules of law, making by consent of autonomous states; it reflects commitment to the principle of laissez-faire as a dominant value of the system. The liberal state believes that "that government governs best that governs least." The international system has resisted all "government"; it has accepted some "governance" through international law (and modest international institutions) but the constraints imposed by that law (and those institutions) have been minimal. *Laissez-faire* and minimal regulation protect and promote state autonomy,[9] akin to a right of privacy in liberal national legal systems—"a right to be let alone" and a conviction that many matters are "not the law's business."[10]

A liberal state is principally a policeman; its purpose is to protect individuals and their property from their neighbors.[11] It enacts laws and imposes taxes for that purpose only. International law has served the same purpose: to police and protect one state and secure its independence, autonomy and inviolability against another. Hence, the basic doctrines of international law, like those of a liberal state, are principles of tort and property.[12] And like domestic law in a liberal state, international law

---

9.   These values of state autonomy, and the need for state consent to any infringement of autonomy, have been shaken, particularly since World War II, but they are still a basic, perhaps *the* basic, value of the system.
10.   "The right to be let alone," Justice Brandeis dissenting in *Olmstead v. United States*, 277 438 U.S. 478 (1928).
11.   The state also protects the society from external enemies, a concern that has no counterpart in the international system since it became universal.
12.   Traditional international law—like the law of the liberal state—has consisted primarily of rules of prohibition and abstention to protect state autonomy and property. Some property-tort principles are buried also in such doctrines as the inviolability of state territory (comparable to the laws of trespass), and freedom of the seas, including the security of state vessels. A state cannot confiscate another state's bank deposits or other assets. Property of foreign nationals is protected as if it were the property of the state. The person of a diplomat is protected by notions of immunity, and foreign nationals are protected by an uncertain standard of justice which in essence applies laws of delict and due process similar to those in domestic liberal law.

developed institutions, procedures and a "due process of law" to protect autonomy and property.

Essential to the liberal state is also the principle of contract: A liberal state is committed to freedom of contract and to the enforcement of the obligations of contract. (According to social contract theory, as expressed by John Locke and the Declaration of Independence, a liberal state is itself made by contract.) The international system, too, is established by consent, by an "inter-state social contract." The principles of consent and *pacta sunt servanda* (agreements are binding) are basic to international law, and in a sense, all international law, including rules of property and tort, is contractual, made by consent of states through practice or treaty. Contract is also basic to international trade: The liberal inter-state system is also a market-economy system. Trade is free except as states agree otherwise.[13]

The liberal state, and the international system, both recognize some limitations on consent; for example, that contracts are not enforceable if they are obtained by fraud or are unconscionable. International law—and the law of a liberal state—both adopted other moral values and equitable principles: under international law, an international standard of "justice" is owed to foreign nationals; the International Court of Justice has invoked "elementary considerations of humanity." [14] Equity as a consideration in international law was expanded when an "equitable" solution was included as guide to the limitation of zones under the 1982 Convention on the Law of the Sea. [15]

In one fundamental respect the analogy to the liberal state breaks down. In the liberal, minimal state, charity is not the business of government. However, men and women who comprise a society are not necessarily selfish, and charity is recognized by many as a religious or other moral obligation. A sense of moral obligation, I believe, probably underlay the movement in Western societies which began a hundred years ago and transformed the liberal state into a welfare state. Today, enlightened states are liberal welfare states. However, the international system has had little analogous development for *state selfishness is the hallmark of the international state system.* "National interest" is commonly seen as the sole motivation of states, and is exalted as a virtue. To this day, even

---

13. As by treaties of friendship, commerce and navigation, or later by the General Agreement on Tariffs and Trade (GATT) or by commodities agreements. Unlike some liberal states that acted to keep the market free by anti-trust laws, the international system developed no anti-cartel norms. Compare the general helplessness before the "oil weapon" in the 1970s.
14. See *Corfu Channel Case*, 1949 I.C.J. 4, 22.
15. See Articles 74(1), 83(1).

international generosity such as foreign aid must be justified as being in the national interest. Occasional reference in recent years to inter-state justice or morality imposing obligations on "have-states" to assist "have-not states," is only rhetoric, and has had no significant normative implications. Selfishness—the national interest—must sometimes bow to competing national interests but is not subordinated to the common good.[16] There is little *Gesellschaft* and even less *Gemeinschaft* in the international system. There is little sympathy for notions of inter-state "utilitarianism"—the greatest good of the greatest number, the maximum of happiness for mankind (or even for the greatest number of states). There is no commitment to "democracy," to the will (and the betterment) of the majority of states, or of human beings.

Cooperation and "Welfare" Principles

In the second half of this century, the state system made significant moves toward a law of cooperation.[17] States, leaders, elites and people in general came to recognize that common interests such as avoiding nuclear war and protecting the environment, as well as the interests of individual states, required not only prohibitions on individual state action but programs of joint action. This new awareness led to the creation of the United Nations and to a multiplication of specialized agencies promoting cooperation in banking and finance, food, health, education and aviation, as well as other international organizations for cooperation in trade, shipping, satellite communication and atomic energy. Various regions of the world organized counterparts to such global organizations for regional cooperation.

Cooperative law was an important development but it did not transform the essential character of the system as a state system, or derogate from fundamental state values. Cooperation was voluntary and was not for the benefit of the "community" but of individual states. In the main, only states were members of the new organizations, only states assumed obligations, and they had only the obligations to which they consented.

---

16. Even in the "commonage" (the high seas, outer space), the stress is on competing national interests; few states stand up for the commonage as such.
17. See, for example, W. Friedmann, *The Changing Structure of International Law* (New York: Columbia University Press, 1964).

Only states were beneficiaries and they received only the benefits which they desired and only those which others would grant.

The cooperative state system is not a welfare system. Occasional suggestions that welfare state principles and justifications should govern international relations could not prevail over the axioms and values of the state system. Even where welfare principles were invoked, they called, at best, for voluntary state generosity,[18] not for binding programs of community action pursuant to community decision. What is more, even states that sometimes invoked welfare principles in claiming aid or favorable trade arrangements, have themselves insisted on state values. External scrutiny and other "interventions" to assure the proper implementation of such programs are resisted in the name of state autonomy and impermeability.

From State Values to Human Values

The traditional values of the international system have been state values—state autonomy and benefits to the state *qua* state. Generally and in principle, the international system did not concern itself with "human values" such as the welfare of the individual human being or of all mankind, neither within any country nor in all countries. It did not consider whether it might be desirable to pursue individual human welfare even if it entailed some cost to state autonomy and some derogation from a state's exclusive responsibility for its own society.

I have set forth starkly both the traditional values of the state system and the traditional purposes of international law. However, the dichotomy between state values and human values may not be as sharp as here implied. States are represented by governments, and governments consist of human beings who cannot entirely and consistently exclude human values from national policy, and who are not wholly immune to concern for human beings in other countries. Moreover, state values— the independence and autonomy of the state, the inviolability of its territory and the impermeability of its society—and cooperative-welfare programs that benefit the state, might also benefit its people. But even when a state's purpose would clearly benefit its people, and not just its governors, its "ruling class," its elites or some other segment of the

---

18. In the U.N., states accepted the principle of "progressive taxation," but such taxation is mandatory only for meeting the regular budget, U.N. Charter, Articles 17-18. Forms of cooperation that would have the wealthy states help the poor, for example, the U.N. Development Program, have special budgets, also based on progressive principles, but participation in them (and contribution quotas) remain voluntary. Special trade arrangements for less developed countries (LDCs) within GATT (Articles XVIII, XXVI-XXVII) and national foreign aid programs, are also voluntary.

population, the people were still only the eventual, indirect beneficiaries, filtered through the state monolith. International law did not presume to penetrate the state monolith, did not directly address people, did not seek to protect individual human beings from governmental indifference, mistakes, misdeeds or terrible repression. The law failed to attend to what we have come to call their "human rights."

International law and the idea of human rights had common antecedents in natural law,[19] but for hundreds of years they did not come together into an international law of human rights. What the state did inside its borders in relation to its own nationals remained its own affair, an element of its own autonomy and "domestic jurisdiction." The first authentic, major movement of the international system to concern itself directly with human values came with the World War II and the birth of the international human rights movement.

Antecedents of International Human Rights

International concern with human rights did not spring full-blown at mid-century.[20] Neither the international political system, nor international law, had totally ignored what went on inside states in areas that were of special interest to other states. Those areas sometimes included concern for, or at least served the welfare of, individual human beings. But what was of interest and considered to be of *legitimate* interest to the international political-legal system was limited *a priori* by the character of the state system. Of course, states were legitimately concerned with the "human rights" of their diplomats. States were also concerned, and developed principles of law to assure, that their nationals living abroad were treated in accordance with an international standard of justice. Sometimes two states entered into agreements, usually on a basis of reciprocity, promising protection or privilege (for example, freedom to reside, to worship and to conduct business) to persons with whom the states identified on the basis of common religion or ethnicity. A growing network of bilateral treaties of friendship, commerce and navigation commonly included provisions benefiting nationals of one state in the territory of the other state on a reciprocal basis.

Concern for individual human welfare seeped into the international system in the nineteenth century. European and American states

---

19. And common intellectual progenitors in Grotius, Vattel and Locke.
20. See, for example, H. Lauterpacht, *International Law and Human Rights* (New York: Garland Publishers, 1973); Sohn and Buergenthal, *International Protection of Human Rights* (Indianapolis: Bobbs-Merrill, 1973); also Henkin, *The Rights of Man Today* (New York: Center for the Study of Human Rights, Columbia University, 1978) ch.3.

abolished slavery and the slave trade. Leading states began to pursue agreement to make war less inhumane by outlawing particularly cruel weapons and by safeguarding prisoners of war, the wounded and civilian populations.[21] Following World War I, concern for individual human beings in particular countries in special circumstances was reflected in several programs put forth by the League of Nations, notably its minorities treaties and mandate system. The International Labour Office (now the International Labour Organisation, ILO) was established and launched major programs, including a series of conventions setting minimum standards for work conditions and other social needs.[22]

In general, these principles of international law and special agreements addressed what happened to people inside one state only when another state was particularly concerned with their welfare, and when such concern was considered that state's proper business in a system of autonomous states. One may question whether those developments reflected an authentic concern for human rights. The principal values pursued were state values—systemic interests in peace and in international trade, or the national interest of the state involved. The human value—the welfare of particular human individuals—was an indirect beneficiary. The international system had no general concern with justice, with equal protection of the laws, or with freedom of religion for all human beings. The international norm that was upheld in giving effect to bilateral agreements that provided protection for individuals was not a human rights norm but the principle *pacta sunt servanda* (agreements are to be kept) the general norm protecting state values on which the system of international relations depends.

I do not suggest that previously states, governments or "the system" were in general less humane or caring than their successors in our day. Concern for individual human beings inside another country encountered many obstacles, not the least of which were the conception and the implications of statehood in a state system. The treatment of individuals by their own government was not commonly known abroad and was not included in the main sources of information of the time. Only dramatic events, not daily repression, were noteworthy. International information

---

21. Even less-than-democratic states began to attend to these human values, even at some probable cost to the state and to its military interests.
22. These continue to be highly impressive and important. More than 100 of these conventions have come into force, and many of them have been accepted by many states.

was filtered through the state system, through diplomatic media, and human values as such were not the business of diplomacy. There were few non-governmental human rights organizations to pressure governments and to sensitize and activate those that might have cared.

For these reasons, and for others flowing from the state system, the veil of statehood was impermeable and there was no effective concern in the political system for what governments did to their own citizens.[23] Moreover, as regards any but the most egregious violations of what we now call human rights, few if any governments had either the moral sensitivity or the moral standing to protest. Few states had effective protection for individual rights at home; torture and police brutality, perversions of law and denial of due process were not abnormal. Clearly few states provided political freedoms (voting, political activity, speech, association), religious freedom, or religious, social or gender equality.

The International Human Rights Movement

A watershed came with the Allied victory in World War II.[24] Wartime atrocities in occupied countries and full realization of the enormity of the Holocaust led to the inclusion of "crimes against humanity" in the Nuremberg Charter.[25] Human rights undertakings were included in peace treaties with Italy and Central European Powers, though they appear there, in effect, as realizations of war aims, not as universal legal norms; the treaties did not impose any human rights obligations on the victors.

Human rights achieved a prominent place in the U.N. Charter, the fountainhead of a new international law of human rights. Unlike Nurem-

---

23. If occasionally something particularly horrendous happened, such as massacres or pogroms, and was communicated by the media of the time, it usually evoked from other states more or less polite disapproval, not on grounds of law, but of something like "noblesse oblige," or common "princely" morality wrapped in Christian charity the violation of which would give princes (and Christians) a bad name.

24. Roosevelt's Four Freedoms address (January 1941), calling for a world in which all enjoyed freedom of speech and religion and freedom from fear and want, later became an articulation of Allied war aims. Roosevelt's catalogue of rights did not anticipate the inconceivable, ineffable atrocities that were later revealed.

25. At Nuremberg there was some sensitivity to claims that the Tribunal was *ex post facto* law, so that no one was punished for that offense alone.

berg, the Charter made law not only for the vanquished, but also for the victors. Indeed one might argue that law was made, in a sense, only for the victors, since the Charter was initially open to those declaring war against Germany (and the Charter explicitly denied some protection for the vanquished[26]).

The Charter was politically and legally radical. Perhaps without fully realizing the degree of derogation from state values it entailed, the framers declared the promotion of human rights to be a principal purpose of the United Nations, committing the international system to human values even at some cost to state values. But erosion of and derogation from state values was slow, limited and met continuing resistance; the system's profound, entrenched commitment to state values shaped and limited the human rights undertaking.[27]

Unlike the older international standard of justice for foreign nationals which reflected conceptions of natural right, the Charter avoids any philosophical justification of human rights (which could never have been agreed), but seems to find human rights to be required by human dignity.[28] The normative content of the Charter was strictly limited. Perhaps because we now wish to find in the Charter firm and extensive normative content, we tend to exaggerate what the Charter actually accomplished, and what, I believe, the framers intended. As regards human rights, the Charter penetrated the cloak of statehood in that relations between a state and its own citizens were recognized as matters of international concern and were made a subject of U.N. concern. However, the Charter did not itself impose significant normative human rights obligations, and did not eliminate the requirement of state consent for any future obligations. The purpose of the United Nations was only to achieve international cooperation, that is *consenting* cooperation, "in promoting and encouraging respect for human rights" [Article 1(3)].

---

26. See Article 107.
27. As conceived at least, the Charter itself pays due respect to the axioms of the system: It is binding only on states that consent to it. To justify the unprecedented permeation of state society which concern with human rights entailed, the Charter in effect declared human rights to be a state value by linking it to peace and security. It replaced the protection of minorities, linked to peace under the League of Nations, with its own links to peace for *all* human rights. It was apparently thought that the new commitment to self-determination, in addition to universal human rights, would eliminate the minorities problem. In particular, it was expected that some minorities would achieve independent statehood by self-determination, and that the rest would find their rights protected equally with members of the majority by a universal commitment to human rights for all.
28. See Preamble; see also the preambles to the Universal Declaration of Human Rights and to the principal human rights covenants.

Responsibility for promoting human rights was lodged under the overall jurisdiction of the General Assembly which has authority only "to initiate studies and make recommendations" [Article 13]. The Economic and Social Council (ECOSOC) "may make recommendations" [Article 62(2)], and may prepare draft conventions [Article 62(3)] for voluntary adherence. The Charter also mandated establishing a commission "for the promotion of human rights" [Article 68].[29]

The Charter also contains Article 56: "All members pledge themselves to take joint and separate action in cooperation with the Organization for the achievement of" the U.N. purpose of promoting universal respect for, and observance of, human rights. The phrase "pledge themselves" has normative flavor; does it create a legal obligation, and if so, what is its content? Does a state that practices torture violate its pledge to take action in cooperation with the United Nations to promote universal respect for human rights? Some of us have so argued, and U.N. bodies, including the International Court of Justice, seem to have so interpreted that Article,[30] but that interpretation is not obvious. Surely, the Charter did not state clearly that every member of the United Nations assumes legal obligations not to violate the human rights of persons under its jurisdiction.

The Universal Declaration of Human Rights

The 44 years that have elapsed since the Charter was adopted tell a story of the politics of the system and their impact on law, on law-making, law-applying and law-observing. Under the pressure of events and revelations, and while still basking in the postwar mood, the state system placed human rights permanently on the U.N. agenda and established human rights as a basic ingredient of international politics. Despite reluctance (not least by the Big Powers), political forces soon produced some hard law. Slowly the Charter itself acquired normative vigor for human rights purposes.

---

29. Human rights are prominent in Chapters XI and XII dealing with non-self-governing territories and the international trusteeship system, but those provisions had limited application, and even they are of uncertain normative quality.
30. See, for example, Advisory Opinion of the International Court of Justice on Namibia, 1971 I.C.J. 16.

Following the Charter of 1945, two major instruments were rapidly completed by 1948. The Genocide Convention[31] became the first general human rights agreement, establishing that, in principle, and in one respect at least, how a state treated its own inhabitants was a legitimate, appropriate subject for international law.[32] On the next day, the General Assembly adopted the Universal Declaration of Human Rights, destined to become—after the Charter—perhaps the most significant international instrument of our time. A few governments, and a few people within governments, dared to support the Declaration and insisted upon its adoption; the rest acquiesced, some perhaps out of shame. Like the Charter, the Declaration permeated the state monolith and confirmed both the legitimate place of human rights in international politics and its definition.

The Declaration also reflected the persisting resistances of statehood. Consider its preamble:

> The General Assembly proclaims this Universal *Declaration* of Human Rights as a *common standard of achievement* for all peoples and all nations, to the end that every individual and every organ of society, keeping this Declaration constantly in mind, shall *strive, by teaching and education to promote* respect for these rights and freedoms and *by progressive measures*, national and international, to secure their universal effective recognition and observance.... [emphasis added].

This was a declaration, not a treaty; a common standard of achievement, not a legal norm. It was hoped and urged that every individual and every organ of society would strive to promote respect for those rights and secure their recognition and observance, but the Declaration did not constitute commitment by states to respect and ensure them. The states in the system exhorted themselves to try to live up to the Declaration's standard.

The subsequent history of the Declaration also reveals both the radical departure it represented and the continuing resistance of the system. The Declaration launched two distinct but related movements. One, the universalization of the human rights idea. Many states did as they were urged to do and recognized the idea of human rights, and many even

---

31. Which one dedicated, determined man, Rafael Lemkin, badgered and shamed governments to produce as a monument to the Holocaust.
32. It also confirmed genocide as a violation of customary international law, and later of *ius cogens*. The Nuremberg judgment invoked the U.N.G.A. resolution declaring genocide a violation of international law. See UNGA Res. 95(II), 1946; the Nuremberg judgment reproduced at 41 *American Journal of International Law* 172 (1946); Restatement, Third, Foreign Relations Law of the United States (1987) 702, Comments *d, n,* and R.N. 11.

borrowed from the Declaration for their constitutions and laws, or incorporated its provisions by reference.

The universalization of the idea of human rights is not to be depreciated, for it may indeed be the most important contribution of the Declaration. However, it is voluntary and therefore wholly consistent with the traditional values of the inter-state system. The Declaration also launched, and became the heart and the engine of the internationalization of human rights. Adoption of the Declaration confirmed that the international political system had accepted human rights as a systemic value, and had given it a prime place on its political agenda. The international agenda was mostly promotional, as the U.N. Charter had projected, but occasionally, and increasingly, it became also normative and "judgmental." United Nations organs gave the Charter and the Declaration normative interpretation. States charged others with violating the human rights of their own inhabitants, first in such cases as Indians in South Africa and Russian wives of foreign nationals, and later apartheid and other violations. United Nations organs and other international organizations remained constantly available for political action on human rights. And the Declaration even helped inject the issue of human rights in bilateral relations between some states.

International Law of Human Rights

Political internationalization of human rights also led to international law. Both political attention and an international law of human rights penetrate statehood in that they address relations between government and the citizen; both are also consistent with statehood in that political resolutions are hortatory and law remains subject to consent.

The Universal Declaration was not law and was not seen as law at the time of its adoption. Some thought that the system should rest on the Declaration and concentrate on promoting its standards. But some powers, particularly small ones, and non-governmental organizations pressed for a comprehensive legally binding covenant. In time, the Declaration was converted into two principal covenants:the International Covenant on Economic, Social and Cultural Rights and the International Covenant on Civil and Political Rights.[33] It took 18 years to transform the Declaration into legally binding agreements, in part, because decolonization and the proliferation of new states complicated and extended the process, and injected additional divisions of opinion and

---

33. Along the way, other specialized conventions were concluded on the status of refugees, the rights of women, slavery and racial discrimination; the European Convention on Human Rights came into effect early, the American and African conventions later.

values; and in part because states, being asked to make law in a matter penetrating their statehood, were cautious. Although adherence was voluntary, governments knew that they might be subject to internal as well as international pressures to adhere; they wished the Covenant to be such that they could comfortably adhere to it. In any event, they did not wish to be vulnerable to accusations that their behavior was unacceptable in the light of norms that had received international *imprimatur*.

In the Covenants, too, the persisting influence of state values was reflected in forms of varying significance. The Covenants—like all international agreements—are binding only on states that consent to become parties. The Covenant on Civil and Political Rights, in particular, is addressed to states and applies within a state's territory.[34] A state may derogate from observing most rights "in time of public emergency which threatens the life of the nation" [Article 4]. Even in normal times, some rights are subject to limitations necessary for "public order" or "national security" (for example Article 12(3)).

The Covenants reflect the inter-state character of the system and state values, also in that the international law of human rights is superimposed on state law. The international law of human rights was not designed to replace state law, but only to make that law conform to international standards. Implementation of the Covenants is left to state institutions. The obligation in the Covenant on Civil and Political Rights to respect and ensure human rights is for the state to carry out: If it does and if the conditions of human rights are satisfactory, there is nothing for international law to do.

The injection of human values into a system built on state values has had important collateral effects on the international legal system. The natural rights tradition, contemporary moral values, and the constitutional law of leading liberal states, have contributed to the international law of human rights without strict attention to the traditional sources of international law. Ordinarily, the system is committed to *laissez-faire* and would be particularly resistant to limitations on state autonomy in internal matters, yet there has been an unusual disposition to find customary law of human rights. In principle, customary law results from state practice with a sense of legal obligation (*opinio iuris*), but practice contributing to human rights law looks different from that required to produce other customary law. Practice that builds customary law general-

---

34. A state party is obligated to respect and ensure rights of all individuals "within its territory and subject to its jurisdiction" [Article 2(1)], though, clearly, no state could enter another state and violate rights there, or violate rights of human beings on vessels on the high seas. See Buergenthal, "To Respect and to Ensure," in L. Henkin, ed., *The International Bill of Rights* (New York: Columbia University Press, 1981).

ly involves *actions* of states in relation to other states; in human rights, practice is largely internal (in relation to one's own inhabitants) and ordinarily involves no reaction from other states. Here, state practice that is accepted as law-building includes unusual forms, notably statements and votes in international organizations. Although the Universal Declaration originally was not intended as law and was merely a resolution of an international body for which states voiced approval, there has been an increasing disposition to attribute legal character to many, if not all, of its provisions as customary law (or as a concretization of the pledges in the Charter).[35]

The law of treaties has also undergone variations where human rights are concerned. In an advisory opinion on adherence to the Genocide Convention, the International Court of Justice developed new doctrine as to reservations, reflecting an eagerness to increase adherence to such agreements even if on some lesser basis. Therefore, a special rule allows a state to adhere with reservations to which some states object. Such states may be regarded as party to the Convention, and may have rights and obligations *vis-à-vis* non-objecting parties, so long as the reservations are "compatible with the object and purpose" of the Convention.[36]

The eagerness to create law is itself an important and novel phenomenon, deviating from the disposition to *laissez-faire* and minimal governance. It is particularly remarkable in a new area of systemic concern that penetrates the state monolith. It must be that, in general, states have perceived the political utility of new human rights law as outweighing the onus of being subject to that law. This development may owe much to one particular factor: The struggle by African states against apartheid, I have concluded, has provided special impetus and can claim major responsibility for this steady growth of new human rights law. Supported by the rest of the Third World and others, the African states, seeking to have apartheid declared illegal, were eager to find support in human rights law in the U.N. Charter[37] (to which South Africa, like

---

35. There has been also strong argument for deriving human rights law from general principles common to major legal systems, although "general principles" have been a limited source drawn on only infrequently and only for interstitial use.
36. Advisory Opinion, International Court of Justice, 1951 I.C.J. 15.
37. Apartheid (in Namibia) was early declared "a flagrant violation of the purposes and principles of the Charter." See Note 8.

virtually all states was party) and in customary law binding on states generally.

Other states extended the African agenda to cover other "consistent patterns of gross violations of internationally recognized human rights."[38] Perhaps, states that were already committed to human rights by their own constitutions saw no reason to resist some internationalization of the same norms. Perhaps, some states saw international human rights law as a significant weapon in the ideological struggle of the postwar world. Perhaps, the idea of human rights had become part of the *Zeitgeist*, with irresistible appeal.[39] For many states, the human rights idea has been useful in struggles to promote other values, including self-determination, "economic self-determination," development and the New International Economic Order. Perhaps, public opinion mobilized by non-governmental organizations and the media around the world has been difficult to resist.[40]

Enforcing Human Values

Compliance with international law generally depends on the systemic culture of compliance; on the interest of states in maintaining norms they have struggled to develop; on the influence of "horizontal enforcement"— the response, or anticipated response, of the victim of a violation.[41] Contrary to some impressions, international law generally has been respected.[42] International human rights law has been less successful.

The culture of compliance with human rights law has developed slowly. The obligations of human rights law look inward, for the benefit of the state's own inhabitants. Some states that have been prepared to make the international legal commitment to human rights have not yet internalized that obligation and developed the institutions to nurture it. States have not yet wholly assimilated the fact that they have assumed an *international obligation* to respect the rights of their citizens and that an act of torture or a denial of due process is a violation of an *international*

---

38. ECOSOC Res. 1503, 48 U.N. ESCOR Supp. No. 1A at 8-9.
39. Thus lending itself to powerful rhetoric and even to hypocrisy. I have suggested that human rights offers lessons in the benign consequences of hypocrisy, the homage that vice pays to virtue. It is important that human rights is the virtue to which vice is impelled to pay homage; it means public commitment to human rights in principle, and if that leads to a need to conceal and lie, the system can concentrate on determining and proving the actual condition of human rights, and on inducing the state to comply with what it has proclaimed.
40. The United States is virtually alone among major powers in resisting exhortation to adhere to the principal human rights covenants and conventions. See below, p.206, fn. 52.
41. See Henkin, *How Nations Behave*, chapter 3.
42. "It is probably the case that *almost all nations observe almost all principles of international law and almost all of their obligations almost all of the time.*" *Ibid.* p.47.

obligation. Both the violating state and other states have not yet fully shed the traditional attitude that conditions inside the state, including how the state treats its own inhabitants, are no one else's business.

There are other, related obstacles to enforcement of human rights norms. Although the obligations under covenants and conventions run to other states, the real beneficiaries are not the other promisee states, but individual inhabitants of each state party. Other states are not yet politically habituated to responding to violations not involving their own nationals. Other states, many of which are themselves still without an entrenched tradition of human rights observance and are not yet committed to many of the rights established in international human rights law, are vulnerable to charges of violation, and are therefore reluctant to respond to violations by others. What is more, the principal element of horizontal enforcement is missing: "If you violate the human rights of your citizens, I will violate the human rights of my citizens" will hardly serve as a deterrent. The result is that temptations to violate international human rights law are stronger, and fear of reactions and other adverse consequences weaker, than with international law generally.

For these reasons and others, the international system has developed special enforcement machinery. Such machinery has been established by particular human rights agreements, such as the Human Rights Committee under the Covenant on Civil and Political Rights, the Committee on Racial Discrimination under the Convention on the Elimination of All Forms of Racial Discrimination, the Committee Against Torture under the Torture Convention, and the Committee on Discrimination Against Women under the Convention on the Elimination of All Forms of Discrimination Against Women.

Some have suggested that the special machinery was intended not to supplement but to replace horizontal enforcement, that unless otherwise provided, one party to a convention cannot claim against other. I think this view is mistaken: There is no evidence to support it, and some substantial evidence against it. I think it is an unwarranted and undesirable interpretation of the various covenants and conventions. There is a need to encourage taking the legal character of human rights obligations seriously, and not debase or dilute that character. Surely, horizontal enforcement is available to enforce the growing customary law of human rights. The obligations of customary law are *erga omnes*: Every state can act (peacefully) to induce compliance, or may even bring suit against a violator before the International Court of Justice if both states have accepted the court's jurisdiction. There is also "political" enforcement by U.N. bodies, namely the General Assembly, ECOSOC, and, in particular, the Human Rights Commission. This enforcement is sometimes seen as political, not legal, but it invokes norms, including the Charter provisions, and is properly seen as part of the enforcement system. A non-official, non-governmental, but increasingly organized contribution to human rights law enforcement is the role of non-governmental organizations and the media in publicizing violations.

The enforcement machinery established by the covenants and conventions indicates how strong the commitment to state values remains, and how resistant states are to "intrusion" on their autonomy, even for purposes of promoting the human values they have embraced by international legal undertakings. The agreements, developed—like all law— by representatives of states, have eschewed external monitoring of states. The principal covenants and conventions do not provide for any body that might take initiative to monitor compliance.[43] No agreement provides for a body that might receive complaints of violation, investigate them and issue a judgment and a directive to a state found guilty of violations.[44]

Because state values of autonomy and impermeability are deeply imbedded, even states that have adhered to human rights law have resisted external monitoring of their compliance, and have been reluctant to monitor others. The basic element of enforcement is the requirement that state parties report to the committee of experts established by the agreement, at regular intervals or at the request of the committee. The committee studies the reports, hears state representatives, makes such general comments as it may deem appropriate, and issues general reports on its activities.

The reporting system also reflects the tenacity of state values. It is the least intrusive machinery. Reporting is unilateral and inevitably self-serving. State values are reflected also in the kind and amount of attention given to the reports. The scrutiny of reports and "cross-examination" of government representatives often depends upon several "political" factors: relations between the reporting government and the government of particular committee members, the degree of independence from his or her government enjoyed by a particular committee member, as well as the particular issue raised and the state being monitored. However, with experience, growing sophistication and confidence, the committees have grown more active and more effective.

The reporting systems in different treaties, while similar in essence, diverge in small yet significant ways. These differences reflect the extent

---

43. By contrast, such authority was given to the Inter-American Commission of Human Rights.
44. Contrast the commission and court established under both the European and American Conventions.

of the international system's commitment to particular rights and the varying levels of pressure on states that are parties to a particular treaty to accept more intrusive monitoring. The Human Rights Committee under the Covenant on Civil and Political Rights has the kind of authority common to all treaty committees. The Committee on the Elimination of Racial Discrimination has benefitted from the international system's strong commitment to eliminating racial discrimination, and was given some additional authority.[45] The Committee Against Torture is a beneficiary not only of experience under earlier conventions but also of the universal condemnation of torture, shaming states (none of which would admit that states ever resort to torture as state policy) into accepting more intrusive monitoring.

The state system has taken small, more intrusive steps by affording some opening to individual complaint against the state. If states parties agree in advance, each of the three committees may receive and consider private complaints. These procedures, too, are subject to limitations that reflect state values—the need to exhaust domestic remedies, confidentiality and discreet attempts to resolve the issue.[46] In an unusual provision, the Committee Against Torture has been given exceptional authority to act on its own initiative if it receives "reliable information which appears to it to contain well-founded indications that torture is being systematically practiced."

The quest for machinery to help monitor respect for human rights has provided interesting lessons about inter-state politics and about state values. For example, it was expected that states would be less reluctant to submit to complaints by other states than to complaints by their own citizens. Therefore, the Convention on the Elimination of Racial Discrimination provided for state complaints but left submission to private complaints optional. Under the Covenant on Civil and Political Rights, both are optional, but submission to private complaints was excluded from the Covenant and relegated to a separate protocol. In fact, as of 1989, out of 87 states party to the Covenant on Civil and Political Rights,

---

45. The Committee on the Elimination of Racial Discrimination (CERD) can receive complaints ("communications") from other states; the Human Rights Committee can receive such complaints only if the accused state and the complaining state have both agreed by advance declaration to be subject to such complaints.

46. This modest procedure is growing in use and effectiveness. As of 1989 the Human Rights Committee has had 369 "communications," and many more are pending, straining the modest resources of the Committee. See Annual Report of the Human Rights Committee, UNDOC. Al44l40, S.V. Paras. 3, 7.

45 are parties to the Protocol, but only 23 have agreed to submit to another state's complaint. States, then, it appears, continue to be embarrassed by accusations by their own citizens and continue to resist penetration of the veil of their statehood by allowing individual citizens into the international arena. They are even more reluctant, however, to inject "internal matters" into their relations with other states.[47]

Inducing compliance with economic and social rights is a different matter involving different politics. In national systems, economic and social benefits are generally not constitutional rights, or are not enforceable, whereas civil-political rights may be, for example, by judicial review. The degree and level of development of a welfare state depend on its legislature and on political forces, and are usually not matters of right (though some sense of entitlement has grown). In the Covenant on Economic, Social and Cultural Rights, there is little expectation of scrutiny and monitoring.[48] The assumption seems to be that states wish to comply and do so when they have resources; therefore, there is a political preoccupation with development as a method of helping states to comply. The Covenant has served as a justification for the demand for a New International Economic Order, and for foreign aid.

Enforcement by Political Bodies

I have been considering "machinery" designed for the purposes of enforcement. For major violations, other bodies, not built by a particular covenant or convention but specifically assigned responsibility for promoting human rights—for instance, the U.N. Human Rights Commission—also serve to induce compliance with international human rights norms. International political bodies, such as the U.N. General Assembly or ECOSOC, sometimes intervene and add their influence.

---

47. The tensions between state values and human values, and the play of political forces in human rights enforcement, look somewhat different in the regional human rights systems. Even greater differences have appeared in the Helsinki Accord and its aftermath, which have given human rights a significant part in U.S.-Soviet relations.

48. The Covenant on Economic, Social and Cultural Rights did not provide for a committee to scrutinize reports, but fed them into the Economic and Social Council process. In 1985, ECOSOC created a Committee on Economic and Social Rights to consider reports under the Covenant on Economic, Social and Cultural Rights; the new Committee parallels, and looks like, the Committee on Human Rights under the Covenant on Civil and Political Rights. It is still too early to appraise the new committee's performance. Its deliberations may serve to interpret the convention and to develop a jurisprudence. It may in effect advise states on the effectiveness of their programs. It remains to be seen whether it will become an authentic monitoring committee. Will it, in particular, undertake to probe whether a state is realizing the economic and social rights of its people "to the maximum of its available resources" (Article 2[1] of the Covenant), especially if it is spending on armaments, or splendor, or modernization?

Political bodies are subject to their own laws. The larger ones, such as the General Assembly and ECOSOC, are more visible and therefore more "politicized"; they are less likely to be judicious and more likely to subordinate the human rights agenda to other considerations. That has led to the "politicization" of human rights through such means as "selective targeting." Smaller bodies, notably the Human Rights Commission, are somewhat less "political,"and are more activist, and increasingly exert remedial influence.

The character of U.N. influence on the condition of human rights has been shaped by the ideological conflict reflected in the organization and by its transformation as a result of the influx of members and the emergence of the Third World. In general, the Third World has been eager to pursue "non-alignment," and has been reluctant to join in condemnations of communist states for human rights violations; it has also resisted proposals for an active role by the United Nations in monitoring human rights. However, African states led the United Nations in its strong stance against apartheid and made it a perennial issue, with perennial resolutions of condemnation and exhortations to sanctions.[49]

The desire to attack apartheid led to early development of "working group" procedures under ECOSOC Resolution 1235 (and later under ECOSOC Resolution 1503). The working group of the Subcommission on the Prevention of Discrimination and the Protection of Minorities has been given limited authority, for a short time each year, to consider communications, in secret, and the subcomisssion may bring those that reveal violations to the Human Rights Commission. The procedure was originally designed for apartheid, but was generalized to all "consistent patterns of gross violations."

How states have voted on apartheid, and whether they have adhered to the conventions on racial discrimination and on apartheid, have influenced their relations with African states. The Third World has considered racial discrimination the most serious human rights violation and therefore the Convention on the Elimination of Racial Discrimination has the largest number of adherents of all the human rights conventions.

---

49. In 1977, the Security Council determined that developments in South Africa constituted a threat to the peace, and ordered states not to provide South Africa with arms and related materials. S.C. Res. 418 (XXIII), 1977.

National Enforcement of International Standards

Most states incorporate international law and treaties into their domestic legal systems. National institutions—including courts—may therefore be available to enforce a state's international human rights obligations, supplementing (and in some systems superseding) domestic law. Some states have also made their institutions available to induce compliance by other states with international legal human rights standards. Many legislatures have adopted sanctions against apartheid; in the United States, Congressional legislation also denies aid and arms sales to governments guilty of "consistent patterns of gross violations of internationally recognized human rights."[50] By direction of Congress, the U.S. Department of State has a human rights bureaucracy that may exert some influence to improve human rights in various countries and issues an annual report on the condition of human rights in every country.[51]

Some states have criticized others for not acting forcefully against apartheid. On the other hand, states generally have not responded favorably to efforts by other states (such as the United States) to act as unilateral human rights "policeman."[52] The United States would probably respond that it is the responsibility of every state to seek to induce compliance with human rights obligations under customary law which are obligations *erga omnes* (to all states), and that unilateral enforcement is necessary because multilateral machinery has not been effective.

The inadequacy of intergovernmental responses has engendered an additional form of enforcement. This includes the activities of non-governmental organizations (national as well as international), such as Amnesty International, which sometimes work with governments and through international bodies and sometimes work with the media, to mobilize public outrage and create a sense of shame which might help terminate, remedy, or deter violations.

---

50. See 22 U.S.C. 2151 (n)(a), 2304.
51. In an unusual case, a United States court has given a judgment in tort against a Paraguayan official charged with torture. *Filartiga v. Pena-Irala*, 630 F.2d 876 (2d Cir. 1980). The threat of such suits may serve to deny a haven in the United States to serious offenders, but that case is not likely to prove a significant precedent. Such suits require judicial jurisdiction over the defendant; sovereign immunity is generally an obstacle to suit against the state itself.
52. Criticism of the United States is compounded by the fact that it has not adhered to the covenants or to most other human rights conventions. See Henkin, "Rights American and Human," 79 *Columbia Law Review* 405, 420-24 (1979), represented in *The Age of Rights* (New York: Columbia University Press, 1990)

Conclusion

An international system of states is likely to be long with us, and state values—independence, autonomy, impermeability—are likely to remain dominant values of the system. Worldwide communications, ready travel and an interdependent world economy have eroded state frontiers and unleashed drives for modernization and development, but they have not seriously endangered state and national identity, local culture, or state insistence on internal autonomy or sovereignty. Indeed, with the notable exception of Western Europe, economic and political forces seem to favor pluralism rather than integration and homogenization.

The human rights idea has provided a principal counter-current to persisting state values. It is *the* idea of our times, the only political idea that has earned universal (at least nominal) acceptance. The universalization of the human rights idea has contributed to a universal, if modest, human rights culture. Internationalization of this idea and the growing body of international human rights law have penetrated state societies and have injected specific human values into inter-state politics and law and into the life of international institutions.

Human values are not inconsistent with state values but are sometimes in tension with them.[53] Both sets of values, I am persuaded, are here to stay. Tension calls for a *modus vivendi, and a modus operandi*. Tension will be reduced or accommodated as states attend better to their own human rights condition, strengthen their own commitment to constitutionalism and establish their own institutions (for example, judicial or other constitutional review) to make such rights effective. That would reduce the need for international scrutiny and would reinforce state values of autonomy without jeopardy to human values or human rights.

The human rights which the international system has accepted are not the last word on human values, but the assimilation of human rights should make the system less resistant and more receptive to other human values, including those that cry for relief from market forces. If the New International Economic Order is too radical, and does not necessarily embody a human value *per se*, some other kind of new international economic order would promote human values without prohibitive cost

---

53. The inclusion of economic-social rights added an additional source of tension as poor states sought to press wealthier states to help them satisfy the economic-social rights of their inhabitants. In the Covenant on Economic, Social and Cultural Rights, an effort to promote legal obligations to provide such assistance was compromised through ambiguity. The Covenant declares the obligation of states parties to realize the rights of their inhabitants "individually and through international assistance and cooperation." Some may have hoped that the language would be interpreted to mean that state parties to the Covenant were obligated to provide such assistance to other state parties.

to what is authentic in state values. The system has accepted economic and social rights as human rights; it ought not leave the responsibility for "progressively" achieving them to the sovereign state when "the maximum of its available resources" is insufficient. Nor need the system accept state autonomy and impermeability as obstacles to scrutiny of waste and corruption, and of diversion of resources to weapons instead of food.

The decades ahead call for an international politics and an international law that will make strains between state and human values not less tense, but more creative. Bill Fox would applaud.

REASON AND CHANGE IN INTERNATIONAL LIFE: JUSTIFYING A HYPOTHESIS

By Ernst B. Haas

My contact with Bill Fox began when I completed my doctoral dissertation at Columbia University. It was initiated with a long discussion of my final draft, a discussion that proved seminal to me. Its content directly influenced the message embedded in this paper: Because truth is elusive and because many roads lead to it, none of us has the right to proclaim "the" truth with pomp and certainty. Bill proceeded to praise my argument lavishly despite the fact that it could be read as a direct challenge to his book, *The Super-Powers*. He then proceeded to advise me on how to publish parts in *World Politics*, of which he was the editor.

This essay too is about the themes that challenge the causal centrality of structured power in international affairs.[1] I trust nevertheless that it reflects a spirit of which Bill would have approved because I argue that international events are governed by human self-reflection and by self-conscious striving for improvement. He could not but have respected an essay that questions the adequacy of both Hobbes and Kant as theorists of international politics.

Reason, Self-Reflection and International Change

Charles Darwin wanted to establish two hypotheses as plausible. One held that man and mammals had descended from more primitive species, an inference from the more basic claim that all species had "evolved" from more primitive ancestors. In addition, he urged that evolution had occurred *because* of natural selection. Even though the two hypotheses could be considered independently of each other, Darwin wanted to link them. My objective is less grandiose, but similar in some ways. I want to explore the hypothesis that progress has occurred in international politics, but I also want to argue that progress has occurred *because* our conceptions of what constitute political problems, and of solutions to these problems, have been increasingly informed by the form of reasoning we label "scientific." Perhaps the hypothesis suggests a corollary:

---

1. This essay seeks to summarize and justify a book I am attempting to write, provisionally entitled *Understanding Change in International Affairs*. I am grateful to the editor for giving me the opportunity to test the waters, and to Emanuel Adler, Robert Keohane, David Laitin, Rick Doner and John Ruggie for rigorous criticism of an earlier draft.

The diffusion of this mode of thought from its home in eighteenth-century Europe to the far corners of the planet is creating a universal problem-solving technique. Cosmopolitanism may thereby be associated with human progress, and thus transform international politics.

"If my theory of relativity is proved successful," remarked Albert Einstein, "Germany will claim me as a German and France will declare that I am a citizen of the world. Should my theory prove untrue, France will say that I am a German and Germany will declare that I am a Jew."[2] However accurate this observation may have been in 1930, my essay seeks to show why it need not be accurate in general, and certainly not in the future. I advance the immodest claim that theories of international politics ought to recognize the role of the changing knowledge of nature and society that we, as actors, carry in our heads.

My emphasis on knowledge might tempt readers to classify me as an "idealist," an advocate of the force of ideas as the main engine of history. The charge must be laid to rest immediately. I take my stand squarely with Max Weber:

> interests (material and ideal) not ideas directly determine man's actions. But the world views, which were created by ideas, have very often acted as the switches and channeled the dynamics of the interests.[3]

Material interests, according to Weber, are the things people want for their happiness and well-being, for their wealth, health, and peace. Ideal interests cover the things people want for their emotional and spiritual happiness. Both are interests in the sense political scientists use that term: specific demands for action (or inaction) made of the state by its citizens, derived from what people consider their most basic needs. Both kinds of interests are informed by ideologies, by systematized bodies of ideas people carry in their heads. Neither kind becomes politically relevant largely or exclusively *because of* the ideas that legitimate the demands.

I also reject the following "idealistic" notions. The study of progress is not necessarily the most appropriate research program of the social sciences. Nor do I subscribe to a particular view of what progress ought to be. My hypothesis is explanatory and descriptive; it does not seek to advocate a specific future for mankind, not even liberalism. And I eschew any intimation of inevitability, irreversibility, or historical necessity.

Qualifications and caveats come later. For the moment, I claim only this much. I wish to explore how consensual knowledge *can* emerge from

---

2. Remarks made at the Sorbonne, as reported by Robert K. Merton, *The Sociology of Science* (Chicago: University of Chicago Press, 1973) p.120.
3. Quoted in Wolfgang Schluchter, *The Rise of Western Rationalism: Max Weber's Developmental History* (Berkeley: University of California Press, 1981) p.25. The commentary on the quotation is Schluchter's.

the rival claims of various ideologies, not that it is *destined* to emerge. I grant that such a consensus must originate in the personal ideological commitments of the actors on the political scene. But I also insist that the origin of ideas does not determine their eventual shape or influence on policy. If competing scientific research programs can overcome their origins by blending into more comprehensive programs later, so can policy prescriptions with their roots in economics and sociology. Consensual knowledge is best thought of as the confluence of streams of thought that began as ideological knowledge and eventually transcend any personal or class-based characteristics of their founders. Does such a construct also contain *my* ideology of how things ought to work out? It certainly does insofar as my own intellectual commitment is to the notion of a rationality that can be universally practiced, but I hope to demonstrate that this notion is not merely my personal preference and that it enjoys general validity.

If we consider as progress the retreat of the great ancient scourges of famine, death from epidemics and unceasing toil unaided by technology, there is no doubt that the tide turned during the eighteenth century. "What has changed entirely is the rhythm of the increase in life. At present it registers a continuous rise, more or less rapid according to society and economy but always continuous. Previously it rose and then fell like a series of tides."[4] Population rose steadily in Europe and Asia, while remaining more or less stable elsewhere. Hunger receded because people's diets were enriched by the diversification of crops, a change made possible by the improvement in communications. Plague, cholera and typhus ceased to take the toll in lives they had claimed previously. Cities grew to unprecedented size. Improvements in metallurgy, water and steam power made possible a way of life to which we are heirs. The eighteenth century is the watershed of mankind's material progress. Perhaps more importantly, it also invented the *idea* of progress and attributed it to man's ability to reason scientifically.

I hypothesize that progress is global because scientific rationality is being globalized by way of secular cosmopolitanism. I have to show that such a diffusion is taking place and that it penetrates into all corners of the globe, not merely to the bastions of Western culture. I am advancing the risky thesis that we, as a whole, are better off because we know more and that we know more because we use a particular mode of defining and solving problems. Knowledge is a key engine of progress. But it is not the only engine and scientific problem-solving techniques could not find

---

4.   Fernand Braudel, *Capitalism and Material Life, 1400-1800* (New York: Harper Torchbooks, 1975) p.1 and ch.1.

a fertile soil unless material interests and conditions provided appropriate incentives.

A Two-Step Model of Recognizing Complexity: Disappointment as the Trigger of Learning

My thesis is evolutionary. It holds that human collectivities choose more complexly and discriminatingly as they come to know and understand more. It holds that things get better for us as our routines for choosing become capable of searching for solutions that get more sophisticated in recognizing complexity. Modern history seems to me to have unfolded in a direction consistent with this thought. Consequently, a much larger proportion of the global population, as compared with the situation before the eighteenth century, now lives at more tolerable standards of life despite two terrible world wars and almost incessant lower-level warfare since 1945.

Suffering and disappointment are the stimuli that cause collectivities to examine past experiences and reinterpret them. Dissatisfactions with unpleasant events and outcomes, repeated many times, stimulate the search for answers that contain different and more abstract explanatory schemes. The kind of suffering I have in mind always involves experiences for which a social or political explanation is required. If the reason for one's unhappiness lies in the individual psyche, in the will of God or in personal shortcomings, there is no trigger for collective learning. The cause of the unhappiness must be located in society, the economy, the government or the global situation.

My evolutionary thesis is a two-step affair. Progress by way of secular rationality occurs first at the level of the state, turning it into a nation-state. The successful formation of nation-states goes hand in hand with a deterioration of some aspects of international relations. While trade and communications increase, so do war and imperialism. The successful formation of more rationalized national communities entails a greater amount of discord among such communities. Local happiness is achieved at the cost of international strife. The second step is not taken until some elites come to the conclusion that further problems cannot be resolved at the level of the nation-state, that collective action among several (or all) states alone can provide solutions. When this conceptual threshold is crossed the same secular rationality that harnessed knowledge to local political choice will also be applied to relations among nations. However, insights reconceptualizing phenomena in more complex ways may differ among issues; what works in economics and ecology may not work in military-strategic matters.

The historical sequence of concern to me is captured on Figure 1.[5]If this scheme turns out to describe accurately what has gone on at the national level in most countries and places, and if I can show that the growth of international rule-governed life has developed as a result of disappointment with the performance of the nation-state, then I will have shown that things have progressed—that things have gotten better—because of the role of reason in human affairs.

Interdependence, Reciprocity, Rationality, Learning

The persuasiveness of this thesis, of course, depends crucially on a series of assumptions. An increase in interdependence among sections and groups within nation-states and a sharp increase in international interdependence are postulated as real. More than mutual dependence on scarce natural resources and an asymmetrical dependence on trade and money are involved. I also postulate increasing interdependence in the sense of sequential production or sequential decision processes not under the control of a single actor. There is interdependence in the sense of asymmetrical dependence on knowledge in someone else's possession. In sum, interdependence becomes a multifaceted constraint on strategic choice.

Rational choice among self-interested actors in such a situation entails the behavior pattern exchange theorists label "reciprocity." Each encounter among actors is dominated by the assumption that there will be need for future encounters and bargains. This, generally speaking, creates incentives to behave that set up a pattern of sequential exchange in which the benefits will eventually be seen as equivalent (though not necessarily at the time of the exchange) and the actions of each party are contingent on the prior actions of the other in such a way that eventually good is returned for good, and bad for bad.

Reciprocity must be learned. Learning can be said to follow a pattern of "differentiation," then "unification," and then partial decomposition of the solution found. Differentiation means that various role incumbents take apart the constituent elements of a social context in which a decision has to be made. Each element is analyzed in terms of technically appropriate criteria. The complexity of the problem requiring solution is first appreciated and then disaggregated for close inspection of the components. Extreme differentiation without unification mistakes the trees for the forest. The pieces must then be put together again before the

---

5.   The variables in the right-hand column are defined closely and operationalized in my *When Knowledge Is Power* (Berkeley: University of California Press, 1990) ch.4.

most appropriate (rational) solution can be selected in terms of substantive or value-based criteria. When a solution is found, the steps required for its implementation must then be decomposed once more in recognition of the fact that overall unified action seems to be impossible in most human collectivities. As Paul Diesing has written, "A functionally rational structure [for choice] is one which yields adequate decisions for complex situations with some regularity; but only structures which embody the two characteristics of differentiation and unification to a considerable degree will regularly yield adequate decisions."[6] Learning, then, is the ability of a social collectivity to recognize patterns of interdependence, reciprocityand decisional techniques so as to increasingly succeed in attaining desired values. We call the ensemble "progress" when we find historical evidence of such behavior.

The scene is now set for the remainder of this essay. The next task is the establishment of the relative novelty of the very notion of progress, and of the link between that notion and the idea of the intercultural sharing of meanings and beliefs. I must then show that despite the fact that our realities are "socially constructed," there are some beliefs—derived from the very science made possible by the Enlightenment's belief in reason—that withstand the argument about cultural and contextual relativity. There is a selectionist test for establishing "truth," however temporarily. That done, I will address the challenge posed by some sociologists of science who suggest that a social science derived from a relativistic argument about truth can never be more than just another ideology. If they are right, why accept an argument about the relationship between improvements in international life and scientific rationality as more than just another liberal dogma? I shall show that there is a difference between my thesis and liberalism, and then go on to demonstrate how the study of international regimes can become an empirical study of progress in international affairs.

Types of Progress

When the Enlightenment thinkers invented the modern idea of progress, they thought that increased human knowledge about the world will lead to increases in human power to control the world. Moreover, increases in human virtue, also springing from the growth in knowledge about the world, will improve the manner in which that power is exercised. Increases in happiness for all will be the result of this fortunate juxtaposition. Progress in science is thus linked to the improvement of politics and political choice. Scientific progress leads to moral progress.

---

6.   Paul Diesing, *Reason in Society* (Urbana: University of Illinois Press, 1962) p.178.

Figure 1

Key Events Expressed
As Stylized Historical Process

Historical Process Expressed
As Interacting Variables

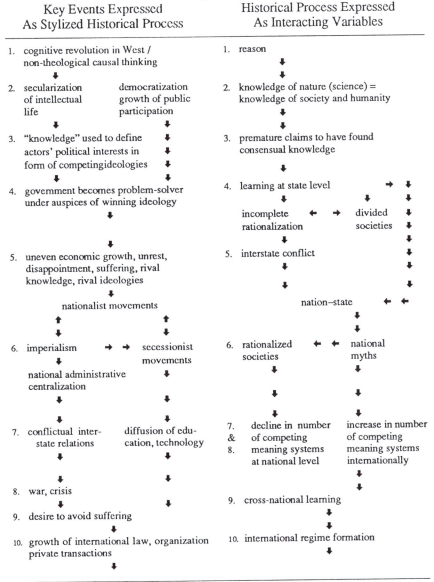

continued

Figure 1 – continued

| Key Events Expressed As Stylized Historical Process | Historical Process Expressed As Interacting Variables |

      ⋮
      ↓

11. repetition of step 5 leads to reiteration
of steps 6 - 10 ↓
  ↓

globalization of ma-   ↓
terial expectations   new states
  ↓   ↓

12. use of diverse   administrative
bodies of   centralization
knowledge   welfare state
  ↓   ↓

   new incentives for international
   problem-solving along with national
        ↓
        ↓

13. new institutions based on
Western codified knowledge
      ↓

14. uneven development, negative externalities from consensual science,
technology, more disappointment,
suffering, competing ideologies
      ↓

15. reiteration of steps 12 - 14
      ↓

16. new consensual knowledge with new
forms of national-international
collaborative problem-solving

                     ⋮
                     ↓

12. fewer number of meaning systems
internationally = international sharing
of meanings
                     ↓

13. international consensual knowledge
                     ↓

14. fragmentary international rationalization
                     ↓

                     ↓

                     ↓

16. rationalized society at international level

Few seemed to worry about the content of the morality, about the specific items that constitute human happiness. Nor was there much concern about whether all, some, or only a few humans subscribe to the particular morality. It is not this version of progress I wish to investigate. Still, I share with the Enlightenment prophets the concern with showing that progress hinges on collective choices to alter the state of the world. I define progress as *directional change for the better*. There is no need to assume that directional improvement is uniform; not all potential beneficiaries of the improvement need benefit at the same time and the trend need not be uninterrupted. Nor does this definition imply irreversibility. We are talking about *net* progress.

Substantive Progress

How can we know what constitutes an improvement without referring to some standard of valuation, some value? While it is impossible to avoid using some evaluative scheme we can still preserve objectivity by not using purely personal moral standards. Change for the better must mean change in terms of something that is valued by all, or almost all, not merely by the observer. All of humankind wants to be wealthy, healthy and live in peace; all of us want to be free of the fear of being killed wantonly, innocently. Desires for a healthy, wealthy and relatively peaceful life can be considered universal substantive values. Even though the hope for peace has almost always been belied by the prevalence of war and violent death, our times differ from earlier ones in that all governments at least profess the necessity for peace, and increasingly act in conformity with their rhetoric. I deliberately exclude the desire for democratic institutions and for basic human rights because these do not appear to me to be universal aspirations, but temporally and culturally specific ones.

Progress: Ends or Means?

Substantive progress is a result, a condition that comes about because of specific antecedents we wish to pinpoint as we talk about reason, knowledge, science, dissatisfaction, democratization, centralization and nation-building. I stress that progress is not the dependent variable of this enterprise; it is a label summing up the direction of the historical process under investigation. The investigation may even disclose that progress is not occurring, or that it can be found only in a few places. There are other connotations of the term that are embedded in the process of change, and these have to be clarified. Progress also means that people entertain expectations of improvement, that they have reason to hope for a better and more secure life. Moreover, these expectations acquire a normative form: people come to expect that they have a *right* to specific improvements. What accounts for such beliefs? Why do people demonstrably hold them now but not before the eighteenth century, even though they surely have hoped for a better life since paleolithic times? The answer is that with the Enlightenment a method for deliberately creating improvements came into being; a procedural (or cognitive) notion of progress emerged. Cognitive progress is the means that makes possible the end of substantive progress.

Who or what creates the improvements? Who makes use of the procedure? The answer varies with culture and geography and political system. Certainly progress can be brought about by private individuals and private organizations. Nevertheless, in our times the progressive use of procedures designed to bring about improvements in people's lives is associated with *public* action, with collective action by government and—in the case of international regimes—by several governments. What concerns me here is the attempt to plan and control change by collective action. This implies regulation or restraint of private actors. The reliance on public collective action in bringing about change is the lesson we learned from the dissatisfactions engendered by the Enlightenment's view of progress.

Cognitive Progress and Its Limits

Apparently, our species is the only one that possesses the power of self-reflection along with an ability for enormously complex symbolic communication. The ability to improve our lot by self-analysis is an aspect of cognitive progress. So is the reliance on abstract concepts, information technology and self-conscious planning. Social pressure that results in the planning of services that give us more health, wealth and peace are part and parcel of cognitive progress, and so is the capacity of the state to control, to plan, to meld social pressures and technology into programs for human betterment. It is only since the Enlightenment that it is considered legitimate to see humans as the sole agents of their own progress, not as subjects of divine or impersonal forces. The world I seek to understand is one of secular rationality in which we make our own future, though not—as Karl Marx reminded us—always just as we wish.

It is therefore time to face some of the limitations of secular reason. Let us recall that the increase in interdependence, global and local, is linked historically to the increase in secularism by way of technology and industrialism. We know that neither technology nor industrialism is considered unqualifiedly progressive: the last decades have been inundated with evidence of the negative externalities associated with science, technology and industry irrespective of their benefits in terms of health and wealth. The non-consensual aspects of reason and knowledge are evident once we recall that philosophers of science as well as scientists are divided on two core issues we will explore in the next section: they disagree over the validity of the fact-value distinction, and they dispute whether the determinants of scientific progress are "internal" to science or due to "external" forces such as government funding, prevalent ideologies and coincidence with non-scientific interests. Many scientists—but by no means all—believe that while the logic of inquiry and the methods used in research are uniform, orderly, systematic and self-correcting, the order of nature discovered by these means need not be equally tidy. Turgot's announcement of the onset of the reign of reason 250 years ago turns out to have been somewhat premature.

That being so I should clarify the semantic context in which I continue to use the words reason, knowledge, science and ideology. My self-imposed verbal conventions are as follows. Reason cannot be distinguished from science. Reason is the human ability to study systematically the order of nature and of culture. There is no guarantee that our reason and our science will discover the "true" and final shape of the reality we seek. Reason and science refer to our minds, not necessarily to what our minds discover. Still, like our intellectual ancestors, I hold that reason is the antonym of passion, faith, intuition and bias. Knowledge is nothing absolute. I see no warrant for identifying the knowledge of nature with the knowledge of morals and of policy. Knowledge is no more than the temporary consensus of a group of practitioners that a "problem" should be defined in a certain manner, the causes and effects arranged in a certain pattern that ends and means of "solving" the problem identified. Collective rational choice is the process of policy making that conforms to and respects such a temporary consensus, including whatever perceived structural constraints may enter into it.

Cognitive Progress and Shared Meanings

Substantive progress can certainly occur at the local and the national level. It does not require cognitive progress on a global scale. Cognitive progress is more easily achieved among collectivities and individuals who already share a common culture, a culturally-mediated set of beliefs about daily life. Ideological convergences occur more readily when the believers are members of the same cultural group. The mutual overlapping of divergent ideologies can occur first at local levels, presumably in response to locally experienced interdependencies following technological innovations, without awaiting the results of the centralized nation-building of the last two centuries.

These possibilities, however, are not what interests me. I am concerned with the following sequence:

1) when intellectual developments combine with political demands to create a market for the claim that systematic research, that knowledge, can improve the problem-solving ability of governments;

2) as knowledge is so used, some material conditions improve and some deteriorate;

3) still, the belief grows that systematically collected and deployed knowledge is able to effect changes in traditionally-sanctioned institutions and pursuits;

4) as a result, basic "meanings" about the features that cause phenomena are "shared" among collectivities and individuals who had little prior contact with each other.

In short, the process we label cognitive progress comes about as the consequence of the gradual sharing of meanings. Eventually, earlier ideological dogmas are also made to overlap as believers find that their original convictions do not withstand the demonstrations contained in the shared meanings. The sharing of meanings brings about the sharing of beliefs. Lessons learned by widely distributed participants in the sharing of meanings, in many parts of large countries or even the entire world, eventually bring about changes in local beliefs.

Cognitive progress is the result of the work of systematic research and scholarship. Groups of professionals doing their normal work elaborate understandings of phenomena relating to human welfare. Decades and centuries of such work can then result in shared meanings—understandings about cause-effect relationships that prove acceptable to members of ever larger communities irrespective of the ideological commitments of their members. Shared meanings are systematic understandings of cause-effect relationships about specific phenomena shared by people irrespective of whether they are Liberals, Marxists, Buddhists, Muslims or Christians.

But: if cognitive progress depends on the successful sharing of meanings, and if that conjuncture, in turn, depends on the acceptance of certain bodies of knowledge considered authoritative, and since we know consensual knowledge to be an elusive quality, how can we be confident of the unveiling of this sequence? How can we hope to recognize "true" knowledge when we see it? The next step is to explain how I conceive scientific knowledge to be "true." Following that, I must address the issue of why this "truth" is more than just personal ideology, mine or someone else's.

Between Absolutism and Relativism in Natural Science

My thesis about political change is indebted to natural science in a dual way. The first debt is substantive and obvious: the political changes of the last 250 years are directly linked to changes in scientific knowledge and dependent on the technological innovations made possible by modern science. This is as true of the changes in politics that enhance welfare as it is of the ones that seem to threaten it. Science and technology, as triggers of social change, are direct causes of enhanced and reduced welfare. Hence they appear in modern times as components of politics.

There is also a less obvious link between science and politics. I claim that we think differently about public affairs than did our ancestors before the Enlightenment. We think in terms of material problems and separable, manipulable solutions. We think of political action as meliorative, as capable of being designed to improve our lot. This has become the situation almost everywhere in the world. First principles which at one time taught mankind to accept its fate, or at best to transcend it in another cognitive dimension, have yielded to first principles which legitimate protest against fate, which encourage us to think that we can change our fate by engaging in politics. These new first principles are rationalistic, centered on thinking humans, not on the superhuman.

Descriptive Epistemology

Debts acknowledged, the difficulty of coming to terms with them must immediately be appreciated. Scientists and politicians entertain widely differing views of what constitutes relevant knowledge; they also disagree about the manner in which knowledge ought to relate to policy. These disagreements give us a spectrum that runs from absolute relativism—there is no consensual or true knowledge based on science—to unyielding absolutism—there is no certifiably true knowledge except that obtained by way of the modern scientific method, lore that can pass the falsifiability test. I identify with neither extreme. To rescue the plausibility of my hypothesis I must sketch a position that distinguishes me from both.

I repeat that no absolutist claim to knowledge is tenable. No epistemology has succeeded in stilling all objections to the possibility of fully "knowing." Disputes among philosophers of science exemplify the situation. The cacophony of real-life ideological claims confirms that no universal standard of truth prevails. But we do not need to be sure of the possibility of knowing before we feel justified in making an ideological claim. "In contrast to the traditional epistemological approach of holding all knowledge in abeyance until the possibility of knowledge is established," says Donald Campbell, "descriptive epistemology addresses the problem of knowledge assuming that the biologists' description of the world-to-be-known, are approximately correct, although corrigible."[7] What Campbell calls descriptive epistemology I make into my first principle of "relative knowing." Two major assumptions must be made in order to have such a basis, which imply distinct analytical positions not shared by all. First, we have to accept that belief about a phenomenon is distinct from the phenomenon itself. Scientific concepts are not necessarily one with their referents. They may fit or not, and therefore they are correctable. Second, despite this dualism the scientist must accept a belief in the existence of an external world. Campbell also thinks that "probably descriptive epistemology must also be an 'epistemology of the other one'... giving up the effort to solve the problem of knowledge for oneself, working instead on the problem of how people in general, or other organisms come to know."[8] This must indeed be our concern if we expect to have anything to say on how culturally diverse groups of political actors arrive at shared meanings about specific problems. Descriptive epistemology is a cautious faith in the possibility of attaining temporary consensual knowledge, not permanent personal certainty. It holds that the attainment of the knowledge depends on an interaction between knower and things-to-be known.

Divergent Accounts of Cognitive Progress

Some scientists and philosophers consider cognitive progress the guarantor of our survival. Others identify analytic problem solving with the crisis of the globe; they, in turn, see survival related to the debunking of scientific knowledge as inherently biased. Understanding the reasons for these differences is crucial for rescuing our notion of consensual knowledge.

These differences characterize the major philosophers of science; they can be compared by highlighting two questions: (1) Are facts independent of human values or is the determination of the facticity of a phenomenon dependent on a prior belief in some value? and (2) Is knowledge accumulated exclusively because of the analytic techniques used in scientific research ("internal" determinism), or is accumulation due to a social context of rewards and punishments, institutional encouragement and hurdles, the involvement of favored and oppressed classes, endorsement by a biased establishment or exclusion by that same

---

7. Donald T. Campbell, "Unjustified Variation and Selection Retention in Scientific Discovery," in F.J. Ayala and T. Dobzhansky, eds., *Studies in the Philosophy of Biology* (New York: Macmillan, 1974) pp.140-41.
8. *Ibid.*, p.141.

establishment ("external" determinism)? Acceptance of any pair of these alternatives by an observer of the process of discovery allows us to predict how that observer will account for cognitive progress. These alternatives are displayed in Figure 2.

Figure 2

Reasons for Cumulative Knowledge

	Internal Determinants	*External Determinants*
Facts and Values are not distinguishable	1. Radical Ecologists Bronowski, Dubos	2. Marxists "Critical" science
Facts and Values are distinguishable	3. Positivists Lakatos Laudan Early Kuhn Toulmin	4. Later Kuhn

The most absolute claim to truth is that advanced by the logical positivists who tend to deny that assertions of knowledge based on softer criteria have any merit (cell 3). They also deny the legitimacy of the coexistence of conflicting bodies of knowledge, the position defended by the adherents of a descriptive epistemology (cell 4). Logical positivists make no strong claims about the relationship of science to progress except to assert that scientific progress thrives under freedom and that political freedom is related to the open-mindedness that is also involved in analytic investigations allowing for falsifiability.

Logical positivism was directly challenged by Marxist and "critical" philosophers of science (as well as by other externalists who nevertheless accepted the fact-value distinction). These challengers believe that it is uncritical attachment to preconceived "ideas of natural order," not self-correcting methods, that determine the success of a given research program. Inhabitants of cell 2 equate cognitive progress with the rejection of the positivist program, with freeing scientific inquiry from the bonds of bias and oppression and dedicating it to the betterment of humankind.[9] All externalists tend to believe that what passes for true

---

9. See Jean Meynaud, *Technocracy* (London: Faber & Faber, 1968); Jean-Jacques Salomon, *Science and Politics* (Cambridge: MIT Press 1973). Many philosophers have condemned science for producing knowledge that subverts religious and cultural values because it stresses analytic techniques over the realization of morally desirable ends. See Jacques Ellul, *The Political Illusion* (New York: Alfred Knopf, 1967).

knowledge at any one time is merely a reflection of the social power of the epistemic establishment.

Those who make up cell 4, because they differentiate fact from value inference, allow for the possibility of cognitive progress just the same because they also believe that scientific discoveries may (or may not) become a part of political choice, depending on the value preference of the choosers. Scientific knowledge, for them, facilitates cognitive progress when political values are consistent with the discoveries of science, but not otherwise. My own position is represented by this alternative.

Such views stand in sharp contrast to those who view science as the guarantor of human progress, as the cognitive breakthrough which will civilize us and make us evolve into a better species (cell 1). This argument was made explicitly by Jacob Bronowski and by René Dubos. Systems theory, as adapted from biology especially, has been pressed into service to make the same point. In some ecological theories of human survival, systems theory is presented as the science of cognition that will make possible a science of physical *and* political survival. Andrei Sakharov foresaw the convergence of capitalist and socialist societies—and a global utopia—based on the application of science to political thinking as well as on the substantive progress due to science.

A Selectionist Theory of Knowledge

Imre Lakatos's notion of research programs (especially as redefined by Larry Laudan in the form of "research traditions") however, offers a bridge to those of us who are impressed with the external determinants of knowledge.[10] Not single theories, but successive sets of theories, must be examined by successive sets of scientists in order to discover the "progressive" content of a research program. Yet all these theories must share common core assumptions to qualify as a set. These assumptions are the equivalent of what Collingwood called "absolute presuppositions," Popper labelled "myths" and Toulmin calls "ideals of natural order." They demarcate one research program from another. Cumulation takes place when one such set is markedly more successful than its rivals in accounting for both old and new observations. This means that work

---

10. The pages that follow depend heavily on ideas derived from Larry Laudan, *Progress and Its Problems* (Berkeley: University of California Press, 1977); Thomas S. Kuhn, *The Structure of Scientific Revolutions*, 2d ed., (Chicago: University of Chicago Press, 1970); Stephen Toulmin, *Human Understanding* (Princeton: Princeton University Press, 1972); Peter L. Berger and Thomas Luckman, *The SocialConstruction of Reality* (Garden City, N.Y.: Doubleday/Anchor, 1967); Clifford Geertz, "The Way We Think: Toward an Ethnography of Modern Thought," *Bulletin of the American Academy of Arts and Sciences* (February 1982); articles of William Dunn and Donald Campbell in *Knowledge* (March 1982).

based on certain presuppositions not only swamps its own discipline in offering acceptable explanations and predictions, but that it is so fruitful as to be taken over as a basis by cognate disciplines. Because more and more diverse phenomena are explained by the program, the legitimacy of the first principles is also reinforced. Since these, however, were dependent on extra-scientific ideals of "natural order" the amended Lakatosian account is no longer exclusively internal to science.

Can this epistemological relativism withstand the critique that all science is externally determined and its truths therefore dependent on the prior cognitive constraints of its discoverers? Stephen Toulmin tackled the job of developing an account of the temporary victory of specific scientific concepts which rejects the absolutist notion that scientific reason is self-contained and accepts the importance of external determinants *alongside* internal ones. I rely on his "population selectionist" argument in grounding my own.

Toulmin urges us to begin "by recognizing that rationality is an attribute, not of logical or conceptual systems as such, but of the human activities or enterprises of which particular sets of concepts are the temporary cross-sections: specifically, of the procedures by which the concepts, judgments and formal systems currently accepted in those enterprises are criticized and changed."[11] Doing science, applying science and criticizing science all are human activities; their fit with the "real" is always provisional and always dependent on the question being asked. Rival concepts in concurrent use and rival interpretive systems that coexist may be fully legitimate and rational if they address different problems, even if they are not parts of the same research program. That insight, however, does not compel us to view the advancement of scientific thinking either as uniform and incremental or as revolutionary and discontinuous. Both may be correct descriptions; all depends on whether we are talking about a set of theories which are part of a program within a discipline (such as particle physics within physics), or whether we are characterizing all of physics. A still different situation exists when the accepted "truths" of a program in one discipline constitute the major hypothetical premises of another discipline. Toulmin insists that external and internal factors constantly influence each other in producing a consensual outcome. Yet he ascribes primary importance to internal forces when accounting for the selection of new concepts capable of yielding more powerful solutions to unsolved problems. He grants explanatory power to sociological and institutional factors only when a given innovation cannot be accounted for in terms of the internal intel-

---

11. Toulmin, *op.cit.* p.133.

lectual process of the profession. Toulmin gives a very contingent summary:

> Typically, then, the task of evaluating conceptual changes in science requires us to consider implications of half a dozen kinds; and this calls for the exercise of judgment, in two separate respects. Not only are the relevant considerations frequently incommensurable—not only may we lack any simple index for comparing the respective 'values' of (e.g., accuracy, scope, and degree of integration)—but, in addition, the decisions frequently involve striking a balance between a profit of one kind and a loss of another. The recognized disciplinary criteria of choice are always multiple, and sometimes point in opposite directions; so that a proposed theoretical change may be highly attractive in one respect, retrograde in another.[12]

In what sense, then, is science the source of true knowledge that is capable of influencing politics? A selectionist view of the matter cannot assert any clear line of demarcation between sound science and pseudo-science even when the institutions of peer review and of unbiased epistemic critique function perfectly. Says Toulmin:

> What is 'sound' in science is what has proved sound, what is 'justifiable' is what is found justifiable, what is 'internally relevant' is what turns out to be internally relevant. Since any strategic redirection of a science may lead to a redrawing of its boundaries, none of these discoveries can ever be absolute or final....[13]

Even though natural science can be said to aim at "representation" and social science-infused public policy at "regulation," the differences between the claims to truth of the two are not absolute. Both remain embedded in the dominant beliefs of their societies. Both are constrained by the institutional characteristics of their practitioners and users and by the prevailing interest of the state. Relativistic criteria for judging the finality of truth characterize both domains. What constitutes a problem worth solving in science is not entirely a matter of internal logic. Even if the program is not determined by the demands of society its form remains indebted to whatever views about natural order happen to prevail, views that have no single origin. The Enlightenment surely broke the beliefs derived from divine first principles. But instead of a single and authoritative substitute it bequeathed us an unending search.

Can we then know nothing? Is science merely a process of selection among the viable and less viable variants of thought while we lack any reliable criterion for saying what is and is not viable? Toulmin argues

---

12.   *Ibid.*, p.227.
13.   *Ibid.*, pp.259-60.

that "whatever works, works." If theories demonstrably lead to greater understanding that results in greater human mastery over nature, something has clearly been learned. Practical success validates the reality of the knowledge.

Toulmin claims to have staked out a middle ground between absolutist and relativist claims to true knowledge. Does the selectionist stance allow the inference that any balance sheet about scientific progress will surely be the victim of the cognitive limits of the balancers, that judgment will still be subject to the nonscientific beliefs of the judges? If so, what is "science" for the West may still legitimately be "materialistic error" for the East, or *vice versa*. Not, says Toulmin, if the respective practitioners agree on "what there is to achieve."[14] If their rational purposes converge, so will their judgments of what works. If the problems of wealth, health and peace are to be solved on the basis of analyses and diagrams that pass rigorous reality tests, causal inferences will be universally similar.

So what? Is the result "true" consensual knowledge or merely a more popular ideology?

Between Ideology and Knowledge:
The Social Construction of Reality

Before answering the question I will summarize the argument.

I wish to position myself in the universe of controversy among rival schools. I claim both that it is possible to make detached judgments, yet grant the problematic nature of truth and the limits on our capacity to map reality in natural as well as in social science. Throughout I must wrestle with a basic tension: Scientists, including social scientists, claim to know and their claims are sometimes taken seriously by policy makers, yet the social life which contains the phenomena about which we claim knowledge remains separate from the conceptual artifacts in which we express our claim to knowledge. Semiotics has sensitized us to the gap between what we say to each other and what those sayings may refer to. We cannot be sure that our words really describe or explain something "real" out there.

To relax that tension we must distinguish between "ordinary" knowledge and "scientific" knowledge. Ordinary knowledge is cumulative social experience about causal relationships. This experience is accessible to any intelligent person; being intersubjectively experienced, it can become "objective" in the sense that this knowledge can be shared by many diverse actors subscribing to many diverse value-defined views. Scientific knowledge, however, is based on analytic procedures practiced

14. *Ibid.*, p.498.

in and by institutions designed to be self-critical and self-correcting. Disagreements among people are overcome by research programs and paradigms intended to make practitioners epistemologically self-conscious, unlike practices associated with ordinary knowledge-seeking.

"Reality" is a temporary truth to be discovered; it is a goal, a standard, not a certainty attained by the unflinching pursuit of research in the positivist manner. I accept the critique of positivism which points to the neglect of the permanently problematic aspects in the pursuit of knowledge, especially that offered by Jürgen Habermas and the sociologists of knowledge who stress the contextual and social determinants of the search for knowledge. However, I also accept the proto-positivist views of Toulmin; he asserts that knowledge claims that survive despite these problems (in the sense that they explain more and permit more comprehensive cumulation of information that results in more extensive manipulation of nature and of society) ought to be accepted as scientific, not ordinary knowledge, that is, as privileged knowledge.

I do not claim that there are no laws of general cognition because the mind cannot objectively study itself. I also reject the opposite claim, the argument that any regularity discovered is merely another social construction, an emanation of our mind, that all theories are temporally limited ideologies advanced to shore up some particular interest. I *do* claim that mind is a process of continuous approximation. Particular theories and bodies of knowledge *are* indeed socially constructed, at least in part. But they are also "objective" in the sense that—if they appear as transculturally shared meanings—they offer universally accepted explanations of phenomena of general interest and universally persuasive solutions to commonly experienced problems. Such knowledge, I maintain, is capable of self-correction because its practitioners grow conscious of its socially constructed aspects. Such knowledge is different from the ordinary knowledge extolled by critics of "scientism"; scientific knowledge is able to grasp increasingly larger chunks of "reality" without ever being certain that the biggest chunk, the whole, can be grasped.

The selectionist view of scientific knowledge just sketched supports my claim that it is possible to have a consensus on what constitutes a problem and a solution at a given time in history. But very often, it is not possible to distinguish consensual knowledge that meets the criterion of "working better" from claims to knowledge that do not, except in retrospect. If this is true in the natural sciences, should we not despair immediately of making any claim for consensual knowledge in the social sciences, particularly for the kind of knowledge that finds its way into politics? I can cope with this question only by explaining how we "socially construct" the reality disclosed by all efforts at gaining knowledge, ordinary and scientific.

Why is it crucial that we collectively persuade ourselves that we collectively know something? William McNeill contends that collective persuasion "is the unique and characteristic human way of acting together. A people without a full quiver of relevant agreed-upon statements, accepted in advance through education or less formalized acculturation, soon finds itself in deep trouble, for, in the absence of believable myths, coherent public action becomes very difficult to improvise or sustain."[15]

In the West, the old myths were shattered in the eighteenth century. In the rest of the world the process of de-mythification of the traditional beliefs is still underway. The idea of rationally planned human change, using the findings and the methods of science, appears as a strong contender for becoming a new global myth. How can that be if science is problematic and its meaning in politics subject to a social construction of the reality it describes, explains and perhaps predicts, not an objective construction? Even a theory of cumulative knowledge in natural science which relies on as relativistic a criterion as natural selection remains subject to the bothersome question as to how we as observers and students can claim to know what reality is. How, to put it brutally, can we possibly claim that scientific knowledge is anything but just another ideology?

If people perceive something as real, it is real in its consequences because people will act on their perception of reality, to paraphrase W. Ivor Thomas. I add that any effort to systematize one's perception of reality into a formal scheme deserves the label "socially constructed knowledge" if one attributes cause to certain factors and identifies effects from those causes, and then proceeds to make predictions, offer advice, or practice therapy (whether religious or medical) on the basis of such attributions. The efficacy of that knowledge in really bringing about the effects desired may well be problematical. Any systemization when applied to action qualifies for the label, whether we call it magic, mysticism, ideology, or science. Does everything count as knowledge? Even though the answer is no, we must acknowledge not only that ideologies are extremely important in energizing political choice but that they do *not* differ absolutely from scientific knowledge.

---

15. William H. McNeill, "The Care and Repair of Public Myth," *Foreign Affairs* 61, no.1 (Fall 1982) p. 1.

Ideologies May Be Steps Toward Real Knowledge

Scientific knowledge and ideologies both can and do influence politics; both are used in making policy and therefore may produce change either for the better or for the worse. If knowledge is merely "the communicable mapping of some aspect of experienced reality by an observer in symbolic terms," then Western science, magic, mysticism and most dogmas can meet this test.[16] Such constructs may well serve as ordinary knowledge in channelling action and giving meaning to political actors.

Ideological statements share with claims based on self-proclaimed scientific knowledge a dependence on a set of symbols sufficiently shared among the adepts and their acolytes to communicate the canon. These symbols include any natural language, any artifacts, pictures, objects, music and dance that evoke shared meanings among the communicants. Claims to knowledge diffuse from the group of originators to whoever seems disposed to better themselves by virtue of becoming a communicant. Even Western science became universal as its symbolic language, not its artifacts and discoveries, became global; these could perhaps be appreciated, but not imitated and augmented until more diffusion had occurred.

Knowledge about any phenomenon cannot be accumulated unless the practitioners share a single frame of reference, "a structure consisting of taken-for-granted assumptions, preferences for symbol systems, and analytical devices within which an observer's inquiry proceeds. This structure specifically defines the relation of the observer to what he/she knows and represents."[17] This is as true for the social sciences as it is for physics and biology. It applies to political doctrine and to religious belief. A frame of reference enables leaders of movements to communicate with each other and with their followers because it distinguishes them from rival leaders and their followers. An observer of these actors, in turn, cannot give an account of their doings without specifying his or her frame of reference (which is what I am trying to do at the moment).

No doubt ideologies are essential for the generation of social and national myths that give coherence to large collectivities. No doubt ideologies convey meaning and purpose to their believers and enable them to act in the face of uncertainty. Their acceptance as knowledge makes possible social action which might otherwise have languished. And there is no doubt that the very idea of science as a harbinger of power

---

16. Burkhart Holzner, *Reality Construction in Society* (Cambridge, MA: Schenkman, 1968) p.20.
17. Burkhart Holzner and John H. Marx, *Knowledge Application* (Boston: Allyn & Bacon, 1979) p.99.

and plenty acted as a powerful ideology. But if ideologies fail to make accurate predictions their logic is questioned and their appeal disappears. Ideologies, too, must pass a selectionist test to remain credible.

Suppose that all knowledge is nothing more than the ideology of the victorious. If that knowledge provides better solutions to commonly experienced problems than rival dogmas, it "wins" in the sense that everybody will want it. We are talking about secular knowledge, lore appropriate for dealing with people's material needs, with aspirations that involve control over the natural and social environment, not about religious knowledge, spiritual solutions to spiritual problems.

Reality Tests and Consensual Knowledge

Ideological knowledge has historically been a powerful shaper of shared meanings among nations and ethnic groups. Whether in the form of religious or secular claims to truth, ideologies have been used to unify people and states and give a unified culture to widely diffused human entities. But ideologies divide, they do not unite. They pit the believers of one kind of truth against the faithful of another doctrine. They do little for increased health, wealth and peace in situations that concern everybody. Scientific knowledge, on the other hand, *being equipped with a different set of reality tests*, has the potential for providing the kind of self-correcting knowledge that need not pit one nation against another. This is especially true when knowledge becomes widely consensual. It too can produce shared meanings among believers by providing symbolic systems, frames of reference and reality tests that appeal to certain values shared by groups and nations who remain at loggerheads on other grounds. That is why consensual knowledge alone, despite its residue of relativistic and subjective content, remains our prime candidate for the exploration of international change.

Neither reliance on symbols nor the use of frames of reference distinguishes scientific from ideological knowledge. Once we introduce the notion of reality tests, however, the vital distinction appears:

> Reality tests are relatively structured occasions in which some symbolic representation claiming the status of fact is subjected to scrutiny in terms of criteria of truth. They are essentially procedures for validating an experience or observation. They constitute occasions for ascertaining whether an idea is valid to the extent that action can be taken that may entail risk. Thus, reality tests always involve a testing of a cognition, a decision, and performance based on the decision.[18]

---

18.   *Ibid.*, p.103.

The reality tests are "rational" and "empirical." They are rational in the sense that the source of the claim to knowledge is examined in terms of its logical cohesion. Tests are empirical in the sense that the *predictions* and *consequences* generated by the claim are subjected to systematic observation and evaluation. In short, reality tests of a rational-empirical kind are able to check the adequacy of the frame of reference to produce what is claimed. A Lakatosian research program combines a specific frame of reference with rational-empirical reality tests. Toulmin's selectionist criteria for distinguishing successful from failed concepts do the same. Any formal knowledge claim that survives rational-empirical testing, for me, is scientific knowledge; claims which fail this test are ideological or ordinary knowledge. Ideology is not designed to be self-correcting. It is not structured to be self-critical; theoretical knowledge is. Science is subject to the limits of the social construction of reality but it must still meet the reality test to be considered superior to ideological claims of knowledge.

Consensual Knowledge in Social Science

What if this scientific knowledge is still just the ideology of the group of experts that has won out for the moment? That group, like its predecessor and rivals, has its own ties to the larger society and it too represents perceptions and interests and plans for the future that cannot be disentangled from its scientific advocacy and observations. We still have to show that the winner has a better grasp on truth.

In the social sciences, at any rate, the elaboration of knowledge takes a more confrontational and indeterminate form, a selectionist form. What is generally taken to be a true reflection of reality comes about by way of institutionalized challenges to the claims and assertions of one's fellow professionals. The protagonists may never achieve agreement on a single perspective or theory, but their students and successors will, because subsequent generations will retain what is useful for solving their new problems and abandon assumptions and theoretical baggage that no longer serve their needs. This can happen only under conditions of academic freedom. The official or *de facto* enshrinement of a single perspective that precludes challenge, whether under the auspices of state, party or professional association, will remove the chief reality test and condemn all claims to the status of ideological knowledge. That was the fate of Chinese astronomy and of Soviet genetics.

One difference between the accumulation of consensual knowledge in the natural and the social sciences may be the matter of reversibility. The natural sciences have been, at least since the European Renaissance, cumulative in their discoveries. As earlier discoveries have been eroded and superseded by later ones, as the better science survived the selection process and as worse science did not, what remained useful in the earlier discoveries was retained and used, even if in modified form. While specific laws and insights were reversed, the overall thrust of the enterprise was not. This claim cannot be sustained in the social sciences. The selection process sketched above may remain reversible, fragile and subject to the buffeting associated with the uses of social science. William McNeill argues that science as a whole may be discredited or reversed as society rebels against the unwanted effects produced by technology.[19] Even if he is mistaken for natural science, he may well be right when it comes to social science. The only thing that is probably not reversible is the expectation on the part of ever more people everywhere that things could be better, that the knowledge for protecting life, improving health, increasing wealth and preserving peace does indeed exist.[20]

What, then, can we mean by "consensual"? What kind of a consensus remains after due deference is paid to the imperfections of knowledge and all the failings of actors and observers, natural as well as social scientists, have been conceded? In the social sciences, consensus does not mean that there is agreement among the members of a given discipline or that final selection among rival claims to theoretical knowledge has occurred; at any single point in time such an agreement is most unlikely (though decades after a controversy it is possible). Nor does it mean that a single research program has found unique favor among all the practitioners. And it certainly does not mean that a single paradigm of "normal science" is the prevailing orthodoxy. Consensus means much less than any of these formulations suggest.

Consensus implies that most members of a profession agree that a problem exists, that the reasons for that problem can be isolated by using an agreed set of criteria and methods, and that these same criteria and methods can be employed in devising solutions to the problem. Such a consensus is not permanent. It is always subject to challenge and reexamination and it is fully dependent on some kind of crisis mentality as a necessary condition. What *is* consensual is the very idea that human solutions to problems are possible, than human ingenuity and systematic analysis is all that is needed to understand the problem, and that planning and design are effective, practical activities. If such an attitude legitimates public policy and if the attitude triggers behaviors that make

---

19. William H. McNeill, "Control and Catastrophe in Human Affairs," *Daedalus* 118, no.1 (Winter 1989) pp.1-15. McNeill makes the general argument that our notions of planning and control are mere *hubris* because the unwanted and unexpected always takes over eventually.
20. Soedjatmoko offers a strong argument directly opposing McNeill's, i.e., that Western science and technology are irreversibly changing the non-Western world for the better. See "Education Relevant to People's Needs," *ibid.*, pp. 211-18.

us better off by our own account, it doesn't matter if one persists in calling such a consensus an ideology. It still derives its legitimacy from the fact that it works better than any previous rationality. Moreover, such a rationality is a shared meaning, a body of thought and public commitment, that has outgrown its ideological origins because of its service as a guide to cope with generally perceived predicaments, no matter its origin in the social construction of reality.

Why Should You Believe My Observations?

The main principle used to justify my hypothesis about scientific knowledge and the improvement of international life is a cognate of natural selection. I have argued (1) that history selects in favor of social collectivities—nation-states as well as arrangements among nation-states—that are willing to employ secular and analytic problem-solving methods based on modern criteria of rationality. (Objection: what about social collectivities in our days that reject secular-analytic reason?) I have also argued (2) that because solutions to social problems are more likely to be found among science-informed formulas than from dogmas associated with ordinary knowledge, history selects in favor of systems of shared meanings that include such formulas. (Objection: if that is so, why are we still assaulted by such a cacophony of meaning systems?) I now ask (3): why should my own interpretive stance be taken any more seriously than the various interpretations whose claim to longevity has been undermined by the principle of selection? I will address each objection in turn.

Secular rationality has clearly not triumphed everywhere. In many industrialized countries we find political movements that challenge the prevailing secularism with fundamentalist religious dogmas that also challenge rational analysis. Right-wing totalitarian movements, of which the Nazis were merely the most successful, flourish in countries were industrialism and secularism have long reigned. Islamic fundamentalism is merely the most prominent large-scale opposition movement to modernism in the Third World, not the first and not the only one. The principle of selection applies just the same: My hypothesis will be falsified if such movements show more staying power than their modernist opponents. So far, at least in the West and in the communist world, my hypothesis remains alive because anti-secularist movements have consistently lost.

Reality is what an actor experiences, as reported by an observer and mapped according to some professional canon whether by shamans, adepts, engineers or sociologists. There seem to be a lot of these around these days because the clash of contending ideologies is formidable. However, consider that clash now as compared to a hundred or even fifty years ago. It seems that the total number of ideologies is in decline and that convergences among antagonistic systems of meaning are occurring. My hypothesis derives support from a diminishing number of meanings systems in the world; it would be challenged if that number were increasing. The fact that almost every elite in every country wants more science, more technology, more industry and more modern medicine strengthens the argument in favor of ideological convergence. As long as the process of sharing meanings selects in favor of the rationalistically-biased systems, my hypothesis remains alive. It would be falsified if the number of systems of meaning increases and/or if the realm of the rational system fails to expand. I stress that the success of my hypothesis does not depend on the actors' acceptance of the rational systems *because* of actor belief in the superiority of scientific over ordinary knowledge, though in fact many actors do believe in that superiority.

But can my interpretive stance, on which in the last analysis the credibility of the other selectionist tests depends be falsified? Holzner and Marx suggest that "All knowledge is that of an observer who communicates a symbolic mapping of some experienced reality so that it is accepted as factual."[21] I am the vehicle of the argument that knowledge influences policy making, but my mapping draws on the prior mapping of other observers who abstracted their claim to knowledge from the experiences of their time, culture and research programs. I argue the facticity of my findings on the basis of the accepted prior facticity of the myriad experiences that make up the bodies of knowledge whose applicability to politics concerns me. I may not stand on the shoulders of giants; but I derive direction from following in the wake of many diligent dwarfs.

Internationally, the test of my assertion is the fate of the arrangements we call international regimes. They provide the laboratory in which all three sets of propositions can be falsified.

International Regimes: Settings for Observing Change

For two hundred years it looked as if there was an evolutionary direction—some considered it progressive as well—in international politics. Territorial jurisdictions became larger, more centralized and more effectively organized for action. The large, sovereign territorial state took the place of fragmented political entities and of human collectivities not usually organized on the basis of firmly demarcated boundaries. Soon thereafter the territorial state became a national state, an entity whose population made the transition from impassive and inert subject to participant; nationalism implied accountability of some kind

---

21.   Holzner & Marx, p.93.

to the populace. Rulers mattered less and people mattered more. The legitimacy of the state was believed to rest on the approval of its inhabitants. The nation-state was seen as a more effective guarantor of human happiness, a better problem-solver. A world made up of nation-states was seen as the harbinger of peace and welfare among nations. The expansion of some nation-states into major empires after 1870 was interpreted as further confirmation of the paean to progress.

International Regimes as Agents of Progress

Since the end of World War II two new trends have shown us the unreliability of this imputed directionality of political evolution. For the most part the empires broke up, giving rise to a large number of new states, a few of which are even nation-states. Territorial jurisdictions multiplied after 1960. At the same time, the meaning of territorial jurisdiction was beginning to be questioned and with it the value attached to territorial sovereignty. A number of new sources of suffering surfaced for which most territorial states seemed to have no answer: endemic poverty defying purely local solution, military weakness beyond the remedy of any national military effort and pollution of the seas and the atmosphere which do not respect political frontiers. Solutions for each of these called into service more complex schemes of intellectual analysis and interpretation than had been enlisted before. More sharing of meanings across borders and within countries surely took place as well. The upshot, however, was the recognition that territoriality itself is a source of the problem, because solutions put in place in one country cannot work unless all others equally afflicted apply the same solution. Nationalism as the principle for organizing human collectivities was enhanced and undermined at the same time.

Newly shared meanings, possibly, transform international life. Historically, shared meanings among literate elites emerged first in large geographic spaces unified by shared high cultures: in the Greco-Roman world, in China, in the Islamic realm, in the cultural-geographic space once occupied by Hindu culture and in the Christian world of medieval Europe. Here shared meanings cut across and often ignored political boundaries. This world came to an end with the emergence of the territorial nation-state which fragmented elites who had been united by common beliefs, but it unified underlying masses who had previously lived in the isolation of villages and towns. The nation-state became the agent for ushering in improvement of man's condition. The nation-state "rationalized" collective life. Nationalism provided several formulas for making local life better for most people. But, quite possibly (and quite certainly if Rousseau was right) it did so at the price of making international life more miserable. One task, therefore, is to determine what kind of nationalism is compatible with international as well as with national happiness.

Once we know the answer to this question, we can then pursue the matter of what kind of international arrangements are most progressive. International life is the result of foreign policies articulated and implemented by nation-states. The arrow of causality runs from the nation to the international system of relations. Given various kinds of national formulas for achieving happiness, what ways of establishing shared meanings across political borders engender international happiness? Is that happiness the same for all aspects of political endeavor, for military security, for assuring economic well-being, preventing disease and giving us a wholesome physical environment? Are the same shared meanings adequate for all these aspirations or does each engender its own set of more complex collective understandings?

International regimes are collections of principles, norms, rules and procedures for resolving conflict around which actor expectations tend to converge. Regimes may be highly institutionalized, as through the medium of one or several international organizations, or they may be quite informal. They may be based on elaborate legal understanding, or on unspoken expectations of reciprocity, or both. Membership may include all states or only a few. Regimes must be concerned with a specific set of concerns, a set which in principle could cover anything on the international agenda. Regimes provide a setting in which shared meaning systems can emerge, where we can observe whether and why knowledge becomes consensual.

International Regimes as Media for Sharing Meanings

When states attempt to create new norms of behavior under the inspiration of some overarching principle and then go on to fashion more detailed rules for implementing the norms and principles, they deliberately design something novel. When they change or abandon those norms and rules later they deliberately alter what they wrought earlier. For the actors, regimes are *willed* constructs, creating orders expected by their members to benefit them; international regimes are intended to be meliorative. For the observer, regimes are "variables" that intervene between actor motivations and expectations associated with earlier disappointment and suffering and some future shape of the international system. Regimes are not true dependent variables for either actor or observer. They may be settings for discovering the conditions under which macroeconomic coordination leads to more equity or a more perfect international division of labor, how arms control can lead to peace or war, human rights to more democracy or more conflict. Therefore, they are appropriate for confirming or falsifying my hypotheses about knowledge as the trigger of international change.

I study regimes because I want to know under what circumstances actors succeed in so adjusting their meaning systems to one another as to order their universes of causes and effects consensually. I want to study international relationships which are already partially ordered to see under what conditions the partial order disintegrates or becomes more comprehensive. This is a more abstract way of saying that I want to find out when governments learn to use scientific knowledge in defining their interests and in bargaining with others about them, and when, as a result of the bargaining, the scientific knowledge becomes consensual. After it does—if it does—the resulting shared meaning system will be an ordered hierarchy of causal understandings about the issues of concern, such as cholera, economic development, nuclear stability, or freedom to seek asylum. In sum, international regimes provide occasions for studying national redefinitions of interest in a setting of repeated interaction with others engaged in the same process. Institutionalized international cooperation in macroeconomics is my illustration.

Efforts to coordinate and combine national macroeconomic efforts into an international package are legion; their successful aggregation into regimes is questionable. However, the contrast is not with some conceivable utopia but with the situation fifty years ago. Instead of a single regime incorporating a single system of shared understandings, we have many partial orders encompassing competing systems of meanings. Each one, however, still represents shared understandings that go much beyond autonomous national doctrines and consequently serves as the basis of commonly pursued policies anchored on a few generally accepted principles—for example, free trade limited by orderly marketing criteria, or monetary cooperation without a powerful lender of last resort. Moreover, there are a number of generally accepted principles of economic behavior which certainly did not prevail before World War II, namely:

- the rich have an obligation to give economic aid and improve the welfare of the poor;
- there are distinct limits on the unilateral manipulation of national monetary policies;
- creditors have responsibilities for considering the welfare of debtors;
- everyone has an obligation to consider the impact of industrialization (and associated trade and investment issues) on the quality of the natural environment.

That said, however, it also remains true that neither the United Nations, nor any of the specialized agencies singly or together, impose rules and procedures sufficient to give consistent practical significance to these norms and principles.

Regimes, Truth, Values

International regimes may serve as settings for the sharing of meanings such that the rational-analytic way of thinking becomes universal. There remains some nagging doubt: what if the shared meaning is inaccurate? What if it enshrines the wrong information and mode of analysis? What if it fails to alleviate disappointment and suffering? How "true" or "correct" must a shared meaning be to be considered progressive? Common sense suggests that shared meanings which seriously misrepresent the nature of a complex problem will not lead to effective solutions, but possibly to more disappointment and suffering. But common sense is not an altogether satisfactory guide here. True, a system of aircraft safety that ignores physical phenomena such as windshear or slights the importance of low morale among airport controllers is not an effective system no matter how satisfactorily it includes and aggregates physical and human factors not taken into account in earlier safety procedures. The improved system is still faulty if it leads to more plane crashes; it may even be more faulty than its more primitive predecessors if the volume of plane traffic rises sharply. Most human problems that engender suffering, however, cannot be reduced to that type of system. Poverty can be explained by several equally plausible schemes. So can war, provided that all the assumptions underlying the competing explanations have some *prima facie* credibility. Things become more ambiguous if successive social experiments based on each theory all bring about some improvement. In this case the reality is still seen differently by different sufferers, depending on the shared meanings they already carry in their heads. One person's reality can legitimately be another's fantasy.

Faced with this conundrum, we must settle for a notion of reality that eschews any final judgment as to the accuracy of any vision. Progress prevails if there is a decline in the number of complex shared meanings about the causes that are associated with undesired effects, regardless of the final "truth" of the meaning. Only one condition must hold: the remedies associated with that consensus must be effective in mitigating the unhappiness being fought in the *short run*.

There is a second nagging doubt. How can we be sure that progress in the short run, in the face of visions whose truth cannot be guaranteed for lengthy periods, is morally desirable? I suggest that my hypothesis about reason and change in international life is substantively amoral, but procedurally moral. If we think of morality as the acceptance of a specific doctrine, a specific set of values superimposed on a set of concrete decisions, we cannot find moral content in my hypothesis about change for the better. The very notion of shared meanings must eschew attachment to a given doctrine, a pre-specified scale of values which is known to be less than universal in its appeal. The consensual evolution of shared values cannot begin with the unilateral assertion of the superiority of a single one. If Western rational thought is held out as superior it must be proven so on the basis of its voluntary acceptance by other cultures. That is what the sharing of meanings through international programs and negotiations is expected to facilitate, and probably hasten. But beyond stipulating the universal preference for secure life, health, wealth and peace, we cannot dictate a moral code.

If the sharing of meanings is to be morally progressive, then, it must "creep up from below," not be decreed from above (as in religiously sanctioned codes). Universalized morality is the bridging and joining of popular ideologies, each the repository of its own code of values. Bridged ideologies may eventually acquire a genuinely shared substantive morality. But we can begin only with a procedure, the rational-analytic mode of inquiry—Western reason. This procedure offers us both the possibility of attaining consensual understandings of problems requiring solutions and is an incremental step toward achieving a universal morality yet to be conceived.

ABOUT THE AUTHORS

ANNETTE BAKER FOX received her Ph. D. in political science from the University of Chicago in 1941. She married William T.R. Fox in 1935 and is co-author with him of *NATO and the Range of American Choice* (1967).

ERNST B. HAAS is Robson Research Professor of Government at the University of California, Berkeley. A specialist in international relations theory with an emphasis on the concepts and process of international integration, he has authored many books on international organizations and world order including *When Knowledge is Power: Three Models of Change in International Organizations* (1989).

ELIZABETH C. HANSON is associate professor of political science at the University of Connecticut. A specialist in international relations and international organization, she authored *Science, Politics and International Conferences: A Functional Analysis of the Moscow Political Science Congress* (1989).

LOUIS HENKIN is University Professor Emeritus and Special Service Professor at Columbia University. A specialist in international law, human rights, and constitutional law and foreign policy, he is the author of *How Nations Behave: Law and Foreign Policy (1968);The Rights of Man Today (1978); The Age of Rights* (1990) and *Constitutionalism, Democracy and Foreign Affairs* (1990).

ROBERT JERVIS is Adlai E. Stevenson Professor of International Relations and professor of political science at Columbia University. A specialist in international relations theory, deterrence theory and nuclear strategy, he has written many articles and books including "Cooperation under the Security Dilemma" (*World Politics,* January 1978), "Deterrence and Perception" (*International Security*, Winter 1982-83), *The Illogic of American Nuclear Strategy* (1984) and *The Logic of Images in International Politics* (1989).

DONALD J. PUCHALA is Charles L. Jacobson Professor of Public Affairs at the department of government and international studies at the University of South Carolina. A specialist in international politics, international organization and the history of international relations, he is the author of *Fiscal Harmonization in the European Communities: National*

Politics and International Cooperation (1984) and editor of *Issues Before the 39th Assembly of the United Nations* (1984).

ROBERT L. ROTHSTEIN is Harvey Picker Professor of International Relations at Colgate University. He is the author of *The Third World and U.S. Foreign Policy—Cooperation and Conflict in the 1980s* (1981), "The Rise of the Periphery: The Challenge of the NICs" (*The Jerusalem Journal of International Relations*, Fall 1989) and "Getting to Maybe: Large Steps to End a Large Stalemate in the Arab-Israel Peace Process"(*The Jerusalem Quarterly*, Fall 1989).

GLENN H. SNYDER is professor of political science at the University of North Carolina, Chapel Hill. He is the author of *Conflict Among Nations: Bargaining, Decision-Making and System Structure in International Crises* (1977).

KENNETH N. WALTZ is Ford Professor at the University of California, Berkeley. A specialist in international relations theory, he is the author of *Man, the State and War; A Theoretical Analysis* (1959), *Theory of International Politics* (1979) and "Toward Nuclear Peace" (*Strategies for Managing Nuclear Proliferation*, 1983).

MARK W. ZACHER is professor of political science at the University of British Columbia. He is co-author of *Pollution, Politics and International Law: Tankers at Sea* (1979) and will soon complete *The Patterns and Political Foundations of International Regimes: An Analysis of the Regulation of the International Shipping, Air Transport, Telecommunications and Postal Industries and Common Enemies* and *International Change: International Collaboration in Response to Nuclear, Environmental, Health and Translation Crime Threats.*

WILLIAM ZIMMERMAN is professor of political science at the University of Michigan, Ann Arbor. He is the author of "Mobilized Participation and the Nature of the Soviet Dictatorship" (*Politics, Work and Daily Life in the USSR*, 1987) and *Soviet Perspectives on International Relations, 1957-67* (1969).